The Words of the Imams

The Words of the Imams

Al-Shaykh al-Ṣadūq and the Development of Twelver Shīʿī Hadith Literature

George Warner

I.B.TAURIS

LONDON • NEW YORK • OXFORD • NEW DELHI • SYDNEY

I.B. TAURIS
Bloomsbury Publishing Plc
50 Bedford Square, London, WC1B 3DP, UK
1385 Broadway, New York, NY 10018, USA
29 Earlsfort Terrace, Dublin 2, Ireland

BLOOMSBURY, I.B. TAURIS and the I.B. Tauris logo are trademarks of Bloomsbury Publishing Plc

First published in Great Britain 2022
Paperback edition published 2023

Series design by Adriana Brioso
Cover image: The Prophet Muhammad Encounters the Angel Half-Fire Half Snow, 13/2012v. Photo by Pernille Klemp. Courtesy of The David Collection, Copenhagen

A catalogue record for this book is available from the British Library.

A catalog record for this book is available from the Library of Congress.

ISBN: HB: 978-1-8386-0560-5
PB: 978-0-7556-4557-2
ePDF: 978-1-8386-0563-6
eBook: 978-1-8386-0561-2

Typeset by Deanta Global Publishing Services, Chennai, India

To my parents

Contents

Acknowledgements viii

Introduction 1

Part I Placing al-Ṣadūq

1 Living without an imam: Imāmī thought in the age of al-Ṣadūq 31
2 Legal theory and the living imam: Al-Ṣadūq as a scholar of hadith 46
3 Hadith as literature: Al-Ṣadūq, *adab* and Imāmī traditionism at the Buwayhid court 65

Part II Reading al-Ṣadūq

4 *Al-Tawḥīd*: Theology and its limits 91
5 *Kamāl al-dīn wa tamām al-niʿma*: Looking for the imam 117
Conclusion: Hadith literature and Twelver Shīʿism 149

Appendix I 153
Appendix II 157
Notes 160
Bibliography 210
Index 224

Acknowledgements

Between 2008 and 2009, I lived in the Sayyida Zaynab suburb of Damascus, so named because of the shrine of Muḥammad's granddaughter Zaynab that dominates the area. While there I was fortunate enough to study Shīʿī hadith in and around some of the many seminaries that dot the area. Without the generosity of the scholars who gave their time to teach me, and without all those with whom I spent evenings and some very early mornings reading venerable texts, this book could not have been written.

The project that became *The Words of the Imams* began life as my doctoral thesis at SOAS in London, and I am immensely grateful to my supervisor Jan-Peter Hartung, upon whose tranquil sagacity the project never ceased to depend. A huge debt of thanks is also due to Augusta Macmahon, Sîan Hawthorne and Nicole Brisch, who got me started with doctoral work, and to Hugh Kennedy, whose continued advice and encouragement after I submitted the thesis was a tremendous help. I must also thank David Stonestreet, Sophie Rudland and Yasmin Garcha at I. B. Tauris for their abundant support and patience in seeing the project through.

Along the way I have depended upon the freely given advice of countless friends and colleagues, whom I can only hope to enumerate to a point of comprehensiveness no less lamentable than that of my bibliography; I remain gratefully indebted to James Montgomery, Amjad Shah and the staff of the Shīʿah Institute, Sajjad Rizvi, Hassan Beloushi, Toby Mayer, Rob Gleave, Stephen Burge, Andrew Newman, Ruth Mas, Devin Stewart, Harith bin Ramli, Martin Worthington, Julia Bray, Najam Haider, Edmund Hayes, Nuha Alshaar, Tamima Bayhom-Daou, Marianna Klar, Hasan Al-Khoee, Helen Blatherwick, Stefan Sperl, Ali Rida Rizek, Alexandra Cuffel, Adam Knobler and Omid Ghaemmaghami.

I owe to my wife manifold thanks for manifold things, only two of which are her sustaining help and presence while I wrote this book.

Introduction

Hadith, occultation and compilation

The truthful master

This book is a study of the fourth/tenth-century Imāmī Shīʿī scholar Abū Jaʿfar Muḥammad b. ʿAlī b. al-Ḥusayn b. Mūsā b. Bābawayh al-Qummī, better known as Ibn Bābawayh or by the honorific al-Shaykh al-Ṣadūq, 'the truthful master' (hereafter al-Ṣadūq). Al-Ṣadūq is best known as an important early hadith collector of the Imāmīya, the author of *Man lā yaḥḍuruhu al-faqīh* ('Every Man His Own Jurist'), the second oldest of what became the four canonical books of Imāmī hadith.[1] This study of him will accordingly focus upon his significance as a scholar of hadith – a *muḥaddith* (pl. *muḥaddithūn*). Through examination of al-Ṣadūq's extensive writings, most of which are collections of hadith, the following also aims to shed light on the broader development of a distinct Imāmī – latterly Twelver – Shīʿī hadith literature.[2]

Hadith is as central to Imāmī thought as it is to Sunnī thought, and, indeed, the fact that Imāmīs refer to a hadith corpus different to that consulted by Sunnīs is one of the most consistent points of difference between Imāmīs (along with most other Shīʿī groups) and their Sunnī brethren.[3] Amidst the immense, overlapping variety of ideas between different groups in different times and places, the question of whether a particular Muslim author is citing al-Kulaynī and al-Ṣadūq or al-Bukhārī and Muslim is a crucial component of where they fall in the spectrum of Islamic identities.[4] This is not a case simply of parallel bodies of texts that function in identical ways; as al-Ṣadūq will show us, underlying the Imāmī hadith corpus are a set of concerns and assumptions that are very particular to the Imāmī view of the world – of God, of prophecy and of scripture. Though hadith literatures have continued to develop from their origins to the present, al-Ṣadūq's career represents a time when foundational aspects of Imāmī hadith took the form that they have retained ever since.

Furthermore, al-Ṣadūq's value as a source for this period is in proportion to the unprecedented volume of writings that he leaves us. Prior to al-Ṣadūq, it is a very rare Imāmī scholar from whom there survives more than a single work. Al-Ṣadūq, by contrast, leaves us no fewer than eighteen (though this is a small fraction of perhaps 200 that he wrote).[5] The value of this body of work is not only its size but also its internal diversity – unlike previous authors, even those like al-Kulaynī whose *al-Kāfī* is very large, with al-Ṣadūq we have a chance to survey a real oeuvre, examining how he responds to different challenges and objectives across his many works.

Almost all of al-Ṣadūq's extant writings (especially when measured by volume) consist primarily of collected hadiths.[6] This has led to his works remaining valuable and surviving – even if later generations of Imāmīs disagreed with his thinking, as a source of the imams' hadith they still had cause to be read and copied. By the same logic, however, interest in the hadiths that al-Ṣadūq collected seldom translates into interest in al-Ṣadūq himself, and as a figure he remains little-studied.[7] Subsequent readers could evaluate his hadiths on their own terms for their own use, without considering the message that al-Ṣadūq was originally trying to convey. This gap between al-Ṣadūq and his later readers is all the more important given his antiquity – as we shall see, his approach to the imams' words is shaped by his early context, often differing substantially from subsequent scholarly norms.

What follows is on one level an intellectual portrait of al-Ṣadūq. Observing him across his written legacy and his context, we will discern his priorities and his projects, and what distinguishes him as a thinker. As for al-Ṣadūq's chief preoccupation – Imāmī Shīʿī hadith literature – through his works we will examine a formative stage of this literature's development, and the features and concerns that set it apart from other types of hadith literature. Uniting both of these objectives, meanwhile, is a concern to study al-Ṣadūq as a compiler. The majority of the texts he leaves behind consist not of his own words but the collected words of others (usually the imams), and the present study is underpinned by the conviction that this does not diminish al-Ṣadūq's authorial agency or his capacity for creativity and ingenuity. As we read his works, we will not be seeking to reconstruct the teachings of the imams themselves, nor will we read their collected hadith as mere substitutes for al-Ṣadūq's own views. These compendia enunciate a complex relationship between the compiler and what he compiles, and in examining them we will explore both that relationship itself and how al-Ṣadūq draws upon it to communicate with his readers.

Shīʿī hadith literature

We begin with a brief account of Shīʿī hadith literature and Imāmī Shīʿī hadith literature in particular (Zaydī and Ismāʿīlī Shīʿism have their own traditions of hadith which have much in common with the Imāmī tradition, but not so much that they can be done justice here without the discussion becoming unwieldy).[8] The study of hadith is now a venerable discipline in the Western academy, but it is a discipline overwhelmingly dominated by the study of Sunnī hadith, the multitudinous and detailed accounts of which remain unmatched when it comes to the study of other Muslim groups.[9] The flow of erudite literature from Shīʿī seminaries, meanwhile, has never ceased, but these works are usually inaccessible to Western readers, due to both their language and their terms of reference. While this situation has begun to change over the past three decades, which have seen marked expansion of Shīʿī studies in general, the study of Shīʿī hadith continues to be a discipline under construction. A few books (like the present one) on aspects of Shīʿī hadith or individual Shīʿī *muḥaddithūn* are available, but as yet there exists no book-length survey of Shīʿī hadith literature in a European language, while the subject occasionally surfaces as an addendum to introductions to Sunnī hadith. Similarly, one may purchase several excellent introductions to Shīʿī Islam, but in none of these does one find Shīʿī hadith discussed as a discrete topic. This is in pronounced contrast to introductions to Islam in general (often restricted largely to Sunnī Islam), wherein hadith is usually afforded generous discussion, if not its own chapter.[10]

Those acquainted with Sunnī hadith will find much that is familiar in the Imāmī corpus, in conceptions of both what a hadith is and how hadith should be used. Like the Sunnī corpus, Imāmī hadith is surrounded with debates over reliability and chains of transmission (*asānīd*, sg. *isnād*), occasioning an enormous accompanying literature devoted to identifying and evaluating the narrators of every text (known as *rijāl* – literally 'men' – literature). A canon of four books, including al-Ṣadūq's *al-Faqīh*, was eventually agreed upon by Imāmī scholars, though long after the period under discussion.[11] Meanwhile, inasmuch as hadiths serve as proofs for arguments and doctrines, they co-exist and interact with a spectrum of other proofs, both the other great textual proof, the Qurʾan itself, and dialectic, rational proofs of different sorts. Often Imāmī thinkers will be divided into different shades of 'traditionists' (preferred here), 'traditionalists' or 'textualists', who prefer to rely on the textual proofs of Qurʾan and hadith, and 'rationalists' who place greater weight on reason. Though there is a great deal of truth to such distinctions, they also have their limits, particularly their tendency to obscure the fact that preference for textual proofs need not be opposed to what is rational.[12]

Thus far, Imāmī hadith has little to distinguish it from Sunnī hadith. These questions of how to use hadith among competing proofs can appear as points of difference between Sunnī and Imāmī groups in different contexts, but do not figure as a consistent divergence any more than they do between different trends within Imāmī and Sunnī thought. To give only the most immediate example, it is commonly said today that Twelver Shīʿī law gives a greater role to reason and a correspondingly reduced role to hadith than Sunnī law does, but in al-Ṣadūq's era, conversely, it is common for Imāmīs to condemn Sunnīs and others for their excessive reliance on reason over text.

Despite all these similarities in theory and practice, Imāmī hadith remains a corpus sharply differentiated from the Sunnī one. The most conspicuous point of departure is the different authorities to whom the hadiths are traced. While Sunnī hadith narrates the words of Muḥammad,[13] Imāmī hadith accords equal sanctity to the words of Muḥammad, of his twelve descendants and successors, the imams, and of his daughter, Fāṭima. Often narrations from the imams are presented as what they have narrated in turn from their forefathers or from Muḥammad himself, but not always, and Imāmī thought does not qualitatively distinguish between these different types of text – they are all hadith.[14]

Not only is this a significant divergence of substance from Sunnī hadith, but it also points to a very different process of origins. The eventual Sunnī focus on prophetic hadith is understood to have concretized in the third/ninth century. It emerged from a long negotiation between competing ideas of authority: the independent authority of jurists, that of Muḥammad's companions and later figures of note, the authority of caliphs and so on. Within legal and especially theological circles, prophetic hadith was successfully justified in the face of several groups, notably the early Muʿtazilīs, who were unconvinced by the reliability and utility of these recorded recollections.[15] Early Imāmīs, including many of the imams themselves, were participants in these early debates about hadith, and early Shīʿī polemics made important use of hadith – texts recording Muḥammad's praise for ʿAlī, for example. For Imāmī Shīʿīs in the second/eighth and third/ninth centuries, however, these debates about the Prophet's authoritative precedent, as recorded in hadith, were inextricably tied to ideas of the role and nature of the imams. Each imam was considered the living successor to the Prophet who inherited his full authority to instruct the Muslims in their religion. They were revered as the indispensable proof (*ḥujja*, pl. *ḥujaj*) of God on earth, and were increasingly viewed by Imāmīs as infallible. At the time of al-Shāfiʿī (d. 204/820), an early proponent of the authority of prophetic hadith, and even of al-Bukhārī (d. 256/870), whose *al-Jāmiʿ al-ṣaḥīḥ* became the earliest of the six canonical books of Sunnī hadith, Imāmī Shīʿīs still followed a line of living imams from whom they could expect inerrant guidance. Therefore, while early Sunnīs debated the authority of written and remembered hadith, Imāmīs' intellectual focus remained the inspired, personal authority of their imams.

Accordingly, it is only after this situation changed and there ceased to be an accessible imam that Imāmīs started to devote to hadith the kind of attention that early Sunnīs had been according it for some time. Change came in 260/874, when the eleventh imam of the Imāmī Shīʿa, al-Ḥasan al-ʿAskarī, died aged 29, ostensibly leaving no male heir to be the imam after him. Soon, however, a significant number of the Imāmī faithful and their leaders declared that al-ʿAskarī had, in fact, had a son, who was now the new, twelfth imam but remained in a state of hiddenness or occultation (*ghayba*). This era of the Hidden Imam came to be understood as consisting first of a lesser occultation, when the imam still communicated with a line of four successive emissaries (*sufarāʾ*, sg. *safīr*) who relayed his words to the faithful, and then, following the last emissary's death in 329/941, a second, greater occultation, during which the imam was completely hidden from all until his promised but indefinitely deferred return. It was believed, as it still is by Imāmīs today, that he will one day emerge from this state of hiddenness as the triumphant messiah (*qāʾim* – 'the one who rises up', or *mahdī* – 'the rightly guided one') to restore the rights of Muḥammad's house and bring about a new era of just utopia in prelude to the Last Day.[16]

The complexities of this period of Imāmī history are legion, but for our purposes here it suffices to note that this was a watershed moment for Imāmī hadith literature. In the effective absence of their imam, Imāmīs were now in the same position as non-Shīʿī groups. The teachings of the imams now had to be accessed in the same way as those of the Prophet himself, narrated across the widening gulf of history as hadith. Accordingly, it is from this period that the earliest large-scale Imāmī hadith compendia date, and within a century after al-ʿAskarī's death Imāmīs had begun to adopt complex methods of hadith criticism similar to those characterizing Sunnī thought of the period, accompanied by similar scholarly institutions that based their authority upon the elaboration and application of these methods.[17]

This brief description, however, threatens to obscure the many overlaps and ambiguities in these developments. While many Imāmīs adhered to the doctrine of the Hidden Imam, others continued to promote alternative models of authority of various sorts, often favouring present, charismatic authority over hadith. Even while the idea of occultation was gaining traction among those Imāmīs who would become Twelvers, many Ismāʿīlīs, who had adopted a similar doctrine of a different hidden imamate nearly a century before, were now declaring that their imam had returned, the very corporeal ʿAbd Allāh al-Mahdī (d. 322/934), the first imam-caliph of the Fāṭimid dynasty, who at the beginning of the fourth/tenth century was embarking on a campaign of conquest across North Africa. The Imāmīs' shift towards a model of authority that placed hadith where a living imam had once been thus remained contestable down to its very fundamentals. Sunnī hadith literature developed in a context wherein the fact that Muḥammad was dead was undisputed, long-standing status quo, but Imāmī hadith literature emerged while having still to contend against the persisting ideal of a living imam, an ideal which threatened to condemn the authority of mere recollected text as radically inadequate. This was a hadith corpus with existential doubts, and *muḥaddithūn* like al-Ṣadūq were under continuing pressure to prove that hadith really could guide the faithful just as effectively as a present and living imam had once done.

Against these odds, the occultation, the twelve imams and Imāmī hadith nonetheless prevailed. Imāmī Shīʿism became Twelver Shīʿism, today the most numerous by far of the world's various Shīʿī communities. Though its history has witnessed many a would-be-messiah, Twelver Shīʿism has retained the doctrine of the Hidden Imam, and with it the location of religious authority in a community of scholars, scholars whose authority rests in turn upon their hermeneutic mastery of scripture – of the Qurʾan and of the hadith.

The life of al-Ṣadūq

Al-Ṣadūq thus stands at a critical moment in Imāmī intellectual history. He was collecting his volumes of hadith during the first few decades of the greater occultation, when the Hidden Imam's last emissary was no more. The intellectual endeavours preserved in his works well reflect these transformative and tumultuous times, but they tell us few details of al-Ṣadūq's biography – of events in his life that might constitute a more personal context to what he writes, or even give us some sense of the man beyond his contribution to Imāmī religious learning. Before proceeding to the main body of our examination of al-Ṣadūq's thought, what is known of his life can therefore be set out here. The following relies principally upon the most extensive biography available, produced by the editorial committee of the Imam al-Hādī Foundation (hereafter IHF), and also upon Hassan Ansari's more recent, briefer account.[18]

The richest sources available for al-Ṣadūq's life concern his intellectual associations as a hadith scholar, identifying his students and his teachers, the scholarly networks in which he participated and his travels between them. These sources fall into three main categories, two of which exist primarily in al-Ṣadūq's own writings: first, alongside his collected hadiths, he occasionally comments upon his own activities, almost always as they pertain to the transmission of a hadith, usually where and when he heard it; second, the assembled *asānīd* of his many hadiths offer a detailed map of his intellectual associations, not only telling us everyone from whom he narrated material but also giving a sense of who his main sources were, in turn suggesting his strongest intellectual and geographical links.[19] Beyond what al-Ṣadūq himself tells us, we have a third source in Imāmī prosopographical and bibliographical works. The first to mention him, the *Rijāl* of al-Najāshī (d. 463/1071) and the *Fihrist* of al-Ṭūsī (d. 460/1066–7), were both written within a few decades of al-Ṣadūq's death, each by a student of one of al-Ṣadūq's students. Together they offer a handful of biographical details, but their main value lies in their supplying catalogues of al-Ṣadūq's now mostly lost works, an essential resource that we will explore when we survey his written output later in this chapter.[20]

Al-Ṣadūq was born, probably in 306/918–19, into an illustrious scholarly family in Qum, reportedly as the result of a request made by his father to the Hidden Imam.[21] Al-Ṣadūq's father, ʿAlī b. al-Ḥusayn b. Mūsā b. Bābawayh (hereafter Ibn Bābawayh the Elder), was one of the most important Imamī scholars in the city, which was a major centre of early Imāmī learning, and it was from him and other teachers in Qum that al-Ṣadūq learned his scholarly craft. Alongside Ibn Bābawayh the Elder, the principal masters who emerge from the *asānīd* include Muḥammad b. al-Ḥasan b. Aḥmad b. al-Walīd (hereafter Ibn al-Walīd) and Muḥammad b. ʿAlī Mājīlawayh, both residents of Qum. These details already reveal their own limits, however: while Ibn al-Walīd is a comparatively well-known figure, whom bibliographers both praise and identify as a prominent authority, none of his writings survive; as for Muḥammad b. ʿAlī Mājīlawayh, almost nothing is known of him beyond the fact of al-Ṣadūq's narration from him, and there are other prominent sources in al-Ṣadūq's *asānīd*, such as Muḥammad b. Mūsā b. al-Mutawakkil, concerning whom almost no information survives at all.[22] As we will see in Chapter 2, much can be learned by relating al-Ṣadūq's writings to the meagre remnants that survive from his father, but these more detailed documents of such intellectual relationships appear as oases in a desert of lost books and unknown narrators. Overall, we know that al-Ṣadūq held some status among his scholarly peers, with al-Najāshī informing us that he was the leader (literally *wajh*; 'face') of the Imāmīya in Khurāsān,[23] but more antagonistic relationships with other Imāmīs are also discernible, most conspicuously the less traditionist-minded among them. We will explore these relationships in more detail in Chapter 2.

One area in which al-Ṣadūq's life can be reconstructed in surprising detail is that of his travels. These were both frequent and far-flung, with al-Ṣadūq's occasional references to his whereabouts revealing a scholar who criss-crossed the Islamic east in search of the imams' hadith. A particularly significant journey was his semi-permanent relocation to Rayy between 339/950 and 347/958,[24] the motivation for which is uncertain, but may have been the search for greater influence for the Imāmīya in this great political and intellectual centre of power. Regardless, al-Ṣadūq retained both his scholarly links with Qum and his distinction from pre-existing Imāmī circles at Rayy, but his presence there is an important factor in his work, as we shall see. Further travel seems to have been conducted around three pilgrimages to the tomb of Imam al-Riḍā in Tus.[25] The first of these began in 352/963, precipitating a series of journeys over the next three years during which al-Ṣadūq spent time in Baghdad, Kufa and Nishapur, as well as making a pilgrimage to Mecca. A second journey to Tus in 367/978 ended with a prolonged stay in Nishapur, whence, in 368/979, he again set out for a third pilgrimage to Tus. This time he journeyed eastwards across the Oxus, visiting cities deep into Central Asia and leaving his mark as a teacher and a hadith scholar on Imāmī communities across the region, from Marv to Balkh to Samarqand. It was during these travels that he wrote his legal summa, *Man lā yaḥḍuruhu al-faqīh*. It is likely that this long spell away from Rayy was linked to his probable banishment thence by the powerful vizier al-Ṣāḥib Ibn ʿAbbād, though the nature and exact date of this remains uncertain.[26] In any event, al-Ṣadūq finally returned to Rayy some time after 372/983, whereafter we have no record of further travels (al-Ṣadūq was, after all, in his sixties by this point), and he died there in 381/991. His tomb may still be visited in Ibn-i Bābūya Cemetery, in what has since become the little-adorned suburb of Shahr-i Rayy in southern Tehran.[27]

Though the preceding travelogue can be reconstructed in remarkable, indeed unique detail for an Imāmī of al-Ṣadūq's generation, it lacks two kinds of information in particular that are a frustrating loss for a study of his work. The first of these is a solid chronology for the dates of composition of al-Ṣadūq's works. Such a framework would have allowed us to examine how his thinking may have changed over his career, shaped, no doubt, by the very different environments in which he found himself, but the evidence is simply not available for its construction, with only a small minority of works yielding sufficient data to set a firm date of composition. As far as one can tell, the majority of his major compendia seem to date from the last two decades of his life; most of the surviving works, including the most ambitious (*al-Faqīh*, *Kamāl al-dīn*, *al-Tawḥīd*, *ʿUyūn*) contain hadiths from Transoxianan sources, making it very probable that they were composed after his travels in that region around 370/980, though the addition of new material to older compendia cannot be entirely ruled out. Al-Ṣadūq often cites his other books as he writes, but this cannot be taken as an indication that the cited work is older than the one in which it is cited, since in some cases two of his works cite one another.[28] These mutual citations could be explained by either later editing of previous works or the writing of more than one work simultaneously, but whatever the reason, it renders such citations quite unreliable as a source for order of composition. The possibility of manuscript-based evidence, meanwhile, is a remote one for such an early scholar. This aspect of our sources inevitably imposes certain limits; as we will see, al-Ṣadūq produced works of many different kinds, and to know their sequence – for instance, whether he at some times and places preferred one sort of writing to another, or emphasized one doctrine over another – would certainly allow for a more developed picture of his thought. Nevertheless, though we can detect him engaging different audiences with different approaches, nowhere in his works do we find an outright contradiction, such as would indicate a substantial doctrinal change of heart.[29]

A second hole in the evidence concerns al-Ṣadūq's life beyond his activities as a *muḥaddith*. As we shall see, hadith scholarship was not the limit of al-Ṣadūq's intellectual horizons; though he never departs from hadith altogether, his compilations evidence dense, sometimes hostile interaction with a number of other intellectual traditions, including *adab* literature and Muʿtazilī-leaning dialectic theology. We can see al-Ṣadūq by turns engaging and rebutting such traditions, but we have little sense of the contextual circumstances and personal relationships that lie behind these sides of his work. There are exceptions to this dearth of evidence, such as al-Ṣadūq's documented interactions with potentates at Rayy (see Chapter 3), but these can rarely be confidently tied to the composition of a particular book, particularly given the lack of a firm chronology for his works.

Though the specifics often elude us, there remain broad characteristics of al-Ṣadūq's historical context that constitute a clear and ever-present backdrop to his writing. The period between *c.* 340/950 and 440/1050 is often called the

Shīʿī century, owing to the unprecedented political ascendancy of Shīʿī groups witnessed therein, and Buwayhid Rayy was one of many courts across Western Asia and North Africa that were newly open to Shīʿīs and Shīʿī ideas.[30] We will presently see al-Ṣadūq engaging with the most powerful men in the land, and it behoves us generally to remember that he belonged to a group that was, at least some of the time, newly politically ascendant. When al-Ṣadūq appears especially experimental, even daring in his intellectual ambitions, it is tempting to evoke these circumstances. The Imāmīs, though, were not a unified force, and al-Ṣadūq's intellectual projects are always implicitly at odds with other Imāmīs who do things differently, particularly with regard to the imams' hadith.[31] Meanwhile, the other powerful groups with whom the Imāmīs co-existed constitute a mirror image of al-Ṣadūq's driving preoccupations. The new, confusing reality of the imam's occultation had to be contended against other, non-Imāmī Shīʿīs, such as Ismāʿīlīs and especially Zaydīs, who held a very different view of the imamate.[32] As for the imams' hadith, their sanctity and use was especially challenged by rationalist dialectic theologians, foremost among them the Muʿtazilīs, who were an especially powerful force in Rayy and Baghdad. Traditionist Sunnism, too, was in the ascendant, developing norms and institutions that would ultimately come to dominate Muslim religious scholarship as a whole, while Ḥanbalīs in particular could be violently hostile, and Shīʿīs of this period never lacked the impetus to contend their core, distinguishing beliefs about the imamate against an unbelieving majority.

Such is the available biographical context for our author. Given the scale and complexity of his works, it is certainly a frustration that we do not have a richer personal history to which to relate them. On the other hand, it is not least due to the particular character of these works, largely bereft as they are of lengthy discussions from the author regarding his activities and circumstances, that our knowledge about al-Ṣadūq's life is so laconic. It is to this character of his writings that we shall now turn.

Compilations and compilation criticism

Al-Ṣadūq was a compiler of hadith. While his surviving works are many, they offer us little in the way of theoretical discussions, systematic explanation of theology and jurisprudence or careful delineations of the Imāmīya from other schools. Instead, they present us with thousands of collected hadiths. Al-Ṣadūq's voice appears commenting upon these hadiths, explaining, summarizing and introducing them, but such appearances are spread thin across an immense expanse of transmitted material.

To many eyes this limits al-Ṣadūq's value as an object of study. While his amassed words of the Prophet and the imams are a potential treasure-trove for exploring the mostly second/eighth-century world whence they purport to originate, they are not widely held to offer much information about their compiler, beyond their illustration that he was a traditionist who preferred to deal with texts rather than discursive argument. Analyses of his thought have fluctuated between basing themselves only on those texts where he does speak *in propria persona*, and the problematic assumption that whatever is said in the hadiths he collects may be taken as a verbatim statement of his own view.

Al-Ṣadūq's fate is largely symptomatic of the broader state of the study of hadith and other areas of premodern Arabic literature during the last century and beyond. Scholars reading hadith compendia in the academy have overwhelmingly focussed on the origin of what has been compiled – the hadiths themselves – rather than treating the work and thoughts of the compiler as deserving of interest.[33] More broadly, it has long been assumed that the medium of compilation, widespread in premodern Islamicate literatures, is not worth significant consideration as a vehicle of expression. A Western model of literature that elates the sustained narrative of the epic, the tragedy and the novel, and which celebrates authorial claims to total originality, has little time for the compiler's fragmented, disemplotted relaying of others' words.

This book, conversely, aims to add to the growing body of scholarship that takes compilation seriously as a potent and various literary medium,[34] and in particular engages hadith compilation as an authorial exercise far more nuanced and complex than the simple transmission of historical material. The situation is well expressed in the words of Hilary Kilpatrick (who is speaking specifically with regard to *adab* compilations but could be describing a far broader group of texts): 'the designation "compilation" is no more, and no less, useful in the context of Arabic *adab* literature than the term "novel" is in the context of modern literatures.'[35]

With regard to hadith, a central dynamic has been what one scholar has described as the shift in interest from authenticity to authority. Today's questions are less frequently about what hadith can reveal of Muḥammad himself (and the imams in the case of Shīʿī hadith), and instead are increasingly about how Muslims in different times and places construct these texts as authoritative – how prophetic authority is represented, managed and enacted in hadith corpora. These questions place questions of compilation centre-stage. If we see hadith's authority not as an immutable, inevitable consequence of their prophetic source but as something that is constructed differently depending on the hadith's presentation and use, our attention must be drawn to the mechanics of how Muslims compile them. Especially with regard to hadith, an important corollary of this attention to compilation is its acknowledgement of diversity: rather than adopting a linear narrative of canonization followed by commentary and eventual stasis, more and more studies have shown the continually changing understandings and uses of hadith in different contexts and periods.[36] Many of these studies, in turn, have drawn attention to the diverse analyses of compilation undertaken by Muslim scholars over the past millennium.[37] Stephen Burge in particular has worked towards the theorization of a 'compilation criticism', one that envisages hadith compendia in conversation with literary theory as well as the tools of Biblical criticism.[38]

The pioneering work of this scholarship allows us to begin our study with the assertion not only that the assumption of compilers' lack of authorial agency in their works is theoretically untenable, but that it is also demonstrably false. Building especially on the work of Burge, what follows is a rudimentary outline of compilation criticism as we may apply it to the works of al-Ṣadūq. This rudimentary character is itself worthy of note; these are not revolutionary literary-theoretical propositions. Rather, the most important contention made here is that the basic questions that we train students to ask of literary and historical sources at an undergraduate level should also be asked of hadith compilations. What I offer here is little more than the integration of such preliminary questions into the formal characteristics of the hadith compendium.[39]

While it is hoped that this framework may be suggestive for further studies, there is little in the chapters that follow that is wholly methodologically new. Instead, where the present study is primarily intended to contribute to the study of compilations is in its scale. In surveying the whole oeuvre of a single author, we will be able to see how he compiles differently in different places and according to different objectives. This will give a sense of the richness and versatility of compilation as an authorial mode, but will also deepen our capacity as readers to understand its workings by extended familiarity with our chosen author. We will attain a sense of al-Ṣadūq's habits, his priorities, his nuances and his limits, equipping us with a capacity to anticipate the kind of thing he may or may not do in a given work, the better enabling us to interpret his texts. In addition, the second part of this book will present sustained studies of two individual compendia by al-Ṣadūq, examining them from cover to cover and giving a critical account of how each text functions as a whole.[40]

A framework for the study of hadith compilations

1. Authority and authorial intent

Hadith literature is almost by definition didactic literature of one sort or another. Hadiths are the words of God's appointed authorities on earth, and the act of presenting them to the reader is near-inevitably an attempt to engage that authority – to instruct, to prove, to argue, to argue with the weight of prophecy behind you. A principal role of analysis of the hadith compendium is therefore to discern how it does this, and to proceed with awareness of the compiler's capacity for different types of proof, of argument and of truth-claim.

Due to established reading habits and the immense potential authority of hadith literature, the wide diversity of its modes of address is often caricatured into a homogenizing syllogism: 'The hadith asserts that the Prophet said *x*, the compiler includes this hadith, therefore the compiler is claiming that *x* is true.' The limits of this equation lie not only in the blank hermeneutical truth that a single text may be read in different ways, but also in compilers' awareness of this fact and their efforts to control it, directing the reader to receive different truths and different kinds of truth from a given hadith according to their own authorial priorities. A foundational question for reading a hadith compendium thus becomes that of the compiler's purpose for writing it. What is this book for? What does al-Ṣadūq wish to convey to his reader? How is it supposed to be read – from beginning to end, as a reference work or through random perusal?[41] As we shall see, answers to this question can vary considerably, as, correspondingly, does the construction of his several works. This question of authorial intent is above all a rehabilitation of the compiler as author. The hadiths a book contains are not just hadiths, they are hadiths imbued with the specific purposes for which al-Ṣadūq has collected them.

There appear a number of routes towards answering this question, the easiest of which is to wait for al-Ṣadūq to tell us. Most of his compendia include some sort of introduction, and some of these give clear statements as to what the work is for: to demonstrate the truth of a particular doctrine, to instruct the faithful in a particular area, to refute others' polemics and so on. Less frequently, remarks made later in the work will state what it is for. An important further indicator is genre – if the compilation is structured in a manner associated with a particular type of writing (e.g., a legal manual), this can tell us what it is likely to be for (e.g., instructing the faithful in matters of law). Beyond these more direct indicators, there are many more potential signs of a compiler's purpose that may be found in a work's form and content, which we shall discuss in more detail presently.

Even as these declarations of purpose vary in clarity, an essential component to reckoning with authorial intention is the recognition that it might be more complex than the author admits. The extent of this can vary enormously – a straightforward, declared intent can be occasionally supplemented by other endeavours, or an actually deceptive statement of intent can be integral to a book's real goals. Al-Ṣadūq may not only be doing what he says he is doing, and may even be doing something else entirely.

This necessary readiness to admit incomplete authorial guidance or even deception is particularly counterintuitive to the received strategies of reading hadith literature. The encyclopaedic structure of most canonical works of hadith and their use as mines of information (be it scriptural or historical), not to mention modern search engines, all reinforce an image of the hadith corpus as an entirely open, transparent literature. The compiler is cast as a guileless transmitter, wholly facilitating the reader's access to scriptural knowledge. Conversely, as a growing number of studies have shown, ambiguity, even duplicity of intent and content are not only fully within the capabilities of hadith compilers but something for which the medium of compilation has an especial alacrity. The compiler seldom states her intentions or meaning directly; rather, her voice operates behind others' speech, creating a built-in opacity and deniability. In humility before the imams' words, the drawing of exhaustive conclusions can be omitted or even discouraged; details and clarifications that would be mandatory in a legal treatise are elided.[42] To acknowledge that authorial agency in these texts is less than completely transparent is not to denounce compilers as conspiratorially deceitful; it is merely to acknowledge, as has long been acknowledged of premodern Muslim historiographers' use of similar material,[43] that they write in dialogue with their context and that the truth-claims they construct from hadith are compelled to negotiate both with competing truth-claims and with the practicalities of conveying truth to their readers. As we shall see in Chapter 3, these machinations operate within a rich ʿAbbāsid literary tradition of exploring and experimenting with authorial agency.

Our analysis of authorial intent must therefore take these possibilities into account. An opening, clear statement of what a book is for by the author, though important, cannot be the end of the matter. Attention must be given to how he puts those intentions into practice, and whether there are elements of the compilation that complicate or even contradict its stated goals.[44] In practice this will often work in terms of identifying anomalies in a work. If a given work is meant to be an accommodation to sober rationalism, why is it describing how the universe is balanced on the back of a rooster? If a given work is meant to be instructing the faithful in their religion, why does its structure actively impair any effort to locate information about specific doctrines? Such questions take us into the complexity of purpose that compendia can possess, undercutting simplistic equations between hadith and pious instruction. Sometimes a work's intention is much more obscure to the modern reader than would be the case for its intended audience, but not always, and we must be ready for the possibility and utility of deliberate ambiguity on the part of the compiler.

These questions of authorial intention rest upon a broader methodological question for the study of compilations: that of relative sophistication. When we ask what an author intends to accomplish, this must be underpinned by a sense of what and how much he is likely to be trying to accomplish. Just how much effort are compilers putting into the selection and arrangement of their material? When it comes to discerning the structures that they create between their collected hadiths, how complex is too complex to be plausible? There can be no definitive answer to this question. An imprecise but still useful guideline is simply to accord compilers the same respect, the same estimation of complexity and consciousness that we accord other kinds of author. Again, it is no longer tenable to hold that sophistication is simply beyond their abilities. If al-Ṣadūq seems to do something that inescapably contradicts his stated goals, our default response should not be 'because he is inept'; rather, we should assume complexity, and ask why he is deliberately doing this. This approach may be bolstered by experience. As we read more of al-Ṣadūq's works, those of his contemporaries and works like them, we may accumulate a sense of what is likely – of the kind of thing we may expect al-Ṣadūq to be doing.

A useful concept in this regard is Ricoeur's notion of the hermeneutic wager.[45] Posited in the context of creating a hermeneutics of symbols, Ricoeur's 'wager' is the necessary gamble of assuming that a set of symbols have an internal logic such that they may be interpreted systematically. Only by such an assumption may we begin to decode them, and in turn our assumption may (or may not) then be vindicated by the meaning that we are then able to produce. Compiled hadiths seem a good deal less abstract than the worlds of signification for which Ricoeur devised this concept, but they face the same hurdle of Ricoeur's symbols in that the structures of meaning that govern them are not self-evident to the outside observer. The compiler does not tell us that we can only understand a given hadith properly by first reading those that precede it in careful sequence. If, however, we wager that this might be her intent, and then explore how our perception of a compiled hadith changes when read in its compiled context, we may find that the effect is substantial, possibly to the point where the accidental engineering of these effects by the compiler becomes very unlikely.

Before we move on to the practicalities of this approach, some encouragement may be drawn from the recent history of another immense literary monument of premodern Islamicate culture, that of classical Arabic poetry. For decades, scholars approached the poems of giants like al-Mutanabbī and Abū Nuwās as 'orient pearls at random strung', assuming and even arguing that these works possessed no particular coherence, no authored structures of meaning beyond the individual line. Then, towards the end of the last century, scholars started to wonder whether this really was the case, and began wagering that larger units of meaning could be found, even that whole poems could possess semiotic coherence (such as had long been accorded to poems by European and American authors). Today the validity of approaching classical poetry in this way is wholly established, with no hint that the fruits of this approach and the depth of sophistication that may be uncovered might be exhaustible.[46] Naturally, there is a great deal of difference between a hadith compilation and a polythematic ode, but the success of this approach in betting on coherence where there was thought to be none, of its unwillingness to write off the unfamiliarity of a literary form as mere incoherence, lets us proceed with cautious optimism.

2. Structure

A compilation is distinguished from many other kinds of literature by the way in which it is assembled of components. We are not usually reading the speech of the author himself; rather, we are reading units of others' speech that he has collected and arranged, and it is therefore through the selection and arrangement of the compilation's content that we look for meaning.[47] Indeed, Burge draws a sustained analogy between the function of the individual hadith in a compilation and that of the word in other kinds of literature.[48] Therefore, while our basic assumptions about authorship and intention are largely unexceptional, these units of meaning to which we must apply them merit some introduction. If hadiths are indeed the words of the compiler's discourse, then it is selections from the wider corpus and their arrangement into chapters and sections that constitute the grammar.

The following sets out the main structural elements of the hadith compendium: hadith, chapter, section and genre, along with the main lines of interrogation to which each may be subject. Uniting our approach to all these components as we encounter them in al-Ṣadūq's writings should be an awareness that a compilation's different components have a great capacity to act upon one another. How an individual hadith is read may depend on the chapter or section in which it is placed, and how a hadith, chapter or section is understood is in turn liable to be conditioned by others in the book, or indeed broader discursive dynamics that affect the book as a whole.

i. Hadith

In any given compilation, al-Ṣadūq is choosing which hadiths to include, for reasons (which may or may not be clear) concerning the hadith's content, its *isnād* or both. As he does so, he is meanwhile choosing to exclude other texts. Before we consider how hadiths are presented and located within a work, then, their very inclusion or exclusion can tell us a great deal.[49]

Paying attention to which materials are included in a given text (known as redaction criticism in Biblical studies) is not always easy when it comes to hadith. We do not always have at our disposal a clear picture of the corpus from which a compiler was selecting, and this is certainly the case with al-Ṣadūq.[50] Unlike scholars of later centuries, whose sources we can still consult ourselves, al-Ṣadūq's early dates mean that his are often the first surviving attestations of a given hadith, and even when that hadith is visible earlier, for example in *al-Kāfī*, that does not mean that *al-Kāfī* is al-Ṣadūq's source – rather, the sources he names are almost always lost to us.

Nevertheless, redaction criticism still points to real possibilities with an author like al-Ṣadūq. Though we can seldom see his direct sources, other surviving compendia from the period at least show us the kind of material that was circulating among al-Ṣadūq's Imāmī contemporaries. In al-Kashshī's (d. 385/995) material criticizing narrators, for example, we have the revealing testimony of a large corpus of which al-Ṣadūq seldom makes use but must have been aware.[51] More rarely, we are able to compare how al-Ṣadūq and his contemporaries select from a common corpus, such as the texts on the Hidden Imam discussed in Chapter 5.

It is in a compilation's basic contents that we also see shaped and tested the boundaries of the hadith corpus; what can hadiths be about? What should they be about? Authors' selection of their texts becomes a more or less transparent discourse in which scholars express their intellectual priorities – one scholar will gather hadiths that support his position, while his opponent will gather different hadiths that support his position, each implicitly contending that he is better articulating the true message of the entire authentic hadith corpus (and thus of the imams) on this point.[52] Elsewhere, differences appear over what constitutes a worthwhile topic in which to engage hadith, with one scholar gathering hadiths on subjects in which other scholars have no interest, or at least no interest in hearing what the imams had to say about it.

ii. Chapter

The most common structural unit of the compendium is the chapter (*bāb*, literally 'gate', pl. *abwāb*). When a compendium lacks this most basic organizational principle, it is not uncommon to find bibliographers marking it out as 'without chapters' (*ghayr mubawwab*). Through chapters a compendium becomes more readily legible – the reader who is concerned with a particular topic can go to the chapter wherein that topic is discussed, rather than simply ploughing through hadith after hadith in the hope of stumbling across something of relevance. Even as they are often a help to the reader, chapters are equally a tool of the author by which the reader may be directed, and as such offer a valuable guide to authorial intent.

The chapter in which a hadith is placed can determine how it is read. A hadith in which the imam's disciple Hishām is denounced for attributing false doctrines to the imam might be cited in an attack on Hishām's reliability as a source, but could instead serve in a chapter refuting the false doctrines he reportedly peddled. The oft-cited dictum 'actions are judged by intention', is placed by al-Bukhārī at the opening of his *Ṣaḥīḥ*, a necessary guiding principle to the often-complex instructions that follow. It is, however, part of a hadith discussing the flight from Mecca to Medina; only by al-Bukhārī's placing it as he does, rather than in a chapter discussing those events, does it appear as a governing ethos of the whole compendium rather than as a historical curiosity or legal detail.[53]

This direction of the reader is not limited to the hadith's presence within a given chapter. It has now been demonstrated with regard to a number of compendia that compilers precisely arrange the content of their chapters to various effects, sequencing them to create an explanatory or argumentative process, a particular emphasis and so on,[54] and we shall often encounter something of the sort in al-Ṣadūq's writings. This kind of minute ordering of material is by no means universal, and can vary considerably within a single book, a variety that can itself be illustrative – we may ask why certain chapters merited this extra level of organizational effort and why others did not.

Beyond individual chapters, the collected chapters of a work offer a potential map of which questions a compiler sees as important. Beyond the general concern of the work as indicated by the title and/or the introduction, attention to the number and length of the chapters allotted to given topics can tell us a lot about the compiler's priorities. There may also appear anomalies in this regard. Are there questions that do not have an allotted chapter, despite their apparent relevance to the book's concerns? There may be disharmony between a work's contents in terms of hadith and in terms of chapters, for example if a book contains a great many hadiths on the subject of cosmogony but does not group these into a chapter on the subject. A book may contain chapters on subjects of questionable relevance to its stated purpose, for example the inclusion of a chapter of stories about Indian princes in a book about the Hidden Imam. Similarly, an individual chapter may contain hadiths that seem unconnected to its designated topic.[55]

iii. Section

Large compendia are often divided into separate sections or 'books' (*kutub*, sg. *kitāb*; 'section' is preferred in what follows for purposes of clarity, with 'book' referring to an entire work). Sometimes this is simply a consideration of size, with little semantic content, but often it plays a structural role. A legal manual, for instance, will be divided into general topics – prayer, fasting and so on – on the level of sections, and then the chapters of each section will address the given topic's subdivisions – afternoon prayer, evening prayer, prayer while travelling and so on. As a structural unit, sections can be structured just as chapters can, the chapters they contain arranged to generate meaning in the same way that the hadiths within a chapter can be.[56] Demarcating a set of chapters as a separate section, as opposed to only part of one, can effect a statement of the independent importance of what they address.[57]

In many compendia, meanwhile, the author does not make any explicit structural demarcations larger than the individual chapters, but this does not mean that no such sections exist. When we survey al-Ṣadūq's writing on the scale of whole books, it often appears that he is doing different things in different parts of the book. This may be as straightforward as his answering different questions with different groups of chapters, but may be accompanied by more profound changes in approach – using different kinds of proof, addressing the reader in a different manner or pursuing a different objective.

The positing of sections is thus at the more ambitious end of compilation criticism; where they are left undemarcated, their identification by modern readers must remain hypothetical. Nevertheless, the readiness to entertain the possible existence of such structures represents only the necessary acceptance that some parts of a compilation may work very differently to others. This is of great relevance to the second half of the present study, where we will be examining entire works of al-Ṣadūq sustainedly, but it also matters whenever we read a compilation, for the same core considerations of structure and meaning laid out earlier. Whenever we read a chapter of a compilation or even a single hadith therein, we should be aware that its intended meaning – what aspects of the text are significant, what questions it aims to answer – may be shaped by the author's choice of which part of the book to place it in.

iv. Genre

Many hadith compendia can be fitted into identifiable genres. These may be genres specific to hadith literature, such as collections of forty hadith,[58] but also more widely used forms, such as the *adab* compendium or the legal manual. The genre of a work may influence and/or be identified in all of the preceding structural units to varying degrees.

Genre is another useful marker of authorial intention, real or apparent. This is especially true when it comes to a work's intended audience: a creed-type work may be confidently understood as having been written to educate al-Ṣadūq's fellow Imāmīs, while a compendium that adopts the forms of wisdom literature may be delineating its intended readership more in terms of class or education than by sectarian identity. Similarly, a work's genre engages it in particular literary contexts, bringing it into conversation with works of related genres and potentially insulating it from discourses associated with more distant genres. These associations, too, affect how the work is intended to be read: in the case of a hadith's authenticity, for example, if the hadith is in what is clearly a book of *fiqh*, the compiler can expect its *isnād* to receive the high level of scrutiny that operates in legal settings, but such scrutiny might be spared a hadith in the different generic setting of a biographical work, wherein conflicting narratives are a regular occurrence and standards of *isnād* criticism are different.

Compilation criticism remains a youthful science, and the delineating of genres among these texts is still far from exact. Even when genre seems an overambitious term, however, determining what kind of writing a compilation is constitutes a central part of taking these works seriously as authored texts. Though the components of a text – the hadiths – remain the same, by bringing these components into different discursive spaces a compiler may be aiming for a very different sort of address and with it different sorts of truth-claims. This has much to do with the overall subject matter of a work, but it further rests on the acknowledgement that different subject matter may occasion a different kind of writing. To the extent that we can identify the norms of a work's genre, we may in turn examine the extent to which that work conforms to the expectations of the genre or disrupts them.

The distinctive breadth of al-Ṣadūq's output sees him engaging with a corresponding variety of genres. Only very seldom, however, does he allow this to part him from the imams' words. It is common for writers of the period to compose some kinds of work with hadith alone, but also to compose other kinds of writing admitting different compiled texts or their own prose. In his surviving works at least, al-Ṣadūq is thus notably resolute in his overwhelming preference to include only the hadith of the Prophet and the imams, an authorial choice that acquires different, sometimes disruptive significances as he navigates different genres.

The structure of this book

This book consists of five chapters divided into two parts. The first part (Part I), 'Placing al-Ṣadūq', is a study of al-Ṣadūq as an early Imāmī hadith scholar. Chapter 1 will discuss his situation within the many political and religious factors affecting the Imāmīya in the later fourth/tenth century, most prominently the establishment of the doctrine of occultation among Imāmīs, of the institution of the school of law (*madhhab*, pl. *madhāhib*) as increasingly normative, especially among Sunnīs, and of the political rule of the Buwayhid dynasty. We will see how, amidst these factors, the development of a distinct Imāmī hadith literature becomes a nexus for core questions of how the Imāmīya are to persist as a distinct group.

Chapter 2 then examines the specifics of al-Ṣadūq's approach to hadith. Theoretical literature on the sciences of hadith and related subjects such as jurisprudence are still a rarity among the Imāmīya at this time, and al-Ṣadūq himself wrote no such works. The nature of his approach thus has to be pieced together from the various, more or less indirect kinds of evidence that do exist in his writings and elsewhere. As well as this reconstruction of al-Ṣadūq's thought, the chapter will argue through al-Ṣadūq's example that this dearth of jurisprudential and hadith-critical literature among Imāmīs was not a product of any underdevelopment of Imāmī thought; rather, it simply reflects the very different intellectual priorities of Imāmī scholars and Imāmī hadith literature at this historical moment.

In Chapter 3, we will turn to al-Ṣadūq's engagement with his courtly literary context, showing him to be much more than just a jurist and theologian. The chapter will give an analysis of several of his works that do not primarily address legal or theological topics but instead engage the forms and themes of *adab* literature. Ranging from works on themes of friendship and wisdom to highly miscellaneous compendia, al-Ṣadūq explores how *adab*'s conventions can be adapted to the priorities of an Imāmī scholar like himself, as well as testing how this elite literary space can function as an address to political power. The chapter reveals these hadith compendia as deeply embedded within this context of the Buwayhid court and its tastes, to the point where they are quite nonsensical if read as straightforward manuals of doctrinal instruction.

Part II, 'Reading al-Ṣadūq', embarks on full-length analyses of two of al-Ṣadūq's most complex works. Chapter 4 reads *al-Tawḥīd*, a book of theological hadith focussing on the nature of God, and Chapter 5 reads *Kamāl al-dīn*, a book about the Hidden Imam. These readings will not only take us deeper into al-Ṣadūq's ideas but also aim to shed light on the full complexity of his hadith compilations as authored, carefully constructed wholes. As they do so, they also show how integrally al-Ṣadūq's intellectual projects, as examined in Part I, are enmeshed within the way his books are put together. His doctrines about the nature of God and the imamate are not merely abstract principles to be formulated in credal statements; they are realized as ways of constructing and relating to scripture, in the tripartite conversations al-Ṣadūq choreographs between himself, his readers and the imams' words.

The works of al-Ṣadūq

Before we begin, the following provides an overview of each of al-Ṣadūq's extant books, listing each of his surviving works with a brief description of their contents, as well as a guide as to where they will be discussed in what follows.

- *Man lā yaḥḍuruhu al-faqīh* ('Every Man His Own Jurist'[59]) (*al-Faqīh*) – Al-Ṣadūq's most famous surviving work and also his largest, as already mentioned, it is now counted as one of the four canonical books of Imāmī hadith. Not unlike other members of this quartet, *al-Faqīh* does not entirely resemble the encyclopaedic model followed by the books of the Sunnī canon. For one thing, as its title suggests, it only concerns matters of law. For another, it does not include the *asānīd* of the hadiths it collects. As al-Ṣadūq explains in his introduction, this is a book to guide the faithful effectively and conveniently in matters of law, and including *asānīd* would only make it cumbersome (though he does supply them in *Mashyakhat al-faqīh*, a kind of annex to the work that catalogues its sources). The book follows the customary structure of a legal manual, and while most injunctions are affirmed by collected hadith, many are accompanied by al-Ṣadūq's own clarifications and summaries and some contain only al-Ṣadūq's words with no supporting hadith. Most discussion of *al-Faqīh* is located in Chapter 2, but as an exemplar of al-Ṣadūq writing with the voice of the instructor of the Imāmī faithful it will remain a key point of comparison throughout. *Al-Faqīh* was composed in 372/983 or shortly thereafter.[60]

- *Al-Iʿtiqādāt* ('Beliefs')[61] – Al-Ṣadūq's creed, this invaluable text outlines his opinion of the correct Imāmī belief on a wide range of subjects, including core doctrines like the nature of God, the infallibility of the imam and the punishment of sinners, but also a few subjects less usual in a creed such as how to confront contradictions in hadith. It is one of al-Ṣadūq's best-known works in Anglophone scholarship thanks to Fyzee's translation, and alongside its value to the study of al-Ṣadūq *al-Iʿtiqādāt* still numbers among a fairly small number of early Muslim creeds in English translation. While it is not a hadith compendium, consisting in the main of al-Ṣadūq's prose which he then supports with hadiths, it is an essential point of reference for understanding him, its utility as an example of al-Ṣadūq discussing theological matters in a didactic register corresponding to that of *al-Faqīh*'s representation of his mode of legal instruction. As such, it is a similarly regular point of reference.
- *Al-Hidāya* ('Guidance') – A short work, *al-Hidāya* is a brief guide to being an Imāmī. It begins with a short creed giving central beliefs, followed by a manual of laws. The former is shorter than *al-Iʿtiqādāt*, while the latter is nowhere near as comprehensive as *al-Faqīh*, but overall the work follows a similar model to *al-Iʿtiqādāt*, combining al-Ṣadūq's prose with supporting hadiths, mostly without full *asānīd*. It answers few questions that *al-Faqīh* and *al-Iʿtiqādāt* do not, but nonetheless provides the present study with occasional points of reference and comparison.
- *Al-Muqniʿ* ('Assurance') – This work is very similar to *al-Hidāya* except that it includes no creed section; rather, it consists only of a short legal manual. Accordingly, like *al-Hidāya* it receives little direct study in what follows but serves as a valuable example of a particular style of writing.
- *Faḍāʾil al-ashhur al-thalātha* ('The Virtues of the Three Months') – This little book gathers hadiths extolling the virtues of the months of Rajab, Shaʿbān and Ramaḍān. It is al-Ṣadūq's only surviving exemplar of a common type of

legal writing which outlines and extols various supererogatory devotions, as distinct from the circumscribed delineations of obligatory acts that dominate a work like *al-Faqīh*. Such literature will grow into a mighty tradition in Imāmī writing, but in al-Ṣadūq's corpus and context this book figures as a fairly direct exhortation to piety, and is therefore not much discussed in what follows.

- *Al-Tawḥīd* ('Divine Oneness') – A large and widely read work on theological matters, *al-Tawḥīd* is a lengthy compendium of reports mostly pertaining to the nature of God. It is the subject of Chapter 4's concentrated study.
- *Kamāl al-dīn wa tamām al-niʿma* ('The Perfection of Religion and the Completion of Grace') (*Kamāl al-dīn*) – Another large theological compendium, this time on the occultation of the twelfth imam, regarding which it is al-Ṣadūq's only surviving work. It was probably composed in 368/979 or shortly thereafter. This work is studied at length in Chapter 5.
- *Al-Khiṣāl* ('The Quantities/Numbers') – One of al-Ṣadūq's stranger texts, this long work amasses a very diverse range of hadiths and arranges them according to the numbers mentioned therein. It is an important example of al-Ṣadūq's relationship with *adab* literature, and thus is discussed extensively in Chapter 3.
- *ʿIlal al-sharāʾiʿ* ('The Causes of Laws') (*ʿIlal*) – Very similar in character to *al-Khiṣāl*, *ʿIlal* gathers a very large and diverse body of hadiths under the rubric of causation. It also receives detailed study in Chapter 3. *ʿIlal* seems to be earlier than most of al-Ṣadūq's other large compendia, with little sign in its *asānīd* of his later acquaintances.
- *Maʿānī al-akhbār* ('The Meanings of Traditions') (*Maʿānī*) – this is a third example of the pattern followed in *al-Khiṣāl* and *ʿIlal*, in this case collecting hadiths connected to meaning and interpretation. The book contains both texts with exegetical content and those in need of exegesis themselves, the latter receiving al-Ṣadūq's own interpretations and those drawn from other sources beyond the hadith corpus. *Maʿānī* is examined in Chapter 3.
- *ʿUyūn akhbār al-Riḍā* ('Wellsprings of the Traditions of al-Riḍā') (*ʿUyūn*) – One of al-Ṣadūq's more popular works in the present day, *ʿUyūn* presents a large number of traditions about al-Riḍā's life and death and an even larger number of traditions narrated from him containing his teachings. Aspects of the work are discussed in Chapter 3, though its significance as a history and a hagiography, unusually for a book of al-Ṣadūq, has received extended attention in previous studies.[62]

- *Muṣādaqat al-ikhwān* ('Sincerity Among Brethren') (*Muṣādaqat*) – This small book enjoins the reader to treat fellow believers with respect, collecting hadiths on the subject of the righteous conduct among Muslims. It is discussed in Chapter 3.
- *Al-Mawāʿiẓ* ('The 'Sermons') – This book collects texts from the imams on the basis of their rhetorical and kerygmatic value. It contains not only short aphorisms and maxims but also stirring sermons which exhort the faithful to piety, among them texts that al-Sharīf al-Raḍī would later deem of sufficient aesthetic quality to be included in his *Nahj al-balāgha*. It is discussed in Chapter 3.
- *Ṣifāt al-shīʿa* ('The Attributes of the Shīʿa') (*Ṣifāt*) – This work gathers hadiths in which are discussed and enumerated the distinguishing moral and pious characteristics of the Shīʿa. It is studied in Chapter 3.
- *Faḍāʾil al-shīʿa* ('The Virtues of the Shīʿa') (*Faḍāʾil*) – Subtly different to *Ṣifāt*, *Faḍāʾil*'s hadiths speak of the exalted position of the Shīʿa. It, too, is studied in Chapter 3.
- *Thawāb al-aʿmāl* ('Deeds and their Rewards') – This short work collects hadiths in which are described the rewards for a variety of virtuous deeds. It stands alongside a number of al-Ṣadūq's works that exhort the reader to pious conduct through hadiths arranged around a particular theme, but in comparison to other such works, such as *ʿIlal* and *al-Khiṣāl*, *Thawāb* is relatively straightforward, and its discussion here is therefore subordinated to that of more interesting works of this type. As such, it receives limited discussion in Chapter 3.
- *ʿIqāb al-aʿmāl* ('Deeds and their Punishments') – Very much the sister work to *Thawāb*, *ʿIqāb* is of near-identical length and structure, except of course that the traditions are united by the theme of how wicked deeds will be punished. Like *Thawāb*, this book is discussed in Chapter 3 but not as extensively as other works.
- *Al-Amālī* ('Dictations') – It is common for Buwayhid-era Imāmī scholars to leave works of 'dictations' (*amālī*, sg. *imlāʾ*), wherein are recorded individual teaching sessions in which the author narrates hadiths to students. Alongside al-Ṣadūq, al-Mufīd and al-Ṭūsī also leave collections of *amālī*. Their wide-ranging subject matter makes these books a useful source for the hadiths in circulation in this period, as well as an invaluable document of the oral dissemination and teaching of these texts. With a few exceptions, the genre has yet to receive much scholarly attention, and there remain

important questions about the nature and provenance of these books. Were they collected during a scholar's lifetime, under that scholar's supervision and sanction? To what extent are they an accurate representation of oral teaching practices, as opposed to a schematized representation thereof for literary consumption?[63] Al-Ṣadūq's *al-Amālī* is not much discussed in this book. This is partly as a result of this set of unanswered questions that surround the work, but more specifically because what purports to be a student's record of al-Ṣadūq's dictations has an unclear role in a study of al-Ṣadūq's own practices of written compilation. Not only is an oral dictation session inevitably different than the composition of a book, but it is highly likely that *al-Amālī*'s record of those teaching sessions is extremely partial, giving only the hadiths themselves without the discussions that would have accompanied them.[64] Such factors severely limit any meaningful comparison between the presentation of hadith as preserved in *al-Amālī* and that of al-Ṣadūq's authored compendia. Nonetheless, *al-Amālī* is a valuable work in its providing glimpses of al-Ṣadūq's approach to subjects (the death of al-Ḥusayn, for instance) about which his writings have not survived, and its record of oral teaching practices, however partial, is an important one. It will be an occasional point of reference in what follows.

- *Majālis maʿa Rukn al-Dawla* ('The Councils Before Rukn al-Dawla') – The given title is only the shortest of a number attached to this work, which is sometimes listed as five separate works, each containing one council.[65] These narrated councils take place at the court of the Buwayhid prince Rukn al-Dawla, in which the prince consults al-Ṣadūq on various matters and receives learned answers. This is not the only time we read of al-Ṣadūq's interactions with Rukn al-Dawla; al-Ṣadūq also narrates exchanges with him in *Kamāl al-dīn* and more briefly in *ʿUyūn*,[66] and in these texts the prince appears as a wise and sympathetic sovereign, thoroughly appreciative of al-Ṣadūq's enlightening discourse. Unfortunately, the insight this work promises into al-Ṣadūq's character as a courtly disputant[67] is hampered by serious difficulties of provenance. The work as it survives, in somewhat divergent manuscripts, clearly represents only part of a larger work, and the extent to which what does survive is wholly attributable to al-Ṣadūq or an eyewitness narrator remains unclear.[68] Though it is a fascinating text worthy of greater attention, for now these hurdles make it of limited use to us here, though it is discussed briefly alongside similar texts in Chapter 3.
- (Lost works) – The surviving books listed here are only a fraction of the total number of works that early bibliographies attribute to al-Ṣadūq. Al-Ṭūsī

> states that he wrote around 300 works, and he and al-Najāshī together give the titles of well over 200.[69] The discrepancy between these numbers and the quantity that survive is familiar to any student of the period, but they may also misrepresent the scale of loss somewhat. Later works incorporated earlier ones, an especially important fact given that the great majority of the lost titles recorded concern legal topics, and al-Ṣadūq introduces *al-Faqīh* as encompassing all of his previous legal output. On the other hand, there are titles among the lost works that address topics rarely covered directly in what survives, and any study of al-Ṣadūq must acknowledge that much of his thought regarding history, Qurʾanic exegesis and other key subjects is lost to time. The most significant of the lost works is his *Madīnat al-ʿilm*, a voluminous collection (perhaps 150 per cent larger than *al-Faqīh*) of hadiths on legal and other topics, though perhaps not ordered into chapters – a barrier to its consultation as a reference work that may well have hindered its survival. As with a few other lost titles, its surviving fragments (preserved in citations) have been edited, but these reconstructions, though valuable, give little sense of these vanished compendia as functioning wholes.[70]

This study aims to be representative rather than comprehensive. The first reason for this is the preceding consideration of source availability, which compels us to recognize that however detailed a portrait of al-Ṣadūq's intellectual life we may be able to create, it will inevitably be a partial one. A second reason, meanwhile, is the more modest hurdle of space. While an overall survey of al-Ṣadūq's extant oeuvre is feasible on a book-length scale, in a way quite impossible for the vast output of many later scholars, this still requires sweeping judgements of emphasis. As the preceding outline makes clear, I will be spending much more time on some of al-Ṣadūq's writings than on others, according to what is deemed of more interest to my own chosen focus.

Nonetheless, these constraints of space and ravages of time need not scupper aspiration towards a representative study of al-Ṣadūq. There are many facets of his thought and career that could be studied on their own account: his theology, his attitude to other Shīʿī groups, even his biography. The focus of the present study, however, is what I will argue lies at the very core of al-Ṣadūq's work as a scholar and as a thinker: his compilation of the imams' hadith and his understanding of that task. We will see in what follows a prodigious variety in al-Ṣadūq's writing, and we must be resigned to the fact that there was once more to be seen, but there is also continuity, a nucleus of sustained concerns for the imams' hadith that unite the many writings of al-Ṣadūq studied here, and point to a project grander than any one book or even the nineteen that remain extant.

Part I

Placing al-Ṣadūq

1

Living without an imam

Imāmī thought in the age of al-Ṣadūq

The Imāmīya in transition

The following two chapters give an account of al-Ṣadūq's most immediate and significant context – that of Imāmī Shīʿī law and jurisprudence in the fourth/tenth century. Al-Ṣadūq describes himself as a jurist (*faqīh*, pl. *fuqahā*ʾ), and the majority of his books concern matters of law (*fiqh*), with a significant minority addressing questions of theology, and it is correspondingly within this context of legal and theological thought that al-Ṣadūq's work is most usually studied. Here we will concentrate on his place within legal thought, both because we will deal with theology extensively when we read *al-Tawḥīd* in Chapter 4, and because it was within jurisprudence that Imāmīs of al-Ṣadūq's period produced their most systematic accounts of hadith. Nevertheless, this distinction is not absolute, since Imāmī legal thought at this time remained tightly enmeshed with ideas about the imam and his occultation. This first chapter, then, will give an overview of this intellectual context and al-Ṣadūq's place within it, while in Chapter 2 we will examine his writings on these subjects in more detail.

An account of Imāmī thought in the fourth/tenth century is by no means a straightforward one to give. This was a period of profound change and disruption for the Imāmī community, above all due to the adoption of the doctrine of the Hidden Imam's occultation and the arrival of Buwayhid political rule in Iran and Iraq. The surviving Imāmī literature from the early fifth/eleventh century looks very different to that of the late third/ninth century, but quite how this change relates to the myriad developments of the period, both among the Imāmīya and around them in society, is highly contestable. These uncertainties, meanwhile, are accompanied by a serious dearth of sources. Even when we are comparatively well served with writings from a particular author, such as is the case with al-Ṣadūq himself, these islands of extant material appear out of an ocean of lost works, a circumstance that curtails our ability to read them in proper context.

This chapter will accordingly take stock of these hurdles, both to present an account of Imāmī legal thought in al-Ṣadūq's day and, in so doing, to draw out the key questions that remain unanswered in the study of the Imāmīya at this time, in particular regarding their attitudes to hadith, and how this related to developing ideas about the occultation. The question of the imamate, usually a defining one for Shīʿī groups, is almost always framed both in Shīʿī traditions and in the academy as a theological question – one concerning the nature of God and of revelation. Conversely, in what follows we will see that in this crucial period of Imāmī thought it was primarily through the questions surrounding hadith – questions of transmission, of textual-critical methodology and of epistemology – that al-Ṣadūq and scholars like him worked out their relationship with the imam.

Traditions and survival

In what follows, I shall attempt to make sense of al-Ṣadūq's unusual intellectual character by tracing the intellectual maps within which he may be located. First, however, we must address an essential caveat to such data gathering, namely the question of survival. The ubiquitous problem of the survival of works from the early Islamic centuries (or lack thereof) is of especial relevance to a group like the Imāmīya, who were small and often persecuted and thus frequently at a distance from the centres of knowledge production and transmission. On the one hand, the corpus of available extant Imāmī works from the third/ninth and fourth/tenth centuries is in part a product of accident, such that we might have a different picture if the dice of history were rolled again. On the other hand, our available corpus is also a product of design, of the interests of Imāmī scholarly communities who were eager to preserve some early works even as others ceased to be of use and therefore ceased to be copied. Insofar as this is the case, then, our picture of al-Ṣadūq's era is also coloured by how that era was viewed by the generations of Imāmīs who came after him.

Such considerations are imminently pertinent in the case of al-Ṣadūq's own writings. The nineteen that survive once counted among an oeuvre of hundreds. Some lost works were absorbed into others, for instance epistles on individual legal topics whose material must have been substantially repeated in *al-Faqīh*. Regarding other works, meanwhile, such as al-Ṣadūq's lost commentary on an elegiac poem for al-Ḥusayn, it is not surprising that this was copied less determinedly than his ultimately canonized legal writings. In other cases, however, such as that of al-Ṣadūq's supposed magnum opus, the now-lost *Madīnat al-ʿilm*, we are simply dealing with an accident of history that must leave its unknowable mark on how we understand al-Ṣadūq as a thinker.[1]

These questions of survival are also essential to how we see al-Ṣadūq in context, all the more so due to his importance as a traditionist. Hadiths, by their very nature, accrue value from their antiquity – there is no such thing as a new authentic hadith. Early hadith compendia thus continued to be of great potential value for later generations of Imāmīs. Andrew Newman's work indicates that the copying of al-Ṣadūq's own writings saw a renaissance in early modern Iran under the Safavids, accompanying a broader renewal of interest in hadith that has been well documented.[2] Even early hadith compendia that potentially challenged later orthodoxies have survived in remarkable volume. Such a dynamic is likely to have served al-Ṣadūq's oeuvre well – many of his surviving works are somewhat obscure in purpose and design, but they nevertheless contain a great many interesting hadiths narrated from the imams. Providential though these dynamics may be for the survival of al-Ṣadūq's hadith-imbued writings, they are liable to distort our view of them. Unlike hadith, many other kinds of literature lost value with the passage of time. Legal theory or theological reasoning of earlier generations was only of academic interest to later scholars whose views and methods differed, all the more so if the earlier scholars' views were deemed heretical. It is a point of fact that the overwhelming majority of early Imāmī writings that survive are hadith compendia, and it is also often asserted by premodern Imāmīs and by modern academics that the early Imāmīya were largely traditionist. It is difficult, meanwhile, not to conclude that both this state of the sources and the hypotheses built thereupon are at least coloured by the fact that the writings of less traditionist-minded Imāmīs, who expressed their views in media other than collected hadiths, were less useful to later Imāmīs of whatever persuasion and therefore much less likely to survive.

A corollary of these observations is the need to recognize the plurality of Imāmī thought at this time. The Imāmī tradition of law and theology after the Buwayhid period remains based upon the foremost Imāmī scholars of Buwayhid Baghdad: Muḥammad b. Muḥammad al-Shaykh al-Mufīd (d. 413/1022), ʿAlī b. al-Ḥusayn al-Sharīf al-Murtaḍā (d. 436/1044) and Muḥammad b. al-Ḥasan al-Ṭūsī (d. 460/1067). There is therefore a temptation to see in these figures the culmination of all that came before in Imāmī Shīʿism, but this is to ignore the fact that these scholars were, of course, highly selective in how they drew on their

Imāmī predecessors. When, for instance, we are struck by differences between al-Ṣadūq and al-Mufīd, we are tempted to see a single, linear development, indeed a radical one. Instead, we should see them as representatives of separate, parallel trajectories of change.

Buwayhid and pre-Buwayhid

One of the two principal changes that al-Ṣadūq's Imāmīya were experiencing was the advent of the Buwayhid dynasty.[3] The Buwayhids were a family of Daylamite origin who rose from leading bands of mercenaries to establishing a dynastic federation that ruled over the central ʿAbbāsid heartlands in Iraq and Iran. The three brothers, ʿAlī b. Būya, al-Ḥasan b. Būya and Aḥmad b. Būya, conquered, respectively, Fārs, Rayy and Baghdad – the seat of the ʿAbbāsid caliphate – in the first half of the fourth/tenth century, together establishing a triad of dynasties ruling over these three centres. The brothers were of a broadly Shīʿī persuasion, but Aḥmad b. Būya did not depose the Sunnī caliph following his conquest of Baghdad, electing instead to maintain him as a puppet, for whom the Buwayhids theoretically acted as governors, while in reality they conducted themselves as sovereigns.

Not only did the Buwayhids emasculate the caliphate, humbling the political aspirations of Sunnī Islam, but they also took active steps to enfranchise Shīʿīs within their domains. Shīʿī courtiers could become viziers, Shīʿī scholars could become judges, and in Baghdad in 353/964 the city's Buwayhid ruler Muʿizz al-Dawla sanctioned and encouraged the public celebration (*ʿīd*) of al-Ghadīr, which commemorated the Prophet's designation of ʿAlī as his successor at Ghadīr Khumm, and commemorations of al-Ḥusayn's death on the tenth day of Muḥarram. Never before had Shīʿism had so assertive a presence in the public space of the ʿAbbāsid capital. The Imāmīya in centres like Rayy and Baghdad found themselves transformed from a community subject to state-sponsored persecution to one that was able to access the highest levels of courtly and intellectual life, a circumstance that meanwhile thrust upon them both opportunities for exchange and necessities of polemical engagement with other traditions.[4]

The impact of Buwayhid rule on Imāmī thought is difficult to overstate, and indeed it has become increasingly common to employ the distinction between Buwayhid and pre-Buwayhid when discussing the Imāmīya in this period. Pre-Buwayhid Imāmī Shīʿism, thus formulated, is substantially shaped by its distance from the centres of power and mainstream intellectual exchange. Third/ninth-century Shīʿīs produced elaborate, cosmological visions of the imams and their Shīʿa, visions that are little intelligible to more enfranchised groups and their systems of knowledge, be it Muʿtazilī theology or Shāfiʿī legal theory. The imams have extraordinary powers such as flight or knowledge of the future, and they and their followers are distinguished from non-Imāmīs even on a cosmogonic level, their souls fashioned from the same illumined stuff at the dawn of creation. This intellectual disconnect from the mainstream was accompanied by a readiness both to provoke and express hostility from and towards non-Shīʿīs, both by enunciating doctrines that other groups would find intolerable and by circulating unflattering narratives about Sunnī sacred personages like Abū Bakr and ʿUmar. So it was that when the Buwayhids arrived and the Imāmīs' marginalized condition was altered, teachings that were symptomatic of that condition moved to the margins of what became Buwayhid-era Imāmī Shīʿism. It was in the interests of Imāmīs both to articulate doctrine in a manner intelligible to their interlocutors and to be sure that those doctrines were defensible in the face of others' scrutiny. Buwayhid Imāmīsm therefore substantially dispenses with the now-outlandish-looking theologies of their forbears, such as flying imams and a corrupted Qurʾanic text, with the likes of al-Mufīd and his student al-Murtaḍā denouncing such beliefs as misguided excesses.[5]

Nor were such accommodations confined to the level of abstract doctrine. Imāmī intellectual life saw similar developments on the level of the discursive frameworks in which doctrines were expressed and of the institutional character of the scholarly community. One of the most widely recognized features of Buwayhid Imāmī thought is the rapprochement with Muʿtazilī dialectic theology (*kalām*), with many Imāmī scholars of the period having studied with luminaries of the Muʿtazilī tradition. The extent to which Imāmīs adopted particular Muʿtazilī doctrines at this time is contested, but what is not contested is that these are enunciated in a robust literature of Imāmī *kalām*, arguing Imāmī positions in the terms of dialectic theology.[6] Meanwhile, even as the institution of the school of law (*madhhab*, pl. *madhāhib*) had been solidifying among Sunnī groups over the course of the fourth/tenth century, we see a similar structure being adopted by the Buwayhid Imāmī scholars, accompanied by an expanding literature of Imāmī jurisprudence which was, again, couched in terms and concepts shared by other groups.[7] Indeed, centuries later, some Shīʿī authors would lament the developments of this period as the beginning of a 'Sunnification' of the Imāmī tradition.[8]

Al-Ṣadūq in between

The previous section describes stark contrasts between the Buwayhid and pre-Buwayhid phases of Imāmī Shīʿism, but with all such distinctions there are spaces in between, and al-Ṣadūq occupies just such a space. Active in the second half of the fourth/tenth century, his career covers the beginning of Buwayhid rule, and it is therefore thoroughly debatable how much his work shows the features that are usually considered characteristic of Buwayhid Imāmīsm, and correspondingly how rooted he is in ideas associated with pre-Buwayhid thinking. This ambiguity of his position is one that is firmly reinforced by scholarship on the period. Al-Ṣadūq is a regular appearance in the increasing volume of available studies of the Imāmīya in the fourth/tenth century, but he is almost never the central focus of such studies, despite his formidable extant output. This sidelining is no coincidence; rather, it is the product of categories and periodizations that leave al-Ṣadūq in between, neither of one type/period of Imāmī thought nor quite of the other. A brief survey of some of the language with which al-Ṣadūq is described in recent scholarship tells us something of this liminal position he is made to occupy: we see him condemned as 'clumsy', 'rambling' and 'cryptic',[9] as employing 'arbitrary interpretations' of hadiths,[10] as trafficking in contradictory paradoxical statements and inferior, untutored theological prose.[11]

A book devoted to al-Ṣadūq can only lament the negative tone of such assessments. We may observe, nevertheless, that much of the language just cited focusses on a perceived impenetrability of al-Ṣadūq – he does not write in a manner in which scholars of his kind are expected to write. This, at least, need not be disputed, but where we must part with such verdicts is when they characterize this simply as a product of al-Ṣadūq's ineptitude. Al-Ṣadūq is certainly unusual by most standards of what legal and theological scholarship of the period looks like, but this, we will come to see, is precisely due to the transitional phase that he occupies within Imāmī thinking on these topics. We may see this in a further set of recent descriptions of al-Ṣadūq, descriptions that consistently ascribe to him curious, indeed paradoxical labels: he is a 'semi-rationalist', someone engaging rationalist challenges with a traditionist methodology and a traditionist with Muʿtazilī sentiments.[12]

Such characterizations indicate why some have perceived an incoherence in al-Ṣadūq's work, and they certainly underscore his position as a figure who disrupts usual categories. As an erstwhile teacher of al-Mufīd, a foundational figure in the Imāmī 'great synthesis' of the Buwayhid period, al-Ṣadūq is often overshadowed by his student, relegated to a kind of prehistory with al-Mufīd figuring as the starting point of Imāmī thought proper. This effect is exacerbated by al-Mufīd's oft-cited, highly critical commentary on al-Ṣadūq's *al-Iʿtiqādāt*, the younger scholar's criticisms casting al-Ṣadūq's doctrine as merely an imperfect precursor.[13] Meanwhile, even as interest in Imāmī writings from before al-Mufīd has steadily increased, above all in the early hadith compendia of Aḥmad b. Muḥammad al-Barqī (d. 274/888 or 280/894) and Muḥammad b. al-Ḥasan al-Ṣaffār al-Qummī (d. 290/903), this has done little to foster interest in al-Ṣadūq; studies of earlier Imāmī Shīʿism rarely consider authors after Muḥammad b. Yaʿqūb al-Kulaynī (d. 329/941), a contemporary of al-Ṣadūq's father and author of the magisterial hadith encyclopaedia *al-Kāfī*, the oldest of the 'four books' of Imāmī hadith.[14]

Al-Ṣadūq is thus placed in an ambiguous *barzakh* between Buwayhid and pre-Buwayhid, between al-Mufīd and his successors and al-Kulaynī and his predecessors. It is little surprise that we find him being described with mixed terminology, but more surprising, perhaps, that his role as a transitional figure has not received more attention. The very fact that he is often excluded from accounts of these two often opposed periods of Imāmī scholarship points to his value as a witness to the process whereby one gave way to the other. That he has nonetheless been discounted as a source may well point to a further crucial factor in his relative neglect: that the nature of his writings is seen to detract from their value as historical source material. If, as we have seen, hadith compendia are considered unable to articulate the thinking of their compilers and, indeed, if the hadiths they contain are to be valued primarily as sources for the thought of the imams' themselves, even a hadith compiler in as significant a position as al-Ṣadūq is liable to be ignored.

Pre-occultation and post-occultation

To amend this state of affairs and fully reckon with al-Ṣadūq's position in Imāmī thought, we must turn now to the second transformative force at work in Imāmī Shīʿism in this period: the occultation of the twelfth imam.[15] In many ways, it is an extraordinary coincidence that two such different events – the death of the eleventh imam and the Buwayhid conquests – both happened to disrupt the Imāmīs at such proximate historical moments, to the point where the effects of either one without the simultaneous effects of the other are difficult for the historian to imagine. The same kinds of institution-building that can be attributed to the tolerance of Buwayhid rule can also be explained by the changes in structures of religious authority necessitated by the ongoing absence of the living imam. Similarly, many changes in Imāmīs' theological vision of the imam can be plausibly attributed both to interaction with other groups under the Buwayhids and to the ongoing reconsideration of the imamate brought about by the imam's vanishing.

Nevertheless, these two transformations do not quite overlap, neither entirely chronologically, with the eleventh imam having died many decades before the Buwayhids arrived, nor very much at all conceptually. The new Buwayhid tolerance was an emphatically external circumstance to which the Imāmīya responded, whereas the developing doctrine of occultation was thoroughly internal to the long-term currents and systems of Imāmī and Shīʿī thought. Though the death of the childless eleventh imam may be no less accidental than the arrival of the Buwayhids, the response thereto was wholly couched in the deliberative processes of Imāmī discourse and scholarship, the brute fact of being suddenly without an imam proving instantly malleable in the face of a venerable and rich imamological vocabulary whereby scholars could determine what this should mean.

Crucial to understanding the relationship between the doctrine of occultation and Buwayhid rule is the question of how abrupt this vanishing of the imam really was. Told a certain way, history casts the Imāmī Shīʿa as going to sleep one night in a world in which all their questions could be answered by God's infallible representative on earth, only to wake up the next morning in a world from which that representative was catastrophically absent. The oft-cited hadith, 'If creation were to be without a *ḥujja*, even for an instant, it would cease to exist',[16] gives a sense of the truly cosmic shock and bewilderment that this development meant. Tempering this dramatic picture, however, are the historical and social realities of how the imamate had been working in the earlier third/ninth century, and indeed how it initially continued to function in substantially the same way after al-ʿAskarī's death. The imam, of course, could not be in every place at once (not least when he was confined by the caliphal authorities), and there had long existed a network of agents and scholars who were the real face of people's interactions with the imamate. That these community elites were substantially in control of affairs is nowhere better illustrated than on the two occasions before al-ʿAskarī's demise when an imam was succeeded in his office by an infant son; on both occasions the elites of the community seem to have carried on quite effectively.[17] Meanwhile, though al-ʿAskarī's death and the consequent declaration that the imam was now hidden was a new development in what would become the Twelver line of imams, various other Shīʿī groups over the past century or more had turned to similar doctrines in the face of similar changes in fortune. In al-Ṣadūq's time and beyond, Imāmīs who accepted twelve imams were under pressure to refute other groups, the Wāqifīs or 'stoppers', who had identified an earlier (usually the seventh) imam as the hidden *qā'im* and therefore refused to accept his successors as legitimate. With these factors in mind, then, al-'Askarī's death appears as part of a gradual process whereby the imam himself ceased to be an active presence in Imāmī life, being increasingly replaced by a self-regulating community of scholars.[18]

This picture of the occultation as a sequence of developments rather than a sudden rupture is more formally recognized in the institution of the emissaries of the imam. Imāmīs came to recognize that for the first several decades of the imam's occultation, termed the 'lesser occultation', the imam was represented by a single designated agent, the emissary, who alone was in direct contact with the Hidden Imam and so able to convey his commands to the community, often in the form of letters. At the death of the fourth of these emissaries, however, it was declared in the imam's final missive that this lesser occultation was to end, marking the beginning of the greater occultation in which no emissary existed, and the imam remained wholly and without exception hidden from his Shī'a. The fourth emissary died in 329/941, only five years before the Buwayhids arrived in Baghdad.[19]

The initial development of the occultation doctrine in Imāmī Shī'ism is as beset by difficulties of source availability as any other aspect of the group's early history. Imāmī literature gives various accounts of exactly how these developments unfolded, but they are unanimous that the period following al-'Askarī's death was one of confusion (*ḥayra*), one where many Imāmīs left the fold in bewilderment and frustration.[20] An episode that became particularly infamous was the short-lived claim to the imamate of al-'Askarī's quite unhidden brother Ja'far 'the liar'. Nevertheless, scholarly works arguing for the truth of the twelfth imam's occultation did not take long to appear, and bibliographies attest to works on the subject of occultation as far back as the turn of the fourth/tenth century. The first extant discussion of the occultation comes in al-Kulaynī's *al-Kāfī*, composed a little before the death of the last emissary and the arrival of the Buwayhids. Al-Kulaynī's hadiths already present almost all of the key details of what becomes the standard Twelver narrative of the twelfth imam (excepting the end of the emissaries and the onset of the greater occultation):[21] he is the only son of al-'Askarī, whom his father designated formally as his successor before his death and who is now the imam, though the Shī'a cannot see him. Roughly contemporary with *al-Kāfī*, meanwhile, is Ibn Bābawayh the Elder's *al-Imāma wa'l-tabṣira min al-ḥayra*, which survives only in part, and these are then followed by a succession of works on the topic, not least among them al-Ṣadūq's *Kamāl al-dīn*, in which, amidst a certain diversity of arguments, we see the doctrine solidify. As for the period between al-ʿAskarī's death and al-Kulaynī, we have a number of hadith compendia from the early decades of the fourth/tenth century and possibly some from the third/ninth, but none of these collections give any substantial mention of the occultation.[22]

What these sources unquestionably show is that these decades saw an intense deliberative process that spanned the fourth/tenth century. It needs only a cursory examination of the broader history of Shīʿism to establish that the Twelver doctrine of occultation was not an inevitable consequence of al-ʿAskarī's demise. Other imamologies were available, and indeed were being enthusiastically pursued by both Imāmī and non-Imāmī Shīʿī groups before and after 260/874. The experiments with Jaʿfar and with the four emissaries, before the eventual agreement upon a hidden, twelfth imam with no emissary, bear witness to the context of doctrinal creativity in which the latter solution eventually emerged. In the mid-fourth/tenth century, in the aftermath of the last emissary's death, as the Buwayhids took power in Baghdad and as al-Ṣadūq was beginning his career as a scholar, this creative process was far from over.

Texts, authorities and institutions

Imāmī literature devoted to the occultation is often somewhat idiosyncratic and technical, concerning such specifics as the transmission of the imamate to an infant and how an unseen leader may provide guidance. Though sometimes obscure in character, these debates had far-reaching epistemological and social consequences for the Imāmīya, and their intersections with the changes wrought by Buwayhid rule raise a number of questions regarding this moment of Imāmī life and thought. We may ask how the process of establishing a hidden imam – a concept rarely wholly devoid of miraculous elements – influenced the ongoing debates regarding the imam's nature. We may ask, too, how ongoing, occultation-inspired changes to the imam's authority in theory effected how authority was exercised in practice in the Imāmī community – authority of texts, of scholars and of legal and theological rulings. Even if the scholarly elites of the community remained in charge through the period of occultation's solidification as a doctrine, at the very least they had a new set of questions to answer.

We have observed that an increasing priority of Buwayhid-era Imāmī scholarship was to tone down the miracle-heavy, often cosmologically focussed imamology that characterized some strands of Imāmī thought. Though some historians have sought to trace these trends in pre-Buwayhid thinking back to the imams themselves, others root them more recently in the aftermath of the occultation.[23] It has been suggested that a more absent imam, combined with the repressive environment that brought his absence about, is conducive to more supernatural understandings of the imam. Far removed from the imams' residences in Medina and Samarra, many beleaguered Shīʿīs in centres like Qum certainly did think of their master as an emphatically miraculous being.[24] It has been suggested, too, that the leaders of the Imāmī community, in an effort to engineer cohesion and stem the tide of confused defectors following al-ʿAskarī's death, adopted a more permissive attitude to such matters, bringing into the Imāmī fold beliefs that earlier generations of Imāmīs and perhaps the imams themselves had condemned as heretical excesses.[25] Both views in different ways tie the occultation to the highly miraculous imamological colour of Imāmī literature from the turn of the fourth/tenth century, thus casting the efforts of Buwayhid-era scholars as grappling directly with the legacy of the vanishing of the imam.

More tangible than this theological legacy, however, are the mechanisms whereby doctrines were arrived at. Imāmī Shīʿī thought shares with the wider spectrum of Muslim law and theology a fundamentally hermeneutical basis, with scholars delivering rulings and teachings based on their interaction with texts. As with other groups, the Imāmīya exhibit a diversity of positions in this regard, with some favouring the expansive use of independent reasoning in conjunction with texts, while others advocate the confining of discourse as far as possible to the letter of the texts themselves. Such tendencies are commonly designated by scholars as 'rationalist' and 'traditionist', respectively.[26] A related but not identical variable, meanwhile, concerns attitudes towards the authenticity of texts; the question of whether a particular hadith may be interpreted or supplemented with analogical reasoning must rest on the question of whether this hadith is reliably attributed to the imams or the Prophet in the first place.

These are, of course, central dynamics of Islamic legal and theological thought, and by the turn of the fourth/tenth century questions of hermeneutics and transmission lay at the centre of protracted, complex and often fierce debates. Though the Imāmīya, like other groups, were exercised by these questions, the nature of their approach is, alongside the occultation itself, one of the most distinctive features of the group in this period. They had been robbed of their access to the supreme authority of the imam, and this new circumstance dramatically impacted upon the Imāmīya's attitudes to the more widely recognized authorities of reason and text.[27] The potential for the occultation to disrupt Imāmī thinking on these matters is self-evident. While accounts differ as to whether the imams encouraged their followers to exercise independent reasoning, the possibility that such reasoning could incur the imam's censure was now decisively removed. As for hadith, with the indispensable guidance of God's *ḥujja* on earth no longer available from the imam's immediate presence, the recorded reports of the imams' teachings had the potential to carry greatly increased epistemological weight.

Hadith had been circulating among Imāmīs since the group emerged. Back in the second/eighth century, the imams al-Bāqir and al-Ṣādiq narrated and discussed hadith as did their followers. A significant change, however, is observable at the very end of the third/ninth century, precisely the time of al-ʿAskarī's death: this is the point where we see Imāmī authors compiling large-scale collections of hadiths for the first time. Though the surviving works completed at this time make no mention of the occultation, there thus appears a clear correlation between this change in the circumstances of the imamate and a change in Imāmī attitudes to hadith, one that spurred a new degree of systematic hadith compilation.

Even as it coincides closely with the developments of the occultation, this emergence of large Imāmī hadith collections is distinctly belated when compared with other groups. By the mid-third/ninth century, there had already emerged among Sunnīs not only a literature of voluminous hadith compendia but also a dense critical literature that attempted to delineate a demonstrably reliable corpus. The most famous representatives of these developments were proponents of the *ṣaḥīḥ* ('correct'; 'authentic') movement, such as Muslim b. Ḥajjāj (d. 261/875) (whose *Ṣaḥīḥ* includes a long introduction outlining his criteria for selection) and Muḥammad b. Ismāʿīl al-Bukhārī (256/870), but their works form part of a much broader Sunnī literature that both assembled and critically examined hadith.[28] This growing technical discourse around the hadith corpus and its verification is an especially conspicuous absence from Imāmī writings of the period. Not only do the early surviving Imāmī hadith compendia from the end of the third/ninth century offer no accounts of how their hadiths were selected, but the bibliographical record gives little sign that Imāmīs were producing such literature.[29] Moreover, when we do begin to see Imāmī engagements with these questions in the first half of the fourth/tenth century, these are still extremely brief and vague. A picture emerges of an Imāmī scholarly community in the third/ninth century that was largely unengaged in other groups' debates about what came to be called the sciences of hadith (*ʿulūm al-ḥadīth*), a disinterest that corresponded with the fact that at this point they still had a living imam to consult, and so did not rely upon a codified hadith corpus to the same extent or at least in the same way that many Sunnīs did.

Naturally, these circumstances changed with the eleventh imam's death, but the difference between Imāmīs and their fellows remained emphatic even as Imāmī hadith literature expanded over the course of the fourth/tenth century, as Sunnī approaches meanwhile took on an increasingly structured, institutional character. This was a crucial period in the longer history of Muslim thought in that it witnesses the consolidation of the schools of law as an increasingly dominant force. The looser coalitions of teachers and students of third/ninth-century Sunnī legal scholarship were coalescing into systematizing entities that functioned to train professional scholars, who in turn would propagate correct understanding of the law and how it should be derived, thus wielding considerable authority over religious knowledge production and practice. Hadith, of course, played a pivotal role, with schools differing over the ways in which hadiths should function as legal proof-texts, including the assessment of their reliability. Different *madhāhib* were distinguished by their legal method, notionally traced back to an eponymous founder, and a key part of their institutionalization was the codification of this jurisprudence in manuals that aspiring scholars would have to read in order to be certified by a given school. Devin Stewart argues that by the early fourth/tenth century every group needed a manual of *uṣūl al-fiqh*, and it is certainly true that even some non-Imāmī Shīʿī groups had such texts when al-Ṣadūq was writing.[30] This increasing normativity of the *madhhab* and its methods, meanwhile, could be coercive, the consensus of the community of scholars of law – as accredited by schools of law – becoming a binding measure of orthodoxy, with those who broke with consensus being condemned as heretics and even as apostates. Groups aspiring to any generally recognized legitimacy were therefore under increasing pressure to conform to a *madhhab*-like structure.[31]

It is a starkly distinguishing feature of the Imāmīya, then, that even in the late fourth/tenth century their jurisprudence, let alone any formal Imāmī school of law, remains difficult to pinpoint. The first surviving Imāmī text of legal theory is al-Mufīd's *al-Tadhkira bi-uṣūl al-fiqh*, and while earlier works are attested, they are conspicuously patchy. Old legal theory is not nearly as useful as old hadith, but even so it is remarkable that in the bibliographical record whole genealogies of scholars pass without a single one having composed a book on *uṣūl al-fiqh*.

Occasional figures stand out as having written on the subject, most prominently 'the two ancients' Ibn Abī ʿAqīl (d. mid-fourth/tenth century) and Ibn al-Junayd al-Iskāfī (d. later fourth/tenth century), the latter of whom seems to have unsuccessfully attempted to found a legal school, but they are unmistakeably on the margins of the Imāmī community, either receiving direct condemnation from later scholars or simply leaving minimal trace of sustained engagement with other Imāmīs.[32] Meanwhile, al-Mufīd's most cited teacher in law Jaʿfar b. Muḥammad Ibn Qūlawayh (d. 367–8/977–8), al-Ṣadūq himself, al-Ṣadūq's principal teachers, his father Ibn Bābawayh the Elder (d. 329/941) and Ibn al-Walīd (d. 343/954–5), and al-Kulaynī (who taught Ibn Qūlawayh) are not recorded as having written any works on jurisprudence. These are writers who are very much engaged with *fiqh*, even with technical matters such as *rijāl* (as we shall see in Chapter 2), but they do not produce written accounts of their methods.

This absence of a distinctive Imāmī jurisprudence corresponds with indicators that the structural elements of a school did not appear until the end of the fourth/tenth century.[33] In the absence of a separate Imāmī school, Imāmīs even appear to have participated for a time in the legal thought and institutions of Sunnī *madhāhib*.[34] An appreciable shift, however, is visible by the time of al-Mufīd, who is the first Imāmī scholar whom contemporary sources name 'head of the Imāmīya',[35] echoing the hierarchy of the Sunnī schools of law for which we see evidence in earlier decades. The first named head of the Shāfiʿīs was Ibn Surayj (d. 306/918), who was active a full century before al-Mufīd.[36]

Early Imāmī literature, unsurprisingly, is consistently focussed on the nature of the imam and Shīʿīs' relation to him. The imam, his identity, his rights and his nature are all elaborated in terms of their relationship to theological questions such as the justice of God, and it is regarding these theological technicalities of imamate that Imāmīs differentiated themselves from other groups and vice versa.[37] Conversely, as we survey the profound changes that mark Imāmī intellectual life from the late-third/ninth through to the fifth/eleventh century, it is not only in their theological conception of the imamate that Imāmīs are distinguished. The sources consistently show an Imāmī thought in the first century after al-ʿAskarī's death that continues to keep its distance from the mechanics, both theoretical and institutional, of how emergent Sunnī thought engaged and theorized hadith.[38] No less than their theologies of the imamate, these Imāmī attitudes to proof-texts and legal theory are marked by the unmistakable silhouette of the vanished imam. It would be most surprising to find Imāmīs conforming straightforwardly to the *madhhab* model of authority even as they were still organized around the emissaries of the Hidden Imam until the middle of the century. It would, too, be curious to find Imāmīs pursuing the construction of a codifiable hadith corpus in the manner of the *ṣaḥīḥ* writers at a point when they were still liable to receive written commands from the imam himself.

Conclusion: The first century of occultation[39]

Al-Ṣadūq emerges in light of the above as inhabiting an uncertain and unique moment in the development of Imāmī Shīʿism. The Buwayhids have arrived and the imam has vanished, and yet the consequences of these events have yet to take the forms that they will assume in the decades after al-Ṣadūq, forms that will be definitive of Imāmī Shīʿism forever after. Imāmīs have established that the imam is not as present as he was, but the occultation has yet to engender what for later Imāmīs will be its inevitable conclusion – a *madhhab*-like structure of scholarly authority, whereby epistemic elites mediate the ultimate authority as it resides in scripture, being the words of the imams and of God. The eccentric doctrines circulated by some Imāmīs are in retreat, receiving diminished attention by al-Ṣadūq as by al-Kulaynī, but the intellectual and textual mechanisms by which a given concept should be evaluated remain unenunciated in Imāmī literature. Hadith are a weighty presence in scholarly discourse, but they have yet to be negotiated in the terms already familiar to other groups.[40]

It is hadith, above all, that sits as the nexus between the driving dilemmas of Imāmī scholarship at this time. Not only was it now the only source of the imams' teachings; as such it was also fundamental to the question of how their authority might be accessed and routinized. Amidst a still-patchy record of Imāmī literature, al-Ṣadūq emerges to confront us with a prodigious stack of works, almost every page of which is given over to collected hadith. In keeping with the situation here described, the methodology behind his compendia is seldom obvious, but these compendia are, by the same token, an invaluable source of answers to the very uncertainties that they embody. Al-Ṣadūq and his fellow Imāmīs faced pressure to conform with the intellectual and institutional norms of other groups, while facing simultaneously the puzzle of the imam's lengthening absence and the increasing need to house the imam's (and thus the imams') authority in text.

2

Legal theory and the living imam

Al-Ṣadūq as a scholar of hadith

The scholar, scholarship and the law

This chapter will attempt a systematic account of al-Ṣadūq's approach to hadith, in terms of both how this worked in practice and its theoretical underpinnings. This is not a straightforward task; as discussed in Chapter 1, the first extant Imāmī treatise on jurisprudence and hadith criticism comes from al-Mufīd, and there neither survives any such treatise from al-Ṣadūq nor any indication that he wrote one, a situation held in common with a great many of his contemporary Imāmī jurists. This difficulty is not insurmountable, however, for what we lack in extended confessions of methodology we may try to make up for with other kinds of evidence that are scattered across al-Ṣadūq's own writings and elsewhere. Al-Ṣadūq and his fellows are not silent about the technicalities of their hadith gathering, though their discussions thereof come in the form of brief, often incidental comments rather than sustained theorizing. In addition, some assessments of al-Ṣadūq's intellectual character survive from one or two generations after him. Viewed in tandem, these two principal sources offer a workable outline of how al-Ṣadūq understood and practised his scholarly craft. Alongside these efforts at reconstruction, meanwhile, we must ask the question of why they are necessary – what it was about al-Ṣadūq's approach to hadith that resisted written theorization, and how this related to the unique circumstances of the early occultation discussed in the previous chapter.

We begin with *Man lā yaḥḍuruhu al-faqīh* ('Every Man His Own Jurist'), al-Ṣadūq's largest and best-known legal work. A comprehensive legal manual that is also filled with hadiths, *al-Faqīh* provides our most extensive view of al-Ṣadūq exercising his authority as a scholar of the law, and putting the hadith corpus to its most common and systematic use.[1] *Al-Faqīh* can, accordingly, tell us a certain amount about al-Ṣadūq's approach to these tasks, especially when compared with other legal manuals of the period, but it also exemplifies the reluctance of al-Ṣadūq and his Imāmī contemporaries to answer what are elsewhere essential questions of the nature of the jurist's authority and the expertise that underpins it.

Al-Ṣadūq writes in *al-Faqīh*'s introduction that he was asked to write the book by a respected ʿAlid in Īlāq, who had been impressed by a medical book entitled 'Every Man His Own Doctor' (*Man lā yaḥḍuruhu al-ṭabīb*) and requested a similarly comprehensive manual of the law, one that would encompass all of al-Ṣadūq's previous learning on the subject. Al-Ṣadūq goes on to tell us that he has omitted *asānīd*, partly for convenience, but also because this is not a book of every hadith that he narrates, only those hadiths that he trusts and upon which he bases his rulings. He also tells us that these texts are drawn from 'well-known, dependable books of reference', of which he gives a partial list, a valuable document of his intellectual networks that includes writings of his father, Ibn al-Walīd, and ʿAlī b. Mahziyār, but from which only one work – al-Barqī's partially extant *al-Maḥāsin* – survives. The book that follows is a rather unusual legal manual, comprising a combination of hadiths and al-Ṣadūq's own rulings. Some topics are addressed only by unaccompanied hadiths, and some are addressed in al-Ṣadūq's own words with no accompanying proof-text, while most incorporate a combination of the two; overall, the great majority of *al-Faqīh* is taken up by hadiths. As a collection both of al-Ṣadūq's *fiqh* and his most trusted resources, the book thus presents as a kind of summa of al-Ṣadūq's scholarship, an endeavour that well fits the context of its composition. Īlāq was a city in Transoxiana, a fact that, alongside the book's sources, places *al-Faqīh*'s origins in al-Ṣadūq's travels in that region during the latter part of his life. This book, then, is a self-conscious attempt to synthesize a lifetime's study, one conceived as al-Ṣadūq was labouring to spread his learning to Imāmīs across the Islamic east.[2]

Even as this brief introduction establishes *al-Faqīh* as a monument to al-Ṣadūq's legal learning, it stays silent on three questions that are indispensable for any substantial account of its author's *fiqh*: first, we are none the wiser as to al-Ṣadūq's deeper standards for a hadith's authenticity, beyond its being sanctioned by a revered teacher; second, the introduction offers no epistemological basis for the authority of the scholar (a common, often crucial feature of other legal writing of the period), and does not even mention the occultation of the Hidden Imam, with all its accompanying dilemmas of authority-making; third, the practical relationship between al-Ṣadūq's own rulings and his assembled hadiths is often unclear, producing an awkward fit between this mix of proofs and direct instructions and *al-Faqīh*'s stated objective of providing a comprehensive legal manual.

These ambiguities are in keeping with what we have already observed of Imāmīs' relative silence regarding legal theory in this period. Later Imāmī writers like al-Ṭūsī set out detailed models of the relationship between the sources of knowledge, the scholars who must interpret them and the masses who must follow the scholars, as do al-Ṣadūq's Sunnī contemporaries.[3] To some extent, however, *al-Faqīh* is an outlier even in comparison to earlier Imāmīs. Al-Kulaynī's *al-Kāfī* is also addressed to an interlocutor who has supposedly asked him to write it, but unlike al-Ṣadūq this request evokes core questions of epistemology. Al-Kulaynī's addressee has complained of the near-total abandonment of true knowledge by the Muslims of the day, who languish in ignorance and the futility of their own misguided opinions. Dependable knowledge, meanwhile, is hard to come by because of the confusion of conflicting narrations. The solution, of course, is a book in which reliable narrations are supplied for every need, and this is what al-Kulaynī supplies in *al-Kāfī*.[4] Al-Kulaynī thus firmly situates his authorial act within the economy of salvation, presenting the imams' authentic hadith as the sole, certain source of guidance in the face of catastrophic doubt. A thoroughly traditionist model of authorial self-justification, *al-Kāfī*'s opening is similar in tone to Ḥanbalī scholars of al-Ṣadūq's era such as Ibn Baṭṭa (d. 387/997), who also decry the Muslim community's lapse into division and speculation (the term *istiḥsān* – 'independent discretion' – is denounced by al-Kulaynī and Ḥanbalīs alike) and prescribe hadith as the only remedy.[5]

That *al-Faqīh* offers neither the traditionist self-justification of al-Kulaynī or Ibn Baṭṭa nor the jurisprudential defence of scholarly authority elaborated by his Shāfiʿī contemporaries or later Imāmīs is as good an illustration as any of the difficulties of assessing Imāmī legal theory in this period. In addition, however, it draws attention to the unusual space that *al-Faqīh* occupies between a hadith compendium and a legal manual. Unlike al-Kulaynī, al-Ṣadūq is not content to let hadiths do all the talking, adding his own interpretative and instructive voice as a *faqīh*, the expert authority who has also guaranteed the book's *asānīd*, such that he does not need to include them. Conversely, this independent voice is still very restrained, in comparison not only with many non-Imāmīs but also with al-Ṣadūq's other extant legal writings.[6] Two of his other legal manuals survive, *al-Muqniʿ* and *al-Hidāya*, both of which are much more heavily weighted towards al-Ṣadūq's own voice; a typical chapter in *al-Hidāya* or *al-Muqniʿ* begins with al-Ṣadūq's ruling on the issue, sometimes supplemented with a hadith or other textual proof, while in the case of *al-Faqīh* hadiths take up a good 90 per cent of the whole book.[7]

This predominance of hadith becomes more significant when we observe the only partial extent to which al-Ṣadūq coaxes his compiled texts into offering definite answers to legal questions. Robert Gleave has documented how both al-Kulaynī and al-Ṣadūq arrange their hadiths to simulate legal explanation, for example starting with a general ruling and following it with more specific technicalities, and he observes, too, that al-Ṣadūq is rather less precise than the earlier scholar, despite the presence of his own clarificatory remarks.[8] The overall effect in *al-Faqīh* is considerably patchy. In the section on fasting, for example, al-Ṣadūq addresses some topics with short, neat chapters in which he takes care to explain how his assembled hadiths synthesize to a single, coherent ruling.[9] For other topics, however, such as in a long chapter on the etiquette of fasting and what can invalidate the fast, the reader is afforded less certainty; the chapter begins with a hadith from al-Bāqir: 'The fasting person may do what he likes provided he avoids four things: eating, drinking, women and immersion in water', a text that might be read as categorical given its position, but there then follow thirty more hadiths stating various other conditions, such as avoiding cupping (*iḥtijām*) during the daytime, with no intervention from al-Ṣadūq to denote which and how different texts' stipulations are to be reconciled.[10] Furthermore, *al-Faqīh* integrates many hadiths that are barely legal resources at all. These include such hadiths as those giving the explanations for elements of the law (especially acts of worship), explaining how components of the Ḥajj reflect the deeds of Abraham, for example, and also material that offers more in the way of pious manners than legal rulings. Such texts include chapters on the virtues (*faḍā ʾil*) of particular acts – a common enough sight in legal literature – but also more substantial digressions, such as a long treatise from the fourth imam on rights (*ḥuqūq*).[11] As in many of his other books, al-Ṣadūq is also liable to segue into exhorting reverence for the imams, for example interrupting texts in praise of looking at the Kaʿba with the hadith 'To behold ʿAlī is an act of worship'.[12]

Al-Faqīh is evidently not the same kind of ruling-focussed legal manual that we find in *al-Muqniʿ* and *al-Hidāya*, and the features here described highlight a certain tension within al-Ṣadūq's own opening account of the work. The story of his invitation to write it, and indeed the book's very title, describe a book that may be consulted for legal rulings like a living *faqīh*, but when he elaborates upon the book's contents, al-Ṣadūq describes a book containing the hadiths 'On the basis of which I give rulings and that I judge to be reliable'.[13] *Al-Faqīh*'s title literally translates as 'whoever does not have a jurist to hand', but often its author seems concerned less to bring to hand a jurist's guiding rulings than to bring to hand the resources with which a jurist might construct those rulings.

Overall, the effect is a book that offers both more and less than an actual *faqīh*. It offers less in the sense that the hadiths that fill its pages are incompletely systematized into a sequence of decisive rulings. By the same token, however, al-Ṣadūq makes *al-Faqīh* more than just a source of legal rulings, presenting the expansive guidance of the imams' speech above and beyond believers' day-to-day enquiries.

Al-Faqīh's character may justifiably play a role in characterizations of al-Ṣadūq as an incompletely systematic thinker, and it certainly gives little away in terms of his jurisprudential method or his theology of scholarly authority. Nevertheless, it speaks loudly of the priorities of its author, and can thereby still tell us something about al-Ṣadūq's understanding of his role as a *faqīh*. When invited to supply a book encompassing all his legal output, al-Ṣadūq delivers not a work of comprehensive legal clarity but the maximum possible volume of the imams' words on (sometimes tenuously) related subjects. The separate chapters on how the Prophet and ʿAlī respectively performed ritual ablution (*wuḍūʾ*) do not exhaustively delineate best practice, but they offer a fuller view of revealed knowledge, a diversity of precedents that al-Ṣadūq evidently considers enriching rather than obscuring.[14] His own scholarly expertise serves to interpret, summarize and even supplement the hadiths with independent rulings, but in the main it qualifies him for what he deems the more valuable task of delivering the hadiths themselves.

A question of competence

To determine how and to what extent these priorities were expressed in a systematic method, we need to look beyond *al-Faqīh*, beginning with the early Imāmī accounts of al-Ṣadūq's work. A first notable feature of these assessments of al-Ṣadūq's character as a scholar is their markedly mixed verdict; we had cause in the preceding chapter to note many modern scholars' unease with al-Ṣadūq, and this is an attitude shared by some of his contemporaries, foremost among them al-Mufīd. Such was al-Mufīd's discontent with al-Ṣadūq's views that he authored a 'correction' of al-Ṣadūq's creed (*al-Iʿtiqādāt*), entitled *Taṣḥīḥ al-iʿtiqād bi-ṣawāb al-intiqād* ('Correcting the Creed with Commensurate Criticism'). Though both *al-Iʿtiqādāt*'s contents and al-Mufīd's criticisms thereof are predominantly theological in nature, during the course of these criticisms al-Mufīd frequently expresses his views regarding al-Ṣadūq's selection of proof-texts, views that are rarely complimentary. The recurring sentiment of *Taṣḥīḥ* on this subject is that al-Ṣadūq relies on weak hadiths with inadequate *asānīd*, which he then interprets in an unsophisticated manner, complaints that al-Mufīd usually follows with what he states are more reliable hadiths, upon which he then bases an amended doctrine.[15] As we saw in Chapter 1, it is a criticism that has found echoes ever since up to modern scholarly characterizations of al-Ṣadūq as traditionist, even primitive in his approach to hadith.

Notwithstanding al-Mufīd's displeasure and the dearth of sustained discussion of hadith criticism in al-Ṣadūq's own writings, a substantial body of evidence makes any view of him as an unthinking, uncritical tradent difficult to sustain. On the contrary, the early bibliographical evidence is quite unanimous in documenting and praising his acumen in such matters. Both al-Najāshī and al-Ṭūsī provide a detailed record of al-Ṣadūq's extensive output on the subject of *rijāl*: as well as a commentary on an earlier work of *rijāl* by al-Barqī, al-Ṣadūq is attributed a set of fifteen works concerning those who narrated from Muḥammad, Fāṭima and the twelve imams.[16] While nearly all of his recorded works are enumerated by the bibliographers haphazardly and with purely descriptive titles ('The Book of Marriage'; 'The Book of Pilgrimage' etc.), these books of *rijāl* are listed as a group and referred to by the distinguishing title of 'The Lanterns' (sg. *miṣbāḥ*), suggesting that they held a particular status as notable works.[17]

Alongside this evidence that al-Ṣadūq was a respected author on the subject of *asānīd* and their contents, both bibliographers also counterbalance al-Mufīd's complaints by according al-Ṣadūq unambiguous praise, even though they were both al-Mufīd's students. Al-Najāshī and al-Ṭūsī give descriptions of the standing and reliability of the authors they discuss, including any notable failings, and their comments on al-Ṣadūq are entirely, emphatically positive. Both laud him with such honourifics as 'our master (*shaykhunā*)', 'our scholar (*faqīhunā*)', 'illustrious (*jalīl*)' and so forth, while al-Ṭūsī praises his memory and critical eye for hadith and *akhbār* and his perspicuity in matters of *rijāl*.[18] Both authors are quite capable of heaping praise upon an eminent scholar while including caveats – such as the scholar's excessive reliance upon weak narrators[19] – and the lack of such qualifying criticism in al-Ṣadūq's case is therefore all the more indicative.

It is unfortunate that none of al-Ṣadūq's *rijāl* works survive to be analysed, but his extant compendia do offer glimmers of the expertise that younger scholars describe. Infrequent though they are, there do occur instances in al-Ṣadūq's writing where he gives pronouncements on the *isnād* of a hadith. He may be found remarking that a particular narrator is condemned (*majrūḥ*) by his teachers and should not be narrated from, that a generally distrusted narrator was sanctioned by his teacher in a particular instance, or that a hadith which his teachers did not explicitly sanction may be deemed reliable by independent means.[20] We also see him discuss, sometimes at some length, concepts related to the analysis of hadith, such as the property of a text of being too densely narrated to be forged (*tawātur*),[21] or what it means for a hadith to give general (*mujmal*) or specific (*mufassar*) injunctions,[22] and we can sometimes see him using different kinds of *isnād* in different works.[23]

It is evident not only that al-Ṣadūq was thoroughly conversant in the discourse of hadith criticism but that he was accorded significant praise for his expertise in this subject by subsequent generations. This does not mean, however, that there is no sign in his work of features that might have provoked al-Mufīd's ire. Quite apart from the fact that the evidence here assembled requires assembling due to al-Ṣadūq's apparent reluctance to produce any treatise on such matters, his works also exhibit peculiarities in terms of how the hadiths therein are presented, some of which are quite at odds with other Imāmī writings of the period.

An illustrative example comes in one of the early chapters of al-Ṣadūq's *al-Tawḥīd*, 'That [God] has Neither Body nor Form'. The chapter features a large group of hadiths in which the imam is asked by a disciple about the teaching that God has a body, to which the imam invariably responds that this is blackest heresy. As often as not, these texts identify the propagator of this rejected doctrine as Jaʿfar al-Ṣādiq's disciple Hishām b. al-Ḥakam.[24] Not only do they deem Hishām a teacher of falsehoods, but some hadiths further specify that he attributes these false teachings to the imams.[25] As far as these texts are concerned, then, Hishām is a deeply suspect source. The reader is therefore liable to be surprised to encounter Hishām appearing, unremarked upon, as a frequent feature of al-Ṣadūq's *asānīd* in the rest of the book, indeed in the very next chapter. Scarcely could there be a more iron-clad reason to distrust a narrator than being condemned by the imam as attributing false teachings to him, yet al-Ṣadūq seems unperturbed, an approach all the more striking in a work much of which is devoted to defending the integrity of the imams' hadith.[26] In the context of *al-Tawḥīd*, there is little doubt that these texts are included purely for their theological content. Nevertheless, al-Ṣadūq's willingness to mutely include texts that raise such serious questions about his narrators gives some indication of why some of his peers took issue with his attitude to *asānīd*.[27]

Reports that explicitly evaluate narrators are a rarity in al-Ṣadūq's surviving writings, obscuring the calculations and controversies that may lie behind his thousands of *asānīd*. One of his exact Imāmī contemporaries, however, Muḥammad b. ʿUmar al-Kashshī (d. 385/995), is much more forthcoming with regard to the kinds of evaluation that Imāmī *muḥaddithūn* were applying to their sources. Al-Kashshī leaves us the second extant Imāmī work on *rijāl*, and unlike al-Barqī's earlier text, which survives only as list of names of the imams' companions, *Rijāl al-Kashshī* is a book of *rijāl* as later scholars would understand it, not just identifying narrators but giving detailed descriptive material concerning their integrity or otherwise. This material is greatly illuminating for the study of al-Ṣadūq because so little of what we see in al-Kashshī is to be found in al-Ṣadūq's surviving works. While al-Ṣadūq's comments on narrators' reliability are so scarce, al-Kashshī gives us such information on every page, showing us (as we might have seen in al-Ṣadūq's lost *rijāl* works) that behind al-Ṣadūq's predominant silence on the subject, his narrators are the foci of a dense discourse of evaluation.

There is a frustrating hindrance to the utility of al-Kashshī's text as a contemporary source, namely that it only survives as an abridgement made by Muḥammad b. al-Ḥasan al-Ṭūsī. We cannot know what or how much al-Ṭūsī expunged, and therefore al-Kashshī's overall approach to *rijāl* criticism and his verdict on any given figure remains uncertain – apparently positive entries could have been stripped of negative reports and vice versa. More generally, al-Ṭūsī's abridgement leaves only narrated material, with no commentary from al-Kashshī himself, if there ever was any. Nonetheless, al-Ṭūsī's text is not a commentary but an abridgement, and we can therefore remain confident that the material it does contain is original and was in circulation among Imāmī scholars of al-Ṣadūq's generation.

If, then, we cross-reference al-Kashshī's *Rijāl* with al-Ṣadūq's *al-Faqīh*, the text in which he is most explicit in affirming the reliability of his sources, we find a picture of significant overlap but notable divergences. The most regularly cited sources in *al-Faqīh*, figures like Zurāra b. Aʿyan, Muḥammad b. Muslim al-Ṭāʾifī and Abū Baṣīr, find consistent praise in al-Kashshī,[28] but a set of figures upon whom he relies less regularly but still consistently, such as Ḥarīz b. ʿAbd Allāh and Hishām b. Sālim, receive both praise and censure.[29] As for al-Ṣadūq's more occasional sources, several of these meet stinging criticism in al-Kashshī's narrations, including Hishām b. al-Ḥakam and al-Mufaḍḍal b. ʿUmar.[30] Looking beyond *al-Faqīh*, moreover, al-Kashshī's evidence tells us that even at the points where al-Ṣadūq is most compelled to produce reliable proof-texts – in the defence of the imams' traditions in *al-Tawḥīd*, supporting his own edicts in *al-Faqīh* and affirming the existence and legitimacy of the twelfth imam in *Kamāl al-dīn* – he is still liable to draw upon narrators whose quality the Imāmī scholarly community had reason to doubt. This tendency, moreover, reflects al-Ṣadūq's corresponding unwillingness to dismiss a hadith solely on the grounds of its *isnād*. Across his writings, when al-Ṣadūq confronts a hadith that goes against his stated opinion, he sometimes points to problems of transmission, but this is almost always accompanied by a hermeneutic solution, whereby al-Ṣadūq reinterprets the text against its apparent meaning such that it no longer represents a contradiction.[31] *Isnād* criticism appears here as a tool to be used, but one that seems subservient to other kinds of discernment.

Narrating in the shadow of the imam

The picture of al-Ṣadūq as a naïve tradent is clearly untenable. Despite the absence of any detailed account of his methodology, there is ample evidence that he possessed significant, recognized expertise in the sciences of hadith, both in his own work and in the bibliographical record. At the same time, we can detect elements of al-Ṣadūq's approach that might well have raised the eyebrows of some of his contemporaries (as they clearly did in the case of al-Mufīd), both in his choice of individual narrators and in signs that he did not view questions of transmission as necessarily producing a decisive verdict on a given hadith's valid use.

Beyond this broad outline of al-Ṣadūq's practical approach to his sources, there do exist texts that suggest something of the more theoretical dimension to his methods, even if these are not treatises on jurisprudence as such. The unexpected main source for such material is his creed, *al-I'tiqādāt*. Most unusually for a creed text such as this, *al-I'tiqādāt* ends with a set of chapters purporting to discuss matters of jurisprudence. Chapters 42 and 43 address two questions of scriptural interpretation in extremely brief terms,[32] followed by a particularly incongruous-looking chapter on medical hadith, before we reach the final chapter of the book, which bears the promising title 'Belief Concerning Two Conflicting Hadiths'. For the researcher of fourth/tenth-century Imāmī jurisprudence, such a text is an exciting prospect indeed. Such expectations are to be frustrated, however. Al-Ṣadūq begins the chapter thus:

> Concerning the authentic narrations of the imams, our belief is that they are in full agreement with the Book of God, blessed and exalted. They are coherent in their meanings without contradiction, for they come from the conduit of revelation from God, and were they from other than God they would contradict. The apparent meanings of narrations therefore do not contradict except for a number of reasons.[33]

Al-Ṣadūq has already dashed our hopes in the first line: he is only talking about authentic hadiths that may seem to disagree. How problems of transmission are to be dealt with, let alone how they might relate to this problem of contradicting texts, is not up for discussion. Instead, he offers interpretative strategies to reconcile texts without impinging upon their sources, whether this be a question of linguistic understanding of a text or information about its context. This second strategy includes the possibility that some hadiths were uttered while the imam was in a state of dissimilation (*taqīya*): giving false information to conceal his true position (though how one tells whether or not a hadith was spoken in *taqīya* is not a question al-Ṣadūq discusses).[34]

Viewed in isolation, this passage offers a brief but unremarkable discussion of hadith criticism, in which the exclusion of questions of transmission is less notable than the inclusion of such matters at all in a creed like *al-Iʿtiqādāt*. When, however, we look to the hadith with which al-Ṣadūq follows his summary, the chapter becomes more remarkable. This hadith, which makes up the greater part of the chapter,[35] gives the response of ʿAlī to his disciple Sulaym b. Qays, who is perturbed by the discrepancy between what he has heard the imam attribute to the Prophet and what he hears attributed to him by the masses. ʿAlī roundly condemns the community at large, who attribute falsehoods to God's Prophet and sacrilegiously interpret the Qurʾan's myriad complexities with their own baseless opinions, before enlightening Sulaym with a ubiquitous feature of the literature of hadith criticism: the taxonomy of narrators. Like any good hadith scholar, ʿAlī lays out the different kinds of people who narrate hadith and the different qualities and defects that affect their reliability. There is the hypocrite who lies, the sincere narrator who nonetheless errs by fault of memory, and the one whose memory does not fail but who is ignorant of technicalities. ʿAlī ends the list with its essential component, the narrator who is free of all these faults, and can thus be trusted to transmit the Prophet's words accurately. Were it not for such unimpeachable individuals, the hadith corpus would be unworkable.

In other discussions of hadith, this superlative kind of transmitter is the person who is knowledgeable, possessed of good memory and moral character and so on. In al-Ṣadūq's text, however, ʿAlī emphatically identifies the fourth type of narrator, perfect and reliable, exclusively with himself. He alone attended on Muḥammad every night, questioning him on every aspect of his teachings, writing them down and committing them all to memory. The only other people allowed in the room during this unique instruction were Fāṭima, al-Ḥasan and al-Ḥusayn. At the end of every session the Prophet would place his hands on ʿAlī's breast and pray that his memory be infallible. The Prophet further declared that God himself had assured him that ʿAlī's memory would not fail, nor would those of the imams who would come after him.

Jurisprudence has here collided portentously with imamology. This hadith is not, ultimately, about selecting the best kind of hadith transmitter; rather, it is about asserting that the Imāmī Shīʿī idea of the imam, as the infallible conduit of the prophetic message, is altogether superior to a system of inevitably fallible *asānīd* made up of no more than human intellect and memory. The imam alone is the solution, but of course, for al-Ṣadūq and his fellows, things are not quite that simple. The imam is present but hidden, and the Imāmīya must access the imams' (and thus the Prophet's) knowledge through recollected hadith just like everyone else.[36] Regardless of the text's origins (which are highly likely to predate the occultation[37]), al-Ṣadūq's inclusion of it here serves to forcefully reassert an ideal of the imamate as a solution to problems of authenticity that does not represent the reality that he and his fellow Imāmī scholars confront. This is all the more striking because this lengthy text is supplied in a chapter that conspicuously neglects to discuss problems of narration in its treatment of hadith criticism. Al-Ṣadūq is not merely omitting to talk about the question of authenticity; his omission represents the subjection of that question to an older, more absolute imamology of the present imam that rejects the need to ask it.

We know that al-Ṣadūq is willing and able to engage with *asānīd*. What we see here is not a contradiction of that fact; rather, it shows what al-Ṣadūq wants to emphasize with regard to such questions. Recalling that this discussion is located in a creed, its theologizing/imamologizing emphasis is best interpreted as a rhetorical act. As he instructs the faithful in core doctrines regarding God, the Prophet and the imams, al-Ṣadūq also acclimatizes them to the still relatively new reality of an imam accessed solely via the hadith corpus. So it is that he downplays the awkward technicalities of that corpus that he must face as a *faqīh*, instead presenting a vision of the imams' recorded speech that carries the same indispensable infallibility, the same mysterium tremendum as the imams' living presence. The fact that the imam, the perfect narrator, now himself needs narrating from is an inconvenient truth to which al-Ṣadūq does not want to draw attention here.[38]

With these goals of al-Ṣadūq in mind, we may now make sense of the previous chapter of *al-Iʿtiqādāt*, improbably titled 'Belief Concerning Available Reports About Medicine'.[39] Offering historians a lively insight into the fourth/tenth-century Imāmī community, al-Ṣadūq here supplies a list of reasons why heeding hadiths containing medical advice may be inadvisable for one's health, even though the imam himself is not at fault. The first thing that strikes us about this chapter is that it offers a more substantial discussion of hadith and its potential hazards than that presented in the next chapter, which purports to focus on such matters. Al-Ṣadūq begins with reasons why a perfectly narrated hadith might still have limited medicinal value (the imam, for instance, might know better than the complainant the nature of his disease, and so prescribe a remedy that does not match the named complaint), but he also warns the reader that some hadiths may be incorrectly narrated, be it by mishap or by malice. The problem of narrators is, at least, acknowledged here, but what follows again subjects it to the theological. The bulk of the chapter is dedicated to the broader point that while some hadiths surely do contain medical knowledge, the imams' fundamental teaching on the subject is that the believer should respond to illness with prayer: 'God does not cure whosoever is not cured by [saying] "praise be to God".' As well as illustrating this maxim with a story about King David and a talking plant that made dubious claims to curative properties, al-Ṣadūq states that it is confirmed by sound (*ṣaḥīḥ*) hadiths.

The chapter confirms what we already knew: that al-Ṣadūq has no inherent hostility to discussing the sources of hadith. It also shows, though, that his real emphasis is on protecting the hadith corpus as a locus for the imams' authority. The upshot of the chapter is that believers should not probe into areas of the imams' hadith that are likely to cause confusion and lead to questioning the overall validity of the corpus or even of the imams themselves. Instead, they should abide by that same corpus' stern command: not to deliberate over different narrated remedies involving honey and aubergines, but simply to pray. Medical hadiths serve as a metonym for the imams' hadith in general, which should be revered beyond concerns over the apparent strangeness of an individual text, and this apparently incongruous chapter thus dovetails with the following chapter to deliver the closing message of al-Ṣadūq's creed: to respect the imams' hadith.

The approach that emerges from *al-Iʿtiqādāt* is thus composed of two components. There is the simply practical concern not to involve the Imāmī faithful in the worrisome business of *isnād* criticism, but there is also the theological background to this, the echo of doctrines dating from before the occultation in which the imam was conceived of as obviating the need for such vicissitudes of transmission as troubled non-Imāmīs. The place of this theological anxiety in al-Ṣadūq's attitude to *asānīd* is best explored by turning to the work of his father. *Al-Imāma wa'l-tabṣira min al-ḥayra* ('The Imamate and Insight that Delivers from Confusion') is a small, apparently incomplete text about the twelfth imam and the occultation, and is Ibn Bābawayh the Elder's only certifiable surviving work.[40] Its introduction, however, contains one of the very earliest extant Imāmī discussions of the problems of hadith criticism, and one in which we see the ambivalence of *al-I'tiqādāt* eclipsed by a full-blown theology of textual inconsistency.

Al-Imāma wa'l-tabṣira addresses itself to the confusion (*ḥayra*) brought about by the still-new occultation, an integral part of which is the profusion of conflicting narrations from and about the imams.[41] The central concept at work here, for Ibn Bābawayh the Elder, is *taqīya*. Like al-Ṣadūq in *al-I'tiqādāt*, he explains that contradictory hadiths can arise out of the imams having spoken through *taqīya*.[42] Where al-Ṣadūq's father goes much further, however, is in his weight of emphasis on *taqīya* both as the main source of conflicting texts and as something utterly, existentially necessary. Ibn Bābawayh the Elder does not deny that the imam is compelled to hide for fear of persecution, but he also argues that hiddenness and the withholding of information are an indispensable part of God's benevolent guidance of humanity. Concerning the End Times, for example, prophets and imams have always asserted that the Day of Judgement is near, thus motivating their followers towards righteousness, and yet, infallible as they were, they knew that in fact it would not occur for centuries. Similarly, Jesus could not tell his disciples that in a few hundred years the *sharī'a* he preached would be abrogated by that of Muḥammad, as this would doubtless deflate their enthusiasm somewhat. Similarly, Ibn Bābawayh the Elder explains, the time of the twelfth imam's reappearance is concealed, even as the imams' hadiths are often difficult to understand, for the believers' own good.[43] When it comes to individual texts, meanwhile, Ibn Bābawayh the Elder attempts to manage even the most troublesome reports by means of suggested, rationalized *taqīya* rather than resorting to source criticism. Even the proof-texts of rival Shī'ī groups, such as a hadith in which Imam Mūsā al-Kāẓim declares himself the *qā'im* (as per the beliefs of the Wāqifīya), are not dismissed as forgeries as they will be by later Imāmīs, but instead adduced as further examples of an imam deceiving his followers in accordance with God's plan.[44]

Ibn Bābawayh the Elder's text epitomizes the capacity of Shī'ī thought to reimagine totally the dynamics of authority at work in other groups. He is writing in the first half of the fourth/tenth century, when most non-Imāmīs are debating conflicting hadiths in terms of jurisprudence, *asānīd* and catalogues of narrators. For Ibn Bābawayh the Elder, however, these texts are also part of a quite separate set of ideas: the force of mystery whereby God, in his wisdom, guides and guards humanity against the perils of too much knowledge. Moreover, *al-Imāma wa'l-tabṣira* contains several arguments refuting other Imāmīs who explain divergent hadiths not through *taqīya* but *badā'* – the notion that God can change his mind – indicating that Ibn Bābawayh the Elder's model was only one of several such theological solutions to textual–critical problems. Like al-Ṣadūq, it is inconceivable that Ibn Bābawayh the Elder was not engaged in the usual business of analysing the sources of his hadiths, but the epistemological ideals of the imamate irrupt into these processes, demanding that they be reimagined or even imagined away, the better to fit the promise of a just God dispensing inerrant guidance.

In the previous chapter, we observed that al-Ṣadūq marks the tail end of the first century after the imam's occultation. We now see how that historical dynamic plays out in the details of his approach to hadith. Still embedded in this approach are the echoes of an impulse that we find much stronger in the work of his father, an impulse to preserve the idea of the imam as a means of theologizing away the textual instabilities of hadith literature in all its cumbersome vastness. It was only natural that this aspiration would not perish in the same instant as the eleventh imam, even as it was inevitable that it would gradually cease to be plausible – that the occultation would retreat from questions of jurisprudence, even as jurisprudence took on the systematic character of the *madhāhib*.[45] In al-Ṣadūq's writings, accordingly, these echoes appear more as rhetoric than as a committed theology, but still rhetoric that profoundly affects his attitude to systematic jurisprudence.[46] Al-Ṣadūq acknowledges the *isnād* and its vagaries, in which he has some expertise, but this acknowledgement co-exists uneasily with the desire to portray a hadith corpus that is untroubled by such things, still maintaining the guaranteed access to prophetic knowledge embodied by the imams themselves.[47]

Tradition, reason and rhetoric

The early history of Imāmī jurisprudence, as with many other areas of Islamic thought in this period and beyond, has predominantly been understood as a dialogue between traditionists and rationalists of various colours. Accounts both by modern scholars and by Shīʿī authors centuries ago portray a spectrum with the dialectic-shunning, literalist reader of scripture at one extreme and the hadith-spurning partisan of unfettered reason at the other end, with the inevitable 'great synthesis' between reason and revelation inevitably emerging in the middle.[48] What the preceding analysis suggests is that this model requires an additional, complicating factor when it comes to the Imāmīya at this time: the rhetorical stance towards *isnād* criticism adopted by different scholars and scholarly factions. A full analysis of this period of Imāmī thought must recognize the degree to which *isnād* criticism, as practised by other groups, was felt by some Imāmīs to threaten the hadith corpus' capacity to retain the infallible character of the living imam. Such an analysis, accordingly, must acknowledge different Imāmī scholars' relative (un)readiness to elaborate upon matters of transmission and *asānīd* as a significant variable between different Imāmī approaches to jurisprudence.

A survey of how Imāmī authors in this period present their collected narrations confirms this rhetorical dimension as an important differentiating factor. Faced with the dearth of Imāmī jurisprudential treatises from the era, we can instead turn to smaller, often introductory remarks with which Imāmī hadith collectors do or do not emphasize the quality of transmission of the narrations they present. An important first text to examine is the only surviving work of al-Ṣadūq's exact contemporary Ibn Qūlawayh. *Kāmil al-ziyārāt* is a manual for pilgrimage to the imams' tombs that is almost entirely made up of hadiths. Accordingly, in his short introduction Ibn Qūlawayh announces the following:

> I have not included herein any hadith narrated from anomalous persons (*al-shudhdhādh min al-rijāl*),[49] narrated as their traditions are from those who have been mentioned but who are not among those known for narration, famed for hadith and knowledge.[50]

Brief as it is, this declaration is a striking departure from al-Ṣadūq's occasional, brief remarks. Not only is it a guarantee of authenticity, but it elaborates on this assertion with a discussion of the kinds of narrators who have been used and the kinds who have been avoided. It is not the discussion of narrators per se that distinguishes Ibn Qūlawayh's remarks, nor, indeed, is *Kāmil al-ziyārāt* entirely devoid of self-evidently weak *asānīd*. What is significant here is that he frames his work in these terms, foregrounding strength of transmission in a manner more forceful and detailed than in any of al-Ṣadūq's introductions, and quite unlike the theological treatments of hadith criticism used by him and his father. Though Ibn Qūlawayh's remarks are especially detailed, briefer affirmations of reliability are also found introducing compendia by Imāmīs of earlier generations. ʿAlī b. Ibrāhīm al-Qummī (d. after 307/919) states at the start of his *tafsīr* that it comprises hadiths 'from our masters and those we trust (sg. *thiqa*)';[51] al-Kulaynī himself presents *al-Kāfī* as offering knowledge based on 'sound traditions from the truthful ones and established *sunan* upon which one can act'.[52] Again, both books are their author's only extant work, but each gives in these meagre sentences a more definitive guarantee of the reliability of their contents than all but one of al-Ṣadūq's surviving introductions. Moreover, the one text in which he does give such an assertion is *al-Faqīh*, a book that omits *asānīd* and often gives rulings without proof-texts at all; al-Ṣadūq's introductory affirmation of his sources is thus as much an assurance that his abbreviated and elided proof-texts are, indeed, available elsewhere as it is a guarantee of the quality thereof.[53]

Another variable between al-Ṣadūq and his contemporaries is the use of hadiths which themselves address problems of conflicting hadiths and faulty narration (another peculiar aspect of Shīʿī hadith – unlike the Prophet, the imams lived in times when such matters were much discussed). A common description of the traditionist Imāmīs before al-Mufīd, among whom al-Ṣadūq is consistently numbered, is that they only engaged with jurisprudential questions to the extent that such questions were explicitly enunciated in hadith.[54] Al-Kulaynī seems the clearest instance of such an approach, giving a long chapter in *al-Kāfī* about conflicting hadiths and their reconciliation that is itself composed entirely of hadiths. The chapter does include al-Ṣadūq's hadith of ʿAlī and Sulaym, but accompanies it with many other narrations that together reconcile its absolutist message with the realities of the occultation. Al-Kulaynī's most detailed hadith outlines quite a procedure: if a believer is confronted by differing narrations of the imams' hadith, she should follow the most just, the wisest and the most trustworthy narrator, but if no distinction is to be found on those grounds, then she should seek corroboration first from the generally agreed practice of the imam's followers, then from the Qurʾan and the Prophet's established *sunna*, and then, if all else fails, follow whichever narration least resembles what non-Imāmīs are doing.[55]

The extent to which al-Kulaynī himself would follow this elaborate process is debatable, given that he places the hadith alongside many others with slightly differing instructions.[56] What his use of these texts does show us without a doubt is that al-Ṣadūq's relative silence on jurisprudence cannot be explained simply by a traditionist desire not to overreach the letter of the imams' hadith. In *al-Kāfī*, we see that hadiths that described *isnād* criticism were available, even while al-Ṣadūq can be found using technical terms for which he does not supply any proof-text.[57] Al-Ṣadūq and his father's concern with how the hadith corpus should be represented thus disrupts the traditionist–rationalist axis: al-Kulaynī may be said to be more 'traditionist' in that he shows more interest in the letter of traditions in his discussion of *isnād*-criticism; al-Ṣadūq and his father, however, often eschew the same 'rational' means of differentiating hadiths that are outlined in al-Kulaynī's texts, thus appearing more 'traditionist' by another metric. Their reason for doing so is that the content of these hadiths describing *isnād* criticism clashes with their view of the hadith corpus as a conduit to the certain knowledge of the imam – their 'traditionism' is thus embedded within elaborately reasoned (that is to say, 'rational') responses to the occultation.[58]

The contrast between the two Ibn Bābawayhs and al-Kulaynī is also significant in that it points to these varying attitudes to the representation of *isnād* criticism as a point of differentiation not just between individual scholars but between scholarly genealogies and even different schools. One genealogy, naturally, is constituted by al-Ṣadūq and his father, who was also among his principal teachers, but those Imāmīs who exhibit a contrasting approach are also closely genealogically linked around the figure of al-Kulaynī. Al-Kulaynī was a principal teacher and source of hadith for Ibn Qūlawayh, who was, in turn, a principal teacher and source of hadith for al-Mufīd. When al-Mufīd narrates hadith from al-Kulaynī, whose work he praises as reliable in the same breath as criticizing al-Ṣadūq, he routinely does so through Ibn Qūlawayh.[59] Another of Ibn Qūlawayh's teachers, meanwhile, was his father, who also taught al-Kashshī. Beyond their genealogical links, these two groups of scholars map precisely onto the intellectual centres of gravity of Qum and Rayy respectively, with al-Ṣadūq and his father representing Qummī circles, while al-Kulaynī and his circle were based at Rayy (and subsequently represented in Baghdad by al-Mufīd).[60] Relative willingness to foreground *isnād* criticism thus constitutes a consistent axis of distinction between the principal surviving Imāmī works from this period, a division that was transmitted through scholarly networks and may even have been a defining contention between regional centres.[61] This conclusion, furthermore, highlights the fact that al-Ṣadūq belonged to a scholarly network and intellectual trajectory distinct from that which became the core of Imāmī thought over the next few centuries, a circumstance that has an inevitable bearing upon the poor preservation of the writings of his principal teachers and students. Viewed from the Baghdad-centric perspective of our surviving sources, al-Ṣadūq can look like an eccentric outlier in his own time, but to a perspective corrected for these imbalances in our evidence, he appears instead as part of a robust, profound diversity of Imāmī attitudes to hadith in the early Buwayhid period.[62]

Conclusion

We ended the previous chapter by observing the unique, transitional moment that al-Ṣadūq inhabits. It is now apparent how deeply this is reflected in his approach to the hadith corpus. To a greater extent than any extant work of his contemporaries, al-Ṣadūq's writings show the complex meeting-points of a new, post-occultation Imāmī thought, one that was increasingly in conversation with broader developments in the nature and role of systematic *uṣūl al-fiqh* and with older intellectual currents that remained suspicious of such developments. Al-Ṣadūq is certainly a traditionist (albeit one with more critical expertise than is sometimes accorded him), but his is a traditionism that goes beyond simply preferring text over fallible reason. His devotion to the hadith corpus is paradoxically driven by a vision of authority for which systems of transmission and recollection always risk being inadequate. The infallible imam promises authority right here right now, authority that does not need to be remembered because it has never gone away. To the extent that al-Ṣadūq does resist critical examination of the sources of his hadiths, this resistance is driven by reasoned theology – the just God's promise of his ever-present *ḥujja*, which means that such ambiguities simply should not exist. Rather than simply lagging behind non-Shīʿī groups, among whom al-Ṣadūq's contemporaries were writing great volumes of jurisprudence and hadith criticism,[63] Imāmī thinkers of his persuasion were approaching their hadith corpus from a quite different perspective, their jurisprudence and theology still merged through the hidden person of the imam.[64] In some ways, there are parallels between al-Ṣadūq's concerns and those of the Sunnī traditionists of the previous century, who also sought to uphold the capacity of the hadith corpus to give meaningful access to the prophetic message. For such Sunnī writers, however, from Ibn Qutayba to al-Shāfiʿī, this was a process of demonstrating the efficacy of *isnād* criticism, not of avoiding it.[65]

Al-Ṣadūq's attitude to hadith was not as idiosyncratic in his lifetime as it appears in hindsight, and it may well have endured within his intellectual circles for another generation or two after his death. Nevertheless, his was an approach that did not outlast the Buwayhid period, and one that remained rooted within ideas of the imamate that were becoming awkward in the post-occultation world.[66] For subsequent generations of Imāmīs, the occultation of the imam became a purely theological problem, distinct from the practicalities of jurisprudential hermeneutics. No doubt the intellectual pressures of the Buwayhid era played their part, but the passage of time was almost certainly an important factor, the conceptual shadow of a present, accessible imam fading even as *madhhab*-style scholarly institutions gained ground. It is precisely because of these subsequent developments and, indeed, their apparent incompatibility with al-Ṣadūq's understanding of hadith and hadith criticism, that make his works such an important source for the nature of Imāmī thought in the century following al-ʿAskarī's demise. Though he did not produce a written jurisprudence or any integrated account of the role of the legal scholar during the occultation, al-Ṣadūq's works display the lucidity with which Imāmīs reckoned with the new stakes of hadith scholarship in a world without an imam.

3

Hadith as literature

Al-Ṣadūq, *adab* and Imāmī traditionism at the Buwayhid court

Beyond the law

As a *faqīh* and as a compiler of the imams' hadith, al-Ṣadūq's writings constantly engage the key question facing the Imāmī scholarly community in the aftermath of the occultation: how to manage authority in the absence of the imam. In the previous two chapters, we have learned something of the highly unusual attitude to hadith criticism that prevailed during this period in some Imāmī circles, including al-Ṣadūq himself, even while many details regarding exactly how Imāmī scholars constructed their own authority remain mysterious. What is certain is that none of these trials and ambiguities prevented scholars like al-Ṣadūq from continuing to act as *fuqahā'*, wielding their scholarly status to guide the Imāmī community in matters of law and theology. This fact is built into the architecture of works like *al-Faqīh* and *al-I'tiqādāt*, which are constructed unmistakeably as reference works in which the Imāmī faithful can seek answers to their questions of belief and practice; scholars' rulings and imams' hadiths are arranged according to subject matter, and proof-texts are supplied in answer to clearly identified and arranged questions. Such features are, of course, entirely in keeping with Muslim manuals of belief and practice from the 'Abbāsid period and far beyond, and their instructive format seems so objectively born of their didactic purpose as to seldom merit comment.

Most of al-Ṣadūq's surviving compendia, however, are not structured as creeds or as legal manuals. In this chapter, we will examine a set of works in which al-Ṣadūq and the hadiths that he compiles go beyond the usual parameters of theology and law, both in terms of their subject matter and in the way they address the reader. These books contain such curiosities as the signs of human ageing and why the bull that supports God's throne hangs his head,[1] but even if the reader sets out in search of these topics, the books' design is more a hindrance than a help, their hadiths and chapters arranged around obscure metrics with little deference to the encyclopaedic ordering of *al-Faqīh* or *al-Hidāya*. These compendia make little sense in a legal framework, but they alert us instead to another formative context of al-Ṣadūq's writing: that of *adab* literature. *Adab* literature was a pillar of the high culture of the Buwayhid age, a milieu in which prominent Imāmī scholars were involved in increasing numbers over the latter half of the fourth/tenth century. Just as Imāmī legal and theological thought in this period was shaped by the group's increased enfranchisement, so Buwayhid-era Imāmī writing is deeply influenced by Imāmī scholars' access to the centres of power, and thus to the concerns, ideas and manners of the political and cultural elite. To be an Imāmī was no hindrance to participating in literary salons, to writing poems to rulers or to appointment to the kinds of posts from which men of letters often drew their income. Imāmīs became viziers, librarians and judges, participating diversely in courtly intellectual life, and forming a rich chorus of voices within the literary legacy of the period.

Al-Ṣadūq is received by posterity entirely as a *muḥaddith* and as a scholar of law and theology, yet the marks of these circumstances of expanding courtly engagement, and of *adab* literature in particular, are clearly present in his work.[2] Many of his books bring the imams' hadith into conversation with *adab* literature's conventions, interests and aims, just as non-Shīʿīs were doing with the hadith of the Prophet in similar contexts. This undertaking shapes these compendia in ways that are inexplicable when removed from an *adabī* context, revealing new elements of al-Ṣadūq as a compiler, and of the creative possibilities that compilers in general have at their disposal. Al-Ṣadūq can be seen adapting the tools of *adab* literature to explore various authorial addresses and readerly expectations, often taking the imams' hadith in surprising directions. Though the literary context in which these works operate is clear, their nexus between *adab*, Shīʿism and hadith is a strange and unpredictable one, and the results of these experiments are some of al-Ṣadūq's most unusual works.

Adab literature in the Buwayhid period

Described in one recent assessment as a 'loose, baggy monster', *adab* literature is notoriously difficult to define.[3] It is a literature that comprises a great many forms, a great many subjects and a great many objectives; in the broadest, briefest sense, these may be grouped by a shared concern with 'manners' or 'culture'.[4] Works of *adab* literature are books that set out to improve the reader, in terms of their moral character, in terms of their knowledge of history, of literature and of anecdote, in terms of their rhetorical skill and in terms of their mastery of societal and courtly norms. Beyond these expansive objectives, *adab* literature in the ʿAbbāsid period is characterized by the particular ways in which it pursues them. At its heart is the *adab* compendium – a collection, sometimes brief, sometimes voluminous, of material intended to impart some or all of the virtues just listed. A typical such compendium may contain gobbets of poetry, anecdotes about any number of different characters from kings to beggars, from figures of recent history to legendary personalities such as Alexander the Great, aphorisms of prophets and philosophers, jokes and theological arguments. Some compendia are organized around a more or less narrow theme (such as friendship or flowers); others are encyclopaedic. Some restrict their sources in some way (e.g., only poets); others quote from an immense variety of sources.[5]

Beyond the eccentric encyclopaedism of the larger *adab* compendia, other genres are usually understood to participate in *adab* literature to varying extents. A universal history, for example, may be written in a way that both shares many of the usual sources of *adab* literature listed above, and participates in *adab* literature's accustomed priorities, such as education in morals, the past and even poetry (e.g., the *Murūj al-dhahab* of al-Masʿūdī). On the other hand, it may be weighted towards other concerns usually deemed less dear to the *adīb* (the writer of *adab* literature, pl. *udabāʾ*), such as salvation history or *isnād* criticism (e.g., al-Ṭabarī's *Taʾrīkh al-rusul waʾl-mulūk*). Similarly, any anthology of poetry likely shares *adab* literature's customary concern with poetic erudition and philology, but may be distanced from *adab* literature by a lack of overt engagement with questions of mannered behaviour. These variables, in turn, might depend upon the intentions of the anthologist, which might be expressed or unexpressed, or upon the contents of the poems themselves.[6]

Adab literature flourished under Buwayhid rule. The fragmenting of ʿAbbāsid power resulted in a plurality of competing political centres, and with them competing courts, each eager to foster their credentials as patrons of learning and of culture. This was the age that produced no less a literary titan than the poet al-Mutanabbī, and the Buwayhid courts hosted a corresponding wealth of *udabāʾ*, among them Abū Ḥayyān al-Tawḥīdī (414/1023), Abū Hilāl al-Ḥasan

b. ʿAbd Allāh al-ʿAskarī (d. circa 400/1010) and al-Muḥassin b. ʿAlī al-Tanūkhī (d. 384/994).[7]

As expansive and precariously defined as *adab* is, one definition which has recurrently been attached to *adab* literature concerns its relationship to religious literature. Scholars have often defined *adab* literature as belletrist or even as secular, to be contrasted to the religious space inhabited by jurists and theologians. The *adab* compendium's exuberantly expansive approach to the texts it includes has even been explicitly contrasted with the hadith compendium, the former outward-looking and open to knowledge and its advancement from a potentially infinite range of sources, and the latter closed, devoted to delineating knowledge in its finite parameters as determined by scripture.[8] This sounds like bad news for al-Ṣadūq's participation in *adab* literature, but recent scholarship has problematized this stark separation of *adab* from the religious. After all, *adab* literature's vision of the cultured man included such virtues as piety, generosity and asceticism, virtues that were of just as much interest to legal and theological discourse. Kilpatrick draws attention to figures like Ibn Abī al-Dunyā (d. 208/823), whose works share *adab* literature's concern with ethical education, but who, like al-Ṣadūq, use a narrower range of sources than many *udabāʾ*, maintaining a focus upon Qurʾanic verses and hadith.[9] Stefan Sperl, too, has pointed to common conceptual ground and exchange between *adab* and hadith scholarship, exploring the understanding and use of the term '*adab*' in Sunnī hadith compendia, which he finds to encapsulate very similar goals to those of *adab* compendia.[10] Other studies, meanwhile, have underscored the legal and theological concerns at work in what have elsewhere been considered 'purely' *adabī* writings.[11]

The relationship between hadith and *adab* literature in this period may therefore be understood as 'a continuum covering the vast religio-cultural legacy inherited and codified by classical Arabic letters',[12] in which the boundaries of what constitutes an *adab* compendium are thoroughly porous. While many *adab* compendia contain authorial remarks that identify them explicitly as such, many others do not.[13] Similarly, while some authors work overtly to distance their books from the priorities of legal and theological writing, constructing accounts of wisdom that transcend any particular parameters of religion or culture,[14] most *adab* compendia, both in their pedagogical outlook and in their sources, exhibit strong continuities with the kinds of writing explored in the previous chapter. This, then, is not a category that inherently excludes either the imams' hadith or al-Ṣadūq's compilations thereof.

The Imāmīya, *adab* and al-Ṣadūq

Quite apart from al-Ṣadūq, the Imāmīya as a group have a distinguished presence in Buwayhid *adab* literature, counting among their number such distinguished *udabāʾ* as the philosopher and historian Aḥmad b. Muḥammad al-Miskawayh (d. 420/1029), the bibliophile Ibn al-Nadīm (d. 380/990), and the brothers al-Sharīf al-Raḍī (d. 406/1015) and al-Sharīf al-Murtaḍā (d. 436/1044). The latter pair, as well as their significance as poets and anthologists, were prominent students of al-Mufīd, with al-Murtaḍā in particular counted as a foundational figure of Imāmī theology and jurisprudence. Another figure of note is the poet and vizier Manṣūr b. al-Ḥusayn al-Ābī (d. *c* 421/1030), who, though almost certainly a Zaydī, is named by some sources as a student of al-Ṣadūq.[15] Like *udabāʾ* in general, some of these Imāmī writers of *adab* literature were equally comfortable writing jurisprudence, while others appear disinterested in and even ignorant of such matters.[16]

Though the breadth of Imāmī presence within this literature is clear, al-Ṣadūq's place, as usual, remains ambiguous. His dates contribute to this uncertainty, with most of the figures just listed being at least a generation younger, and thus part of a more established Buwayhid milieu. Nonetheless, there is a substantial body of evidence in al-Ṣadūq's oeuvre and elsewhere that firmly places him within the orbit of Buwayhid *adab* literature, and indeed of the Buwayhid courts that were such active centres thereof. We will first survey these connections before exploring how they play out in detail in individual works. A first, central factor is al-Ṣadūq's location in Rayy, a city that had attracted many of the period's most illustrious *udabāʾ* including al-Miskawayh and al-Tawḥīdī. Not only that, but al-Ṣadūq is connected to the court at Rayy, with various accounts recording his interactions with both the Buwayhid amir Rukn al-Dawla (d. 366/976) and his vizier al-Ṣāḥib Ibn ʿAbbād (d. 385/995), one of most important and powerful intellectual patrons of the age.[17] He is even cited twice in an *adab* compendium written by his contemporary al-Tawḥīdī, and also appears in his satirical account of life at Ibn ʿAbbād's court.[18] As for the content of his works, al-Ṣadūq is distinguished from earlier Imāmī hadith compilers by his range of citations. Notwithstanding the central place he accords to hadith, he also gives occasional reference to lexicographers, litterateurs, historians, grammarians and poets, among them the feted courtier and chess player Abū Bakr Muḥammad b. Yaḥyā al-Ṣūlī (d. 335/947)[19] and the pioneering philologist and lexicographer ʿAbd al-Malik b. Qurayb al-Aṣmaʿī (d. 213/828).[20] Such voices are staples of *adab* literature, and clearly place al-Ṣadūq's compendia within a conversation far broader than that of an exclusive 'Imami thought'.

As well as his references, al-Ṣadūq's range of subject matters across his works also points to his engagement with the concerns of *adab* literature. He was, of course, a *faqīh* first and foremost, but a significant minority among his works, both extant and lost, address areas quite beyond this purview. Among his lost works are recorded a book on history, a book on poetry, a commentary on an ode, a book on 'firsts' and one on 'lasts'.[21] His extant works, meanwhile, include five in particular that constitute substantial engagement with *adab*, and will be the focus of this chapter: *al-Khiṣāl*, *Maʿānī al-akhbār*, *al-Mawāʿiẓ*, *ʿIlal al-sharāʾiʿ* and *Muṣādaqat al-ikhwān* (a number of others certainly contain *adabī* elements but in a less formative capacity, as will be discussed in what follows). *Al-Mawāʿiẓ* ('The Counsels') presents an Imāmī rendering of the *adab* staple of wisdom literature,[22] collecting the insights that the Prophet and the imams imparted to their successors. *Muṣādaqat al-ikhwān* ('Sincerity amongst Brethren') treats another central topic, namely that of friendship.[23] *Al-Khiṣāl*, *ʿIlal* and *Maʿānī*, meanwhile, are structured in a manner typical of *adab* compendia, each gathering an immensely various set of reports around a more or less eccentric theme.[24]

Though there is much to connect al-Ṣadūq's engagements with *adab* to the specifics of the Buwayhid moment, when it comes to these formal parallels between his works and *adab* compendia he does have a noted pre-Buwayhid predecessor in the form of Aḥmad b. Muḥammad al-Barqī.[25] Among the books of al-Barqī's mostly lost magnum opus *al-Maḥāsin*, both those that survive and those that do not, we find a number of titles evoking *adabī* themes like those of al-Ṣadūq.[26] Moreover, some of these not only echo the shape of monothematic *adab* compendia but are also based on the same themes as those of works by al-Ṣadūq. Al-Ṣadūq's *ʿIlal* and his *al-Khiṣāl* are mirrored, respectively, in al-Barqī's *Kitāb al-ʿilal* and *Kitāb al-ashkāl wa'l-qarāʾin*, a fact entirely in keeping with al-Ṣadūq's widely observable interest in and indebtedness to his third/ninth-century predecessor.[27] Unlike in al-Ṣadūq's case, al-Barqī's work has been subjected to extensive study by Roy Vilozny, whose description of one of al-Barqī's books as 'a collection of hadith with an *adab* style and message'[28] is certainly apt for many of the works of al-Ṣadūq discussed in this chapter.[29]

Virtue and friendship

We will now turn to explore in some detail these five works in which al-Ṣadūq's engagements with *adab* literature are at their most substantial, beginning with *Muṣādaqat*. As a book on relations with one's fellows, this work has two close parallels in al-Ṣadūq's writings: *Ṣifāt al-shī ʿa* ('The Attributes of the Shīʿa'), and *Faḍā ʾil al-shī ʿa* ('The Virtues of the Shīʿa'). All three address questions of communal identity and ethics, questions that by al-Ṣadūq's time had exercised Shīʿīs of various colours for centuries.[30] What was the status of non-Imāmī, indeed non-Shīʿī Muslims? Why, despite its luminous truth, did Imāmīsm not command more adherents? If Muḥammad was God's last prophet, how was his mission allowed to be so comparatively unsuccessful, with the majority of the Muslim community having deviated from the true path? How, meanwhile, should the enlightened few conduct themselves as a minority for as long as these complex, troubling realities continued to be the case?[31]

Much of the extant pre-Buwayhid literature (nearly all of it hadith literature) engaging with these questions is devoted to metaphysical solutions, solutions that enunciate the exclusivist attitude often deemed characteristic of this period of Imāmī writing. Both al-Barqī and al-Ṣaffār narrate a voluminous body of material describing how Shīʿīs were pre-created as such before even the creation of the world; their pre-existent souls were created from the light of Muḥammad and his family, or from the same special clay, thus distinguishing them from the rest of humankind.[32] As well as reinforcing ideas of the Shīʿa as an enlightened few set apart, this projection of sectarian identities onto a pre-existential past removed the potentially wearisome concern that the wider *umma* remained unpersuaded of the truths of Shīʿism. Shīʿīs, these texts taught, were ultimately born, not made, and those who did not understand the imams' truth never would and never could. The Shīʿa were to live as a tight-knit minority among a larger Muslim community who were unaware of their special status, interacting with others only when necessary and doing so with both the caution and the inner condescension appropriate for their own innately superior spiritual nature.[33]

Muṣādaqat, *Faḍā ʾil* and *Ṣifāt* offer a fascinating reflection upon the adaptation of these ideas in the new circumstances of Buwayhid rule. Al-Ṣadūq draws upon the abundant discursive resources concerning friendship and intellectual brotherhood offered by *adab* literature, selecting hadiths to absorb and adapt these concepts alongside long-standing Shīʿī ideas. Of the three works, *Faḍā ʾil al-shī ʿa* is closest in tone to the discourse of al-Barqī and al-Ṣaffār. There is little of the cosmological in its pages, but it offers a more sober recension of the same message, with most of its hadiths affirming the Shīʿa's unique status as the enlightened community of salvation. With dicta such as 'The one amongst you with his foot most firmly on the path is whosoever is fiercest in his love for my house', and 'Love for ʿAlī b. Abī Ṭālib consumes sins even as fire consumes firewood', the reader is repeatedly assured that Shīʿī fealty to the Prophet's house is the way to paradise.[34]

Ṣifāt al-shīʿa, meanwhile, places the emphasis differently. Though it contains no dearth of hadiths asserting the special soteriological status of the Shīʿa, this book also holds those seeking that status to a certain standard of behaviour. The following hadith begins with Muḥammad al-Bāqir addressing his disciple Jābir al-Juʿfī:

> O Jābir, is it enough for one who would be counted among the Shīʿa to declare his love for us, the Prophet's house? By God, no-one is among our Shīʿa save one who is mindful of God and obeys him, who is known only for modesty and humility, for keeping trust and frequent remembrance of God, for fasting and prayer, for piety towards his parents, for taking care of the poor amongst his neighbours, of the wretched, of debtors and of orphans, for speaking the truth, for reciting the Qurʾan, for holding his tongue from addressing people except with what is good, and who is the guarantor of his kinsfolk.
>
> Jābir replied: 'O son of God's messenger, we know nobody who matches such a description!'[35]

Any reader accustomed to the message of *Faḍāʾil* has already received a nasty shock. The love that leads to paradise is revealed in *Ṣifāt* as a dauntingly exacting one, transmuting the Shīʿism of *Faḍāʾil* from a broadly confessional identity (one easily conceived as determined by distant metaphysical events) to an identity predicated on rigorous practice and observance. *Muṣādaqat* takes this trajectory further; in terms of its content, it can be read as a straightforward ethical work on how Muslims should treat each other, with no sign of its Imāmī authorship apart from its being a collection of the imams' hadith, and with distinct echoes of *adab* literature. Among its injunctions are al-Ṣādiq's words: 'The Muslim is his fellow Muslim's brother, neither wronging him nor forsaking him', and those of the Prophet: 'If one of you meets his brother, let him greet him and wish him peace. God has blessed the angels with this practice – do you then as the angels do.'[36] The tone closely resembles the discussions of friendship that were a cornerstone of *adab* literature, most notably al-Tawḥīdī's compendium *al-Ṣadāqa wa'l-ṣadīq*, which actually cites al-Ṣadūq.[37] Alongside *Ṣifāt*, *Muṣādaqat* thus bridges *adabī* discourses of friendship and the vision of Shīʿī brotherhood offered in *al-Maḥāsin*. To look again at the second hadith cited, for the general reader 'brother' reads as 'fellow Muslim', but for a Shīʿī reader it could certainly be understood to refer to one's fellow Shīʿī, enabling different addresses to different readerships.[38] To a non-Imāmī reader, *Muṣādaqat* has an apologetic value, presenting the imams as wise authorities on fashionable philosophical questions, while to an Imāmī reader it articulates fealty to the imams and between their followers in terms of contemporary ideals of ethical conduct.

Read in sequence with *Faḍā ʾil* and *Ṣifāt*, *Muṣādaqat* thus shows al-Ṣadūq exploring how the discourses of *adab* can mediate between exclusivist, metaphysically idiosyncratic accounts of Imāmī salvation and contemporary philosophical speculations on the nature of society, to suggest an expansive communal ethics for the Shīʿa of ʿAlī. Al-Ṣadūq does not directly invoke the vision of universal human brotherhood explored by his philosopher contemporaries, nor the exclusive, pre-existentially determined Shīʿī community of salvation found in al-Barqī's hadiths; rather, he explores through careful selection of hadiths how the two may overlap, enriching the image of the saved sect with an exacting ethics of piety and brotherhood.

Miscellany and persuasion

A more ambitious engagement with *adab* can be seen in *al-Khiṣāl*, *Ma ʿānī* and *ʿIlal*. These three works parallel widespread norms of *adab* compendia, both in their miscellaneous subject matter and in their common structure. As described earlier, each of these works unites diverse hadiths somewhat loosely around a single governing theme-concept. In *ʿIlal al-sharā ʾiʿ* ('The Causes of Laws'),[39] this principle is that of causation, but it is far from being restricted to matters of law. We read hadiths explaining phenomena as diverse as why the sky is called the sky, why corpses weep, why the sunset prayer contains only three bowings, why pregnancy interrupts menstruation, why the world's peoples differ in appearance, why ʿAlī was unable to lift the Prophet on his shoulders when smashing the idols in the Kaʿba and why Jaʿfar al-Ṣādiq stopped brushing his teeth two years before he died.[40] *Al-Khiṣāl*'s organizing principle, meanwhile, is based on a pun in the title, which can mean both 'The Numbers (or Quantities)' or 'The Qualities'. The book is structured according to the first of these meanings, each chapter being devoted to a number and containing traditions in which that number appears (first giving chapters on each from 1 to 20, and then rather more sporadically chapters covering higher numbers up to 100). The contents, however, recall the second meaning, with most of the book's traditions enumerating qualities of some sort: the five virtues that guarantee paradise, the four marks of a Shīʿī and so forth. In *Ma ʿānī al-akhbār* ('The Meanings of Traditions'), the theme is meaning, sometimes in a lexicographical sense, addressed in traditions that either explain obscure vocabulary in other texts or contain obscure vocabulary themselves, but often in a conceptual sense, regarding the different kinds of drunkenness or what the 'ornament of the afterlife' might be.[41]

The structural pattern of these works would not appear wholly dissimilar from some of al-Ṣadūq's more straightforwardly pietistic books, especially *Thawāb* and *ʿIqāb*, were it not for the extraordinary variety of their subject matter. The title of al-Kulaynī's *al-Kāfī* translates as 'Sufficiency;' it is a religious encyclopaedia that sets out to tell believers everything they might need to know from the teachings of the imams. *ʿIlal*, *al-Khiṣāl* and *Maʿānī* undoubtedly present an expansion of what such 'sufficiency' might entail, widening the boundaries of knowledge over which the imams can lay claim to include such things as the ten qualities of the watermelon.[42] Buwayhid literary culture was infused with a spirit of polymathy,[43] and al-Ṣadūq has much to gain from presenting the imam as the supreme polymath. These books, then, can be read as portraits of omniscience, but they remain profoundly obscure portraits, with the knowledge that they contain rendered stubbornly difficult to access. A reader may have use for hadiths relating to the legal status of praying in marshland, wearing skins of unusual creatures or drinking from silver goblets, but she has no way of knowing where they are; there are no demarcated sections on garments, ritually pure surfaces or table manners to which she may turn, leaving extreme patience or good fortune as her only recourse.[44] Moreover, these books not infrequently narrate conflicting answers to a question: on a matter as important as prayer, for example, the number of *rakaʿāt* in the sunset prayer are in *ʿIlal* attributed both to a divine command given during the *miʿrāj* and to Muḥammad's joy at the birth of Fāṭima; similarly, the prohibition of wearing gold rings in prayer is attributed variously to their being worn by the inhabitants of hell and their being worn by the inhabitants of paradise.[45]

These works' combination of the imams' hadith with so eclectic a form seems deeply counterintuitive, all the more so given that similar topics were regularly given far more systematic treatment by al-Ṣadūq's contemporaries.[46] The semi-navigable polyphony that they present raises important questions regarding what al-Ṣadūq is trying to communicate and to whom, questions that were treated with great seriousness in scholarly writing, as the following quotation from Ibn Qūlawayh makes plain:

> I have divided [this book] into chapters, and each of those chapters concerns one topic, such that I have not placed therein any hadith that does not concern that

> topic. Were I to do so, this would distract the reader, rendering him unsure of what he sought, and of how and whence to seek it. Other authors have composed works in just such a manner, presenting chapters wherein the contents are contrary to the title, chapters in which they cite hadiths that do not concern the topic of the chapter, even to the point where a chapter does not contain a single hadith of clear pertinence to the title, filled instead with those that have no relevance at all!
>
> My purpose [in avoiding such practices] is to make it easy for the reader who seeks a particular hadith in this book, such that he may go straight to the chapter relevant to the hadith he seeks and find it therein. In this way the reader will not tire of this book, nor will the one to whom it is read, and they thus may learn what God has in store for his devoted servant.[47]

Ibn Qūlawayh outlines the way in which his and al-Ṣadūq's conventional legal and theological manuals are structured, the reason for this and its necessity. This is the business of guiding the faithful in their religion, and the onus is upon the scholar to facilitate this. It is, therefore, no small matter that the labyrinthine structures of *ʿIlal*, *Maʿānī* and *al-Khiṣāl* dramatically flout Ibn Qūlawayh's stated ideal. These works evidently do not aspire to the same kind of didactic address as *al-Faqīh*, but this does not mean that they contain no didactic address, only that it works differently. Not only are such structures common in *adab* compendia, but writers of *adab* compendia offer a wealth of discussion regarding how and why they are useful. Al-Ṣadūq's contemporary al-Tanūkhī, for instance, tells us exactly why his *al-Nishwār wa'l-muḥāḍara* is no less navigable than it needs to be:

> I present what I have written of things long-remembered mingled together with things heard only recently, neither rendered into chapters nor ordered into categories. For the book contains reports each one of which merits consideration from several angles. Most of them would appear cold and tiresome were I to spend time arranging, categorising and ordering them. Moreover, when the reader had perused the first item in a chapter, he would then know that those making up the rest of the chapter would be similar to it, stymieing his enthusiasm to enjoy reading them all . . . Lost, too, would be the many gobbets and poems, epistles and proverbs secreted herein.[48]

Al-Tanūkhī makes it clear that restricting readers' ability to navigate his book has a clear and considered educative purpose. While Ibn Qūlawayh strives to facilitate consultation by readers who know what's good for them, many writers of *adab* literature, like al-Tanūkhī, outline schemes to force readers to read in a particular way, readers who might otherwise get it wrong. The author of the *adab* compendium is often cast as a benevolent puppet master, using obscure structures to prevent readers from choosing what to read, and strategically placing curious, eye-catching material to lure them towards more improving fare. Al-Ṣadūq does not confess to such a strategy in *ʿIlal*, *Maʿānī* or *al-Khiṣāl*, but elsewhere in his writings he enunciates something very similar: in *Kamāl al-dīn*, following his counterintuitive decision to include stories about the Buddha in a work about the Hidden Imam (more on which in Chapter 5), al-Ṣadūq explains that people are drawn to such exotic tales and that they will attract readers who may then read the rest of the book.[49] Though *Kamāl al-dīn* is openly a book of theological instruction, there is no reason to suppose that al-Ṣadūq is not deploying similar ruses elsewhere, not least in works that are structurally proximate to *adab* literature, where these devices are most frequently discussed.

Close examination of *ʿIlal*, *al-Khiṣāl* and *Maʿānī* quickly reveals that objectives of moral and doctrinal instruction do, indeed, lie beneath their improbable assemblages of reports. As al-Ṣadūq's readers meander between the five ways in which white roosters are similar to prophets and the reason wherefore pruned palm trees don't resprout,[50] they regularly find themselves being told how to behave and what to believe. In *ʿIlal*, the 'cause' that many chapters undertake to explain turns out to be a proverbial moral truth, such as that concerning 'the reason why two men may enter a mosque, one worshipful, one corrupt, and yet when they leave the pious one is corrupted and the corrupt one has become righteous' – the answer is that the worshipful man was conceited in his worship, while the corrupt man lamented his faults.[51] In other chapters, explanations can be a diagnosis of a religious difficulty, such as inability to perform the night-time prayer being caused by sinful conduct during the day.[52] *Maʿānī*'s guiding theme adds a further dimension, whereby apparently complex, obscure hadiths are interpreted to yield basic pieties. The worrying hadith 'Whoever, whilst riding a beast of burden, falls to the ground and dies will enter the fire', is, al-Ṣadūq reassures us, only a warning against riding without holding the reins.[53] God's dislike of houses in which meat is consumed is similarly glossed as referring to the metaphorical cannibalism of speaking ill of the absent.[54] In *al-Khiṣāl*, likewise, chapters discussing 'the five marks of the believer', 'the four qualities that a believer never lacks' and 'the believer is he in whom are gathered seven qualities' are made of fairly similar stuff.[55]

The heady diversity of these works' contents thus often homogenizes down to a simple, repeated message of piety, a pedagogical strategy totally familiar to readers of *adab* compendia. Where they become less typical of *adab* literature, however, is when this obliquely delivered guidance pertains to details of Imāmī doctrine. As expected, *al-Khiṣāl* includes a section devoted to the number twelve. This contains a range of twelve-related hadiths, addressing the existence of twelve worlds, twelve months and twelve seas, and the significance of twelve dirhams once given to Muḥammad,[56] but in the middle of the section we also find a chapter of hadiths declaring that Muḥammad will have twelve rightful successors.[57] Not only has the subject shifted from trivia and manners to a cornerstone of Imāmī theology, but structurally this is also a very different kind of chapter. Most chapters in *al-Khiṣāl* contain only one report, and almost never more than three, but the chapter on Muḥammad's twelve successors lists forty-five hadiths, with a concluding note that even more may be found to the same effect in *Kamāl al-dīn*.[58] Al-Ṣadūq has decisively jumped from the language of curiosity to that of doctrinal assertion, interrupting *al-Khiṣāl*'s noncommittal miscellany to deliver a barrage of evidence in support of core imamological convictions. Though the subject matter alone might be attributed partly to accident – it is an odd collection of Imāmī hadith that contains no reference to the imamate – this distinct, argumentative tone makes plain al-Ṣadūq's very active policy here.

This is not an isolated instance; rather, *Maʿānī*, *ʿIlal* and *al-Khiṣāl* are filled with such devices, their engaging whimsy sporadically giving way to sudden, deftly asserted proofs and polemics. *Maʿānī* includes a chapter on the meaning of Muḥammad's words at Ghadīr Khumm, providing a discussion of this pivotal moment in Shīʿī salvation history that is as densely substantiated and contested as any in al-Ṣadūq's writings.[59] *ʿIlal*'s sixty-first chapter, meanwhile, purportedly concerns why ʿAlī more than once delayed his afternoon prayers until after sundown, and accordingly offers reports in which ʿAlī is prevented from praying at the normal time for legitimate reasons. In each case, however, the imam repairs the fault by successfully commanding the sun to come back up, so that he can pray in the right legal conditions.[60] The miracle is substantiated by several hadiths and multiple *asānīd*, turning what started off as a minor curiosity of ʿAlī's career into a robust set of evidence for the imam's legitimacy and power. Sometimes these chapters' argumentative objectives obliterate the book's guiding framework altogether. In *ʿIlal*, for instance, a chapter on why it is permissible to combine prayers without cause for dispensation (a standard bone of contention between the Imāmīya and other groups) offers seven proof-texts affirming the practice, two of which give no reference to causation at all, only affirming the practice's legitimacy.[61] Another chapter, concerning the prohibition of praying in black clothing (upheld out of Imāmī animosity towards the ʿAbbāsids), includes not only reports declaring black to be the garment of wrongdoers but also a group of hadiths in which the imam endorses the wearing of black (no reason is supplied). These, al-Ṣadūq then explains, were uttered out of *taqīya*.[62]

A particular tour de force is found in an innocuous-looking chapter of *ʿIlal* devoted to 'The reason why people look down while defecating' (chapter 184).[63] This chapter consists of four hadiths. The first delivers the answer to the title question: that God entrusts an angel with the task of bending people's necks forward, so that they may be shown what emerges from them and whether it is *ḥalāl* or *ḥarām*. The second tradition gives the words of ʿAlī: 'I wonder at the son of Adam, that his beginning is a droplet, his ending a corpse, and while he stands between them he is a casket of excrement. God is great.' This is clearly a departure from the original question, transporting the reader from the further reaches of miscellany to the familiar, stark asceticism of the first imam, with excrement providing a convenient link. The third tradition, however, elaborates on ʿAlī's theme, having now wholly abandoned the title concept: a man asks Salmān, 'Who and what are you?', and receives the reply, 'As for my beginning and your beginning, it is an unclean droplet, and as for your ending and my ending, it is a putrescent corpse. But when judgment day comes and the scales are set, the man with no weight to his worth is vile, but the man whose worth has weight is noble.' This brings us to the final tradition, in which a man seeks to test Jaʿfar al-Ṣādiq's assertion that there is no subject not addressed by the *sunna*, and asks him for a *sunna* concerning defecation. The imam naturally meets his request, supplying a pious formula to be uttered at the opportune moment, at which point his interlocutor remarks, as an afterthought, upon the mystery of this chapter's title: that man is compelled to look down at what issues from him. The imam gives the same reason offered in the first hadith, with the added detail that here two angels chide the defecator, 'See, son of Adam, what you laboured over in the world until it passed thus!'

This last example is only an exceptionally focussed case of what al-Ṣadūq can be seen doing throughout these three works, shifting between different kinds of knowledge, some clearly the stuff of the *adab* compendium, others more germane to theological catechisms. What starts off as the purest miscellany (hadith no. 1) moves swiftly to meditation on the frailty of the material world (hadith nos. 2 and 3); to this moral reflection, in turn, is added an assertion of normative practice (hadith no. 4), before, in the final image of Imam al-Ṣādiq asserting his supreme knowledge of the law in the face of scepticism, we behold the total, expansive sovereignty of the imams' knowledge and Imāmī hadith.

Truth and dissimilation

By now it is evident that al-Ṣadūq creates a dense interplay between Imāmī hadith and *adab* literature in several of his works. While this does much to explain why these books look the way they do, it only exacerbates the question of the audiences for whom they are intended. Their address to the reader, we have established, retains a strongly didactic character; what then does it benefit al-Ṣadūq to adopt this mode of instruction rather than that employed in *al-Faqīh*? It seems safe to assume that this dramatically different style signals a different audience, but the identity of that audience is uncertain. Are *Maʿānī*, *ʿIlal* and *al-Khiṣāl* aimed at a more educated, less pliant class of Imāmī reader, who are perhaps less likely to pick up a catechism like *al-Muqniʿ* and therefore need instructing by more refined means? Are they an attempt to divert Imāmīs from the seductive power of courtly intellectual fashions, showing them that such fads can add nothing to the boundless knowledge contained in the hadith? Alternatively, are these works an attempt to preach the truth of the imamate to non-Imāmī readers of *adab* literature? The books' reception offers few answers. *Adab* literature produced by other Buwayhid Shīʿīs such as al-Ābī, al-Murtaḍā and al-Raḍī have received continued attention in *adabī* contexts, the unmistakeable Shīʿī tone of much of their content notwithstanding.[64] By contrast, there is no evidence that the works of al-Ṣadūq discussed here were consulted by subsequent generations as anything other than sources for the hadith of the imams.[65] This long-term picture may be deceptive, however, inasmuch as it potentially obscures the exceptional circumstances of the Buwayhid context in which al-Ṣadūq was writing. It is not inconceivable that an *adab* compendium made up entirely of the imams' hadith might have enjoyed some currency as an *adab* compendium during the Buwayhid period, but for this to have ceased when Imāmīs and their ideas fled the centres of power in Iraq and Iran following the fall of the Buwayhids to the Seljuqs. Though far from conclusive, the apparent citation of al-Ṣadūq by al-Tawḥīdī indicates that some of his works initially enjoyed a more diverse readership than they have come to have in later centuries.

Some compendia offer more clues in their introductions. *Al-Mawāʿiẓ*, al-Ṣadūq's short collection of wisdom-filled testimonies from imams to their sons, possesses the clearest appeal to a broader audience. The transmission of knowledge and status from one imam to the next is of vital importance in Imāmī imamology, but this book of father-to-son advice gives no hint of such a group-specific conceptual framework; it is introduced in distinctly detheologized tones, promising 'precious glimmers and iridescent jewels, counsels from the house of prophecy', focussing rather on the supremely *adabī* concern of rhetorical excellence. The introduction also refers to the Prophet's 'successors' (*khulafā'*, sg. *khalīfa*), conspicuously avoiding Shī'ī vocabulary (*imām*, *waṣī*, etc.) that might alienate non-Imāmī readers.[66] By contrast, *Ma'ānī* departs from *'Ilal* and *al-Khiṣāl* in that its opening directs it to specifically Imāmī concerns. The first chapter is entitled 'The Reason Wherefore We Have Entitled This Work "The Book of the Meanings of Traditions"', and describes the dizzying polyvalence of the imams' inspired speech and the consequent importance of being able to understand it correctly. In this case, at least, al-Ṣadūq's use of *adab*-like techniques remains directed at Imāmīs, serving only to explore a long-standing theological-hermeneutic conundrum in a new light.

These direct addresses confirm al-Ṣadūq's capacity to seek very different audiences for different works, but they are the exception rather than the rule, and for the other works discussed in this chapter the situation is less clear-cut; *'Ilal* has no surviving introduction, while *al-Khiṣāl*'s is extremely brief and offers few clues as to the book's intended audience. This relative silence, however, may itself be indicative, and the ambiguity it creates may be deliberate. *'Ilal* can be read as a demonstration of the imams' omniscience of causality, but unlike in *Ma'ānī* the reader is not directly invited to approach it in this way, increasing the likelihood that al-Ṣadūq is here courting a broader, non-Imāmī readership.[67] This possibility, in turn, raises the intriguing hypothesis that these works' mixture of curiosity and theological assertion is designed to lure, even trick non-Imāmī readers (who might have no interest in a book that announced itself as Imāmī theology) into ingesting Imāmī arguments, the very device that al-Ṣadūq admits to using in *Kamāl al-dīn*. Such a hypothesis is all the more tempting given *adab* literature's rich and various discourse about authorial acts of deception. Though *udabā'* routinely champion sincerity and truthfulness (the *ṣadāqa* and *Muṣādaqa* of al-Ṣadūq's and al-Tawḥīdī's respective titles),[68] they are also commonly found laying out plans to mislead their trusting readers. Here is al-Ābī introducing part of his *Nathr al-durr*:

> Perhaps someone will say, why has he not devoted an independent book to jesting, or placed it all at the end, giving it a section of its own after the completion of the serious part? He does not realise that I did this in order to trap the ignorant, that he might come upon some knowledge, and to ensnare the jester, that he might fall upon something serious. If I had devoted a separate section to it and had not mixed jest and earnest in this book, most present-day readers would have gone for that one section and they would have considered the serious parts as

> something heavy and dull, even something to be avoided and left alone, in spite of its being valuable like gold and pearls.[69]

We have already observed similar strategies described in other *adab* compendia, but al-Ābī's more explicit language of manipulation ('trap'; 'ensnare') is a reminder that though stealthy proselytization is not a common occurrence in this literature as a whole, the act of deceiving the reader for her own good is entirely at home in the generic space that *ʿIlal* and *al-Khiṣāl* unmistakeably inhabit.

Alongside these discourses of deception within *adab*, Imāmī Shīʿism has its own rich traditions of secrecy, encapsulated in the complex concept of *taqīya* – 'dissimilation'. If al-Ṣadūq is, indeed, seeking consciously to deceive readers in these works, it seems plausible that he does so with some understanding of *taqīya* in mind. We have already explored how *taqīya* served a hermeneutic function for early Imāmīs including al-Ṣadūq, but in the main its role in Imāmī thought is divided into two broad categories: firstly, an expansive notion of initiatic secrecy, inextricable from broader Imāmī doctrinal vistas of an enlightened few guarding hidden knowledge, hierarchical authority structures and messianic expectation; secondly, a practicality, codified in law, for self-preservation in Sunnī-dominated contexts, in which overt Imāmī practice or confession could be hazardous. The first meaning is more dominant in pre-Buwayhid Imāmīsm, increasingly giving way to the second from al-Mufīd onwards.[70] This leaves al-Ṣadūq once again as a transitional figure, and his exact views on the matter are unclear. He gives a strikingly absolute verdict in *al-Iʿtiqādāt*: 'Our belief regarding *taqīya* is that it is obligatory, and the station of one who neglects it is that of one who neglects prayer', but he does not say what this actually involves.[71] Al-Mufīd criticizes this statement for missing obvious points of practicality, making it unlikely that al-Ṣadūq was entirely unaware of such things.[72] The statement itself, however, evokes older, paradigmatic notions of secrecy, in which we have already seen al-Ṣadūq express some interest in Chapter 2 (and will again in Chapter 5).[73]

These accounts of *taqīya* leave us little the wiser regarding the kinds of dissimilation we see in al-Ṣadūq's *adabī* writings – the possibility that he is deliberately but deniably foisting Imāmī teachings upon unsuspecting readers. Studies of the older meaning of *taqīya*, with its initiatic hierarchies and hermeneutic riddles, have noted that this is a feature of a closed system – that *taqīya* thus conceived is inextricable from the broader scheme of early Imāmī cosmologies.[74] Such a concept thus has little currency in a book like *al-Mawāʿiẓ*, which specifically undertakes to bring the imams' hadith into generic spaces and readerships beyond any closed Imāmī discourse. While *taqīya* as a matter of practicality, by contrast, has an obvious relevance here, it remains the case that when later Buwayhid scholars give examples of *taqīya*-worthy situations they give solidly legal examples, such as avoiding specifically Shīʿī ritual forms.[75] This, however, is only to be expected, given that these are jurists writing within a legal framework, their concern being which obligations a believer is allowed to forego in the name of self-preservation. Literary experiments, even if explicitly conceived with *taqīya* in mind, would hardly register with such concerns.[76]

Ultimately, *taqīya* is a troublesome concept to study. The possibility that authors are deliberately concealing the truth is a daunting one for any field wherein scholars rely on those authors' written testaments for their information. For an author to confess to dissimilation is usually self-defeating, and the hypothesis that an author is trying to conceal something is only demonstrable to the extent that this endeavour is not successful, the breaking of authorial ciphers being the only sure way of revealing them.[77] This being the case, our verdict regarding al-Ṣadūq's use of *taqīya* in these works must remain tentative in some respects. The question is one of two parts: the first asks whether al-Ṣadūq is actively trying to deceive readers in the hope of changing their attitudes to the imams' hadith; the second asks whether he understands these attempts as a form of *taqīya*. In answer to the first part, we can affirm with some confidence that in *al-Mawāʿiẓ*, *Muṣādaqat*, *ʿIlal*, *al-Khiṣāl* and possibly other works, too, al-Ṣadūq is anticipating a partly non-Imāmī readership, and is accordingly taking steps to circumvent their prejudices and increase the chance of their taking Imāmī hadith and Imāmī doctrine seriously. With the aforementioned considerations in mind, the evidence of *Kamāl al-dīn* is particularly significant – in this work specifically aimed at other Shīʿīs,[78] al-Ṣadūq admits to devices that manipulate the reader, and it stands to reason that were he to use similar devices in works aimed at non-Shīʿīs he would be less likely to acknowledge them. At least as important, meanwhile, is the context of *adab* literature. These works inhabit a discursive space wherein the exact same manipulations of the reader that they seem to exhibit are an established presence, making their accidental simulation highly unlikely. This same context of *adab*, however, complicates the second part of the question, since it provides a solid basis for what al-Ṣadūq is doing that has little to do with Imāmī *taqīya*. Conversely, one of the key lessons of this chapter has been that these books are experiments of combination, and effective readings of them are ill-served by dichotomies of *adab* against hadith, religious against secular, curiosity against catechism and so on. It may be that al-Ṣadūq thought of his literary deceits as something quite separate from the deceits comprised by *taqīya*, but it seems more likely that this was another potential overlap between Imāmī and *adabī* forms and concepts that he recognized and sought to explore.[79]

The address to power

There were certainly reasons for al-Ṣadūq to consider his situation as potentially hazardous enough to merit dissimilation; regardless of Buwayhid rulers' Shīʿī leanings, anti-Shīʿī riots racked Baghdad in this period.[80] A more pressing danger than rampaging mobs, however – at least in Qum and Rayy – was another facet of *adab* literature's pedagogical ambitions: the address to power. *Adab* literature is yoked to social aspiration, its very building blocks constituting the cultural standards of the educated establishment: lexicographical information, amusing anecdotes, poetry, tales of moral virtue and gobbets of erudition to impress a courtly soirée. *Adab* compendia promise their readers this cultural capital, but their authors' role is not only to dispense empowering knowledge; they also confront potentates who hold power over them. Writers of *adab* literature regularly voice their aspiration to engage the ear of the ruler, a goal supplied with its typical rationale by Ibn Qutayba (d. 276/889):

> For religion to be in order the times must be in order, and for the times to be in order those in power must be in order, and those in power are kept in order – with God's provenance – by guidance and sound understanding. I have put together these wellsprings of reports (*ʿuyūn al-akhbār*) as instruction for the one who neglects manners, as a reminder for those with knowledge, as culture both for those who rule and for those who are ruled over, and as a relaxation for kings.[81]

Ibn Qutayba outlines a top-down vision of societal order and improvement, one that requires *adab*'s educational remit to include the sovereign. 'Culture both for those who rule and for those who are ruled over' smoothly elides the two constituencies, but the first sentence cited places emphasis firmly on those who rule. A century later in Buwayhid Rayy, the recent history of the Imāmīya was an imminent example of how a community's fortunes could be transformed by a change of political regime, and on an individual level, too, personal relations with those in power were vital to success at the Buwayhid court. The stakes of an *adīb*'s attempted instruction of the powerful were thus extremely high, and failure to keep harmony with the economy of manners could be disastrous.[82]

These dynamics provide essential context for the indirect, deniable routes through which works of *adab* literature seek to instruct their readers. The intended addressee cannot simply be told what to do; rather, instruction must be mixed with entertainment, diluted with miscellany and insured with the potential apology 'But I was only joking!'[83] The *adabī* reverence for sincere friendship, meanwhile, was at its most ambitious an ever-thwarted plea for an equal platform of exchange, where culture could flow between kings and courtiers free from imbalances of power.[84]

The image of the author stood precariously before the sultan resonates closely with the cautious, deceptive style of al-Ṣadūq's most complex forays into *adab* literature in *ʿIlal* and *al-Khiṣāl*, and with what we know of his situation in Rayy. Buwayhid rule offered promising circumstances for Imāmīs, but as a traditionist and a sometimes vociferous opponent of dialectic theology,[85] al-Ṣadūq was far from invulnerable in the courtly environment. The hazards facing him are embodied in the person of al-Ṣāḥib Ibn ʿAbbād, the formidable vizier, patron of *udabāʾ* and enthusiastic proponent of Muʿtazilī *kalām*. It was Ibn ʿAbbād who, we are told, banished al-Ṣadūq and others precisely for being traditionists, deeming their views primitive and detrimental to individual enlightenment and the public good.[86] Al-Ṣadūq's traditionism, moreover, sharply distinguishes him from Imāmī authors of the period who attained high office at court.[87]

The opportunities and dangers of bringing the imams' speech before powerful readers constitute a compelling subtext for the full range of al-Ṣadūq's experiments with *adab* explored in this chapter. None of the works examined thus far provides any direct portrayal of al-Ṣadūq's encounters with potentates, but in other writings he offers us precisely that. Twice – in *Majālis maʿa Rukn al-Dawla* and in a shorter passage in *Kamāl al-dīn* – he gives accounts of himself debating at court in the presence of Rukn al-Dawla. Al-Ṣadūq is likely the narrator in both of these texts, and accordingly they present very comfortable occasions: al-Ṣadūq appears wholly in control of the situation, demonstrating his knowledge before a benevolent and grateful amir;[88] there is little sense of danger, let alone cause to exercise *taqīya*. In another work, however, we see another encounter with similar stakes, but in which al-Ṣadūq does not get to write both sides of the conversation. *ʿUyūn*, his book about ʿAlī al-Riḍā, the eighth imam, remains one of al-Ṣadūq's most enduringly popular and well-studied works,[89] valued variously as a history and as a hagiography, but it is rarely remarked upon that al-Ṣadūq addresses this work to none other than Ibn ʿAbbād, the only such dedication in his oeuvre to survive. Ibn ʿAbbād, we read, had composed some elegies to the eighth imam, and al-Ṣadūq therefore presents him with this work on the Martyr of Tus to feed this laudable devotional enthusiasm. Here, then, we have al-Ṣadūq seeking to ingratiate a less-than-benevolent potentate, to ingratiate him, what is more, with the very hadith of which Ibn ʿAbbād was habitually suspicious.

ʿUyūn is not structured as an *adab* compendium; most of its hadiths are gathered in chapters under broadly theological themes, with a sporadic deference to historical linearity (it starts with al-Riḍā's father and birth and ends with his death and tomb). It is, however, replete with the same strategies to which we are now so accustomed, wrapping what al-Ṣadūq wants to say in what his reader wants to read. Chapters devoted to particular aspects of the imam's teaching and knowledge are reliably sanitized for a Muʿtazilī audience, with the first chapter on the imam's teachings (chapter 11) devoted to God's transcendent unity (*tawḥīd*).[90] In the book's chapters on the *dalāʾil* ('signs' or 'proofs;' sg. *dalāla*) of the imam, al-Riḍā is allotted only one kind of miracle, that of pre-emptive knowledge, knowledge which, al-Ṣadūq explicitly clarifies, has been transmitted to him through his forefathers from the Prophet.[91] This is a stark departure from the portrait of the imams' powers in al-Ṣadūq's other works, wherein they exhibit all manner of supernatural knowledge, the ability to command the sun to rise in the afternoon and so on.[92] *ʿUyūn* even sports a chapter affirming the Imāmī imams' high regard for Zayd b. ʿAlī, a claim with minimal discernible relevance to al-Riḍā, but of great relevance for ingratiating the Zaydī sentiments of Ibn ʿAbbād.[93] Outside the demarcated chapters for such topics, however, one is liable to find an imam who is rather less explicable. In chapter 41, a courtier of al-Maʾmūn expresses cynicism at the efficacy of al-Riḍā's prayer for rain. Al-Riḍā responds by commanding two attendant statues of lions to devour the man, which they obligingly do.[94] *ʿUyūn*'s readers, like those of *al-Khiṣāl*, also encounter unsignposted instruction in Imāmī doctrine, with miscellaneous material about sorcerous angels providing cover for forthright accounts of the necessity of the *ḥujja*, the fact of the occultation and the coming of the *qāʾim*.[95] *ʿUyūn* thus makes full use of the tools we have surveyed across this chapter, tools that it reveals as perfectly suited to its goal of presenting the imams' words to an inimical potentate.

Unlike *ʿIlal* or *al-Khiṣāl*, *ʿUyūn* accompanies the imam's collected teachings with some sustained narrative of his life. In this work, as in subsequent Imāmī literature on the eighth imam, a lynchpin of al-Riḍā's portrayal in narrative is the corpus of 'council' (*majlis*) texts, which narrate al-Riḍā's debates with various opponents at the ʿAbbāsid court. Al-Riḍā's career was transformed by his appointment as heir to the caliph al-Maʾmūn, but he predeceased the latter, murdered, as Imāmī accounts tell it, on al-Maʾmūn's orders. These council texts depict the cynical caliph (who, whatever his motives, has turned against his appointee) arranging for the imam to debate with some formidable opponent before the court, hoping to show the humiliating limits of al-Riḍā's knowledge. Inevitably, al-Riḍā triumphs in a magnificent display of inspired wisdom, and al-Maʾmūn is left seething with jealous, ultimately murderous resentment. Spread across the text of *ʿUyūn*, these council narratives serve to dramatize the work's own core didactic project. The imam speaks his truth before a hostile sovereign, a sovereign whose ultimate, violent rejection of that truth will lead to his own damnation. The story cannot but ring manifold echoes with al-Ṣadūq's own situation; he, too, seeks to convey the imam's speech to sceptical political power, before whom he must cloak declaration of the imams' truth beneath concessions to hubristic rationalism. Ibn ʿAbbād is unwittingly thrust into the position of al-Maʾmūn – confronted with the imam's voice, facing the fateful decision of whether or not to acknowledge it as he should. Perhaps the book's most daring image comes at its very end when, after offering multiple visions of al-Maʾmūn's final wretchedness, al-Ṣadūq presents the image of the meek, dishevelled poet Diʿbil al-Khuzāʿī, who attains salvation through the beautiful elegies he has composed for al-Riḍā.[96] Ibn ʿAbbād, whose own elegies for the imam al-Ṣadūq praised in his introduction, is here shown his route to salvation in a subversively humble new role model.

We do not know whether Ibn ʿAbbād ever read *ʿUyūn*, or, if he did, how and whether this might have affected al-Ṣadūq's situation in Rayy. What the book nonetheless shows us with especial lucidity is al-Ṣadūq's effort, observable across the works surveyed in this chapter, to bring the imams' hadith to different audiences, and the potential risks and rewards of that effort. Through all these compendia, even as he dextrously negotiates the forms and foci of *adab* literature, al-Ṣadūq's works remain composed almost entirely of hadith. Later Imāmī writers of *adab* will mix the imams' hadith with other material, but not al-Ṣadūq, and in the ill-fated confrontation between al-Riḍā and al-Maʾmūn we see something of the salvific urgency underlying this rather strange compromise of form and content. In the previous chapter we saw al-Ṣadūq as a jurist and theologian seeking a technical approach to the hadith that befitted their status. In his experiments in *adab*, we see a continuation of this same project, introducing (even smuggling) the imams' words into literary spaces inhabited by non-Imāmīs and powerful non-Imāmīs in particular, that they might receive the reverence that is their due.

Conclusion

The first conclusion of this chapter must be that many of al-Ṣadūq's compendia – *ʿIlal, al-Khiṣāl, Maʿānī, al-Mawāʿiẓ, Muṣādaqat* – represent a deep and expansive conversation with *adab* literature. Whether or not they can be considered *adab* compendia themselves (definitions thereof fluctuating as they do), these books of hadith are incomprehensible when removed from that conversation. In them, al-Ṣadūq makes inventive use of *adab* literature variously to reimagine Imāmī concepts, expand the perceived range of the imams' teachings and deliver their hadith to new, influential audiences.

This conclusion, in turn, alerts us further to the importance of compilers' authorial agency. The meaning and significance of al-Ṣadūq's hadiths are transformed according to the contextual and generic spaces into which he compiles them. We have seen the testaments of compilers themselves discussing in detail how different types of compilation should best be done, and we have seen, too, that al-Ṣadūq and others are capable of conducting authorial schemes quite beyond what they openly declare. The apparently anarchic character of books like *ʿIlal, al-Khiṣāl* and *Maʿānī* has played its part in the repeated characterization of al-Ṣadūq as a compiler of imperfect rigour; viewed in his true context, however, the author of these compendia appears as deliberate and flexible, adopting different styles of compilation to suit his purposes, rather than pursuing a single goal with inconstant capability. It is with this understanding of al-Ṣadūq in mind that we proceed to examine his compilations in greater detail in Part II of this book.

A third conclusion pertains to the Buwayhid period. The Buwayhid Imāmī experience led to formative developments in theological and legal scholarship, but this was not the only achievement of Buwayhid Imāmīsm, for Buwayhid Imāmīs did not only write and excel in the fields of law and theology. The same opportunities that fostered theological development also nurtured literary engagement and experimentation, creating an age of Imāmī poets and Imāmī *udabāʾ*. The boundaries between these different intellectual pursuits, moreover, were highly porous, and the phenomenon of a traditionist *faqīh* experimenting with *adab* literature shows us the folly of isolating any one aspect of this effervescent period of Imāmī writing. While jurists like al-Ṭūsī became canonized into a continuing tradition, these literary developments proved less enduring, but al-Ṣadūq's adabesque compendia show us one part of the continued importance that they retain, speaking through collections of hadith that Imāmīs have consulted ever since.

Part II

Reading al-Ṣadūq

4

Al-Tawḥīd

Theology and its limits

Introduction

One of al-Ṣadūq's most widely-consulted works, *al-Tawḥīd*, 'The Book of God's Unity', is a collection of some 580 hadiths concerning the nature of God. It follows a broadly encyclopaedic style, divided into chapters according to subject matter, such that a reader can with relative ease seek out statements from the imams regarding, for example, divine essence, the createdness of the Qur'an or whether or not God is a thing (*shay'*). Enquiries into these and similar subjects were the driving force of Muslim theological debate in the Buwayhid period, and *al-Tawḥīd* is often consulted as a document of al-Ṣadūq's own views and those of the early Imāmīya on such topics, as well as being a source long cherished by Twelver readers.

With *al-Tawḥīd*, we enter our most extensive engagement with al-Ṣadūq's theology, though this must be accompanied by certain terminological caveats. Anglophone literature on Shī'ism has become accustomed to the distinction between theology and imamology, but this was not a distinction that Imāmīs like al-Ṣadūq used; rather, questions about the imams and their nature were part of discussions of belief (*'aqīda*; *i'tiqād*), as were questions regarding God's nature. The imams are, after all, a central part of how God communicates with his creation. Furthermore, God's nature and (for Shī'īs at least) the imams' nature were central topics for dialectic theology – *kalām* – to be debated rigorously with one's intellectual opponents. For some Shī'īs, conversely, and some Sunnīs, such dialectic was a gross impiety to be avoided and condemned. These Muslims were no less possessed of doctrines about God's nature – they had their theologies inasmuch as they had theological beliefs – but they were opposed to dialectic theology as a practice, and often resisted articulating beliefs in terms of the questions it asked.

Al-Tawḥīd, then, is certainly theological in subject matter, albeit no less theological than *Kamāl al-dīn* by some measures. The topics that concern most of its chapters had long occupied the centre of theological controversies between Muslim groups: the tensions between God's transcendence and immanence; the interpretation of certain Qurʾanic verses that described God in anthropomorphic terms; the question of free will and predestination; the nature of God's names and attributes, and how these related to his unknowable essence. Moreover, intergroup disagreements surrounding these issues were frequently articulated in terms of rationalist–traditionist axes, with traditionists adhering more closely to the perceived literal meaning of scripture, meanings that rationalists were more inclined to reinterpret the better to conform with abstract theological schemata. Al-Ṣadūq's introduction directs *al-Tawḥīd* squarely at such debates, announcing the book's purpose to be the refutation of those who denigrate the Imāmīya as heretically theologically inept, and more specifically those who decry the imams' hadiths as theologically unsound, 'Being ignorant of their interpretation and misunderstanding their meanings, removing them from their proper context and failing to compare their words with those of the Qurʾan'.[1] As we shall see, these adversaries are clearly identified as being of a Muʿtazilī orientation, with al-Ṣadūq consistently anticipating friction with the Muʿtazilī teachings of God's absolute transcendence and justice and the reality of human free will.

Though it is al-Ṣadūq's most extensive surviving engagement with core theological matters, *al-Tawḥīd* is therefore not a theological encyclopaedia, nor is it an account of al-Ṣadūq's own theology, though it has frequently been read as if it were.[2] While in *al-Iʿtiqādāt* or *al-Hidāya* we find hadiths on theological topics explicitly committed as proof-texts for a particular tenet for the instruction of the faithful, we find those same hadiths used very differently in *al-Tawḥīd*. This is an apologetic work, as much about the source of doctrines – the hadith – as it is about the doctrines themselves, a work that identifies the sanctity of the imams' hadith as its primary goal. Following what we have seen in Part I, we should expect al-Ṣadūq to pursue such a task with enthusiasm, and indeed we find him in his very element in *al-Tawḥīd*'s pages. This book far oversteps the tone of negotiated apology with which it begins, moving on from attempts to reconcile the imams' hadith with theological arguments to a wholehearted disavowal of theological dialectic in its concluding chapter. While its amassed traditions offer no shortage of answers to theological questions, their ultimate effect is to instruct on how the imams' hadith should be read, presenting a thunderous manifesto of al-Ṣadūq's traditionism.

The structure of *al-Tawḥīd*

This chapter will present a reading of *al-Tawḥīd* as a whole text, analysing in detail how al-Ṣadūq constructs and communicates his arguments. We will proceed through the book from beginning to end, examining its compilation according to the approach outlined in the Introduction. What follows will thus depend a great deal upon the chapters of *al-Tawḥīd* and their arrangement. For the sake of clarity, a complete translation of the book's table of contents is therefore supplied in Appendix I.

The following reading will inevitably be selective, with judgements made as to which chapters and hadiths are most significant for illustrating al-Ṣadūq's endeavours. Where a chapter is not explicitly discussed, this is because it is deemed to fit into the broader patterns already outlined. In terms of larger structural units, the present analysis divides *al-Tawḥīd* into three principal sections. These are not demarcated by al-Ṣadūq himself; rather, they are hypothesized here on the basis of the dramatic shifts in form and content observed between each. In his introduction to *al-Tawḥīd*, al-Ṣadūq singles out two erroneous beliefs that the Imāmīya are often falsely accused of holding: belief in God's similarity to created entities (*tashbīh*), the worst excess of which is anthropomorphism, and fatalistic belief in predestination (*jabr*). It is to these two doctrinal areas that the first and third of *al-Tawḥīd*'s three sections are, respectively, devoted. Section 1, then, concerns *tashbīh*; it runs from chapter 1 up to and including chapter 28, and consistently deals with topics directly related to divine transcendence: that God cannot be confined to place, the meaning of God's anger and so on. Section 2 starts at the point where this direct address of *tashbīh* gives way to something more mysterious. Beginning at chapter 29, this section contains material concerning such things as the meaning of God's names and the distances between angels' wings. While some of its chapters are not unconnected with matters of God's transcendence, the change in tone is consistent and distinct. Section 3 deals with the second of al-Ṣadūq's opening worries, that of free will and predestination, and begins at chapter 53, running until the end of the book. The table of contents given in Appendix I delineates these hypothesized sections. As we shall see in the following text, at least as important as changes in subject matter are the changes in argumentative style that distinguish one section from another. Hadiths in all three sections may sometimes offer similar kinds of information, but how al-Ṣadūq situates them within different compiled structures encourages that they be read in very different ways.

1 *Tashbīh*

The two problem-doctrines of *tashbīh* and *jabr* differ from one another in nature, and these differences and al-Ṣadūq's corresponding differences in approach constitute the principal axis upon which *al-Tawḥīd* pivots. The book's first section is devoted to *tashbīh*, which is by far the easier of the two questions for all concerned. In sharp contrast to questions of predestination, the charge of anthropomorphism can be countered by a wholesale espousal of the opposite position – that God is transcendentally dissimilar to any created thing. By the time al-Ṣadūq is writing, especially within the context of the heavily Muʿtazilī-leaning Buwayhid milieu, to espouse *tashbīh* is considered a relatively fringe position.[3] While this lends urgency to al-Ṣadūq's denial that the imams ever taught such things, this urgency is not a troubling one, for *al-Tawḥīd* showcases his access to a wealth of Imāmī hadiths that affirm the transcendence of God in suitable terms. As for hadiths that might be more troublesome, al-Ṣadūq has no trouble excluding them (at least for now).

In keeping with the simplicity of *tashbīh* as a problem, section 1 is where al-Ṣadūq's compiling most straightforwardly reflects the apologetic aims set out in his introduction. The chapters dealing with *tashbīh* teem with mechanisms and strategies to convince the reader that the hadiths he reads are fully in keeping with theological norms, without any trace of the heresy and intellectual laughing stock of anthropomorphism. Our foremost concern as we examine this section will be to identify these compiler's mechanisms and examine how they work. To begin with a note on sources, it is a conspicuous feature of *al-Tawḥīd* that it has the most restricted set of sources of any of al-Ṣadūq's surviving writings. Al-Ṣadūq narrates here only from his most frequently cited and clearly most trusted teachers, figures like Muḥammad b. ʿAlī Mājīlawayh, ʿAlī b. Aḥmad b. Muḥammad b. ʿImrān al-Daqqāq, his father and Ibn al-Walīd. He excludes more eccentric sources, an obvious defensive device, but also Sunnī sources who, though useful in many apologetic situations,[4] have no bearing on a vindication of the Imāmī corpus. At the same time, a striking absence with regard to source material is that nowhere in *al-Tawḥīd* does al-Ṣadūq mount the defence with which he begins *al-Iʿtiqādāt*: that any tradition ascribed to the imams that compromises God's oneness is a forgery.[5] Instead, as is so often the case in al-Ṣadūq's work, he suspends this most useful (but most compromising) of rebuttals in his quest for a hadith corpus that can be more intact and more sacred.

Explication

In the first two chapters of *al-Tawḥīd*, we already see two sides of al-Ṣadūq's approach. In chapter 1, 'The Reward of Those Who Know and Declare God's Oneness', the title concern is affirmed in 35 mostly short, straightforwardly relevant hadiths: 'God has forbidden to the fire the bodies of those who declare his oneness'; 'O Muḥammad, blessed among your community are those who say there is no god but God, only he, only he, only he'.[6] The result is a specific point clearly made with a large body of targeted evidence. A very different approach, meanwhile, emerges in chapter 2, 'The Oneness of God and the Prohibition Against Likening Him to Created Things (*tashbīh*)'. This chapter is the longest in the book, and presents a hymnic assemblage of what appear to be the most powerfully eloquent attestations of monotheism in the imams' hadith that al-Ṣadūq could find, many of which are of considerable length. Imam ʿAlī sets the tone in the first hadith:

> Praise be to God who cannot die, whose wonders are boundless, since each day he brings into being new things that had not been before. He it is who was not begotten, such that he might share his glory, nor does he beget, such that he might owe inheritance or pass away. Thoughts cannot grasp him to apprehend him with fancies or likenesses, nor do eyes see him, such that he would change with their shifting. He it is in whose primacy there is no end, nor is there edge or limit to his finality. He it is whom no time precedes, whom no age follows, nor does there touch him any excess or weakness.[7]

Al-Ṣadūq has only just begun, but the size and magisterial character of this chapter are such that one might wonder whether he has not already achieved at least half of his stated goals. This is a vision of the imams' speech as sweeping kerygma, as beautiful, total encapsulations of transcendence that brook no response. This kind of presentation plays an important role in *al-Tawḥīd*, but it is tempered and put to work by the very different picture of the imams' hadith offered in chapter 1, which rigorously subdivides their speech to address targeted apologetics and details. The interplay between these two approaches, encapsulated in these two opening chapters, will play out across the work.

After chapter 2 ends, section 1 relies largely upon the latter, more technical approach. Al-Ṣadūq delivers a long sequence of chapters after the pattern of chapter 1, each addressing a particular subsidiary question to the overall theme of refuting *tashbīh*. It is in these pages that *al-Tawḥīd* most resembles a reference work, as successive chapters address such questions as the relationship between God's attributes and essence, whether or not he has a form and whether or not he can be seen. Though this mode of presentation certainly assists a believer seeking specific answers, it also completely fits al-Ṣadūq's stated apologetic goal. Through their exhaustive demarcations, these chapters show the reader that these are all questions to which the imams are wholly able to respond. Their demarcated variety affirms the precision and breadth of the imams' erudition, while their contents exhibit significant efforts to ingratiate Muʿtazilī thought, most clearly in chapter 5, 'The Meaning of Divine Oneness and Justice (*ʿadl*)'.

Al-Ṣadūq's desire to maximize the apologetic potential of these chapters is manifested in an unusual feature of *al-Tawḥīd*, namely the regularity with which we encounter his own voice. Far more so than in most of his other compilations, here he is forever interjecting between the traditions, interpreting and clarifying their contents whenever these might be open to unhelpful, controversial readings. Following the statement that whosoever professes the oneness of God shall enter paradise, wine drinkers and adulterers included, al-Ṣadūq inserts the caveat that such sinners will be admitted only if they duly repent; when the imam tells his interlocutor that God's knowledge is to God as one's hand is to oneself, al-Ṣadūq appends a much more technical turn of phrase ('is among the attributes of his essence'); when Moses expresses repentance, al-Ṣadūq explains how this need not imply that the sinless prophet had done anything wrong.[8] He also regularly abbreviates hadiths, including only the element that addresses the question at hand and avoiding complicating digressions.[9] A further, more heavy-handed form of control is sometimes exerted through lengthy summaries in al-Ṣadūq's own prose, wherein he explains the concepts to which groups of narrations or whole chapters attest. Such summaries are sometimes significantly longer than the collected hadiths of the chapter,[10] and variously employ both the discursive tools of *kalām* ('If it is argued . . . Then our response is . . .') and citations from a range of sources beyond hadith.

This careful hermeneutical policing has obvious utility for *al-Tawḥīd*'s apologetic purpose, and it echoes and responds to a particular complaint from al-Ṣadūq's introduction: that the Imāmīya's detractors condemn them for heresy 'on account of those narrations that they find in [Imāmīs'] books, though they are ignorant of their exegesis (*tafsīr*) and meanings (*maʿānī*)'.[11] Faulty interpretation is a hazard that must be avoided, and al-Ṣadūq therefore takes exceptional care to control how his narrations are understood.

Obfuscation

So far we have seen al-Ṣadūq pushing to the limit his traditions' capacity to attest to their own orthodoxy. He uses a range of compiler's tricks alongside line after line of his own prose to show precisely what the hadiths mean, such that the reader may know the precision with which they are theologically sound. There is, however, another side to these chapters, to all these checks and balances, where we start to see indications that al-Ṣadūq is not simply striving to be as clear as he possibly can.

When *al-Tawḥīd* is placed alongside other works by al-Ṣadūq and his contemporaries, it is clear that there exist other techniques of compilation which would further clarify *al-Tawḥīd*'s contents but which are conspicuously absent from the chapters on *tashbīh* that make up section 1. The first of these is the basic strategy of grouping similar reports. It is common practice among al-Ṣadūq and his fellows (including later on in *al-Tawḥīd*) to group together narrations that have similar content within a chapter. For the duration of section 1, however, al-Ṣadūq consistently neglects to do this: in chapter 9, '[God's] Power', for example, a number of hadiths address the question of whether or not God can put the universe inside an egg without making the universe smaller or making the egg bigger, but these reports are not all juxtaposed but dispersed across the chapter, mixed with those addressing very different questions.[12]

A second absent technique is the sequencing of a chapter's hadiths so as to create a developing explanation or even an argument. The most basic form of this is to begin with reports that straightforwardly state the desired position and then to move to those that treat subsidiary aspects of the question or illustrate it a little more lengthily or colourfully. Once again, as well as in al-Ṣadūq's other works and those of other writers, this technique will appear later on in *al-Tawḥīd*'s own pages,[13] but not in this first section. A third, related strategy is to make sure that a chapter's reports do not contradict one another, an essential ingredient of didactic clarity which is not always applied in *al-Tawḥīd*. Returning to chapter 9, the egg and the universe, al-Ṣadūq's different reports give different answers, varying between affirmation, denial and objection to the question;[14] this knotty little problem is evidently not one to which al-Ṣadūq is interested in giving a definitive answer.

This combination of efforts at clarification with features that undermine those efforts could be read as self-defeating ineptitude. Such a reading, however, denies that al-Ṣadūq might combine these features on purpose, a hypothesis that stands at odds with the fact that he elsewhere shows himself wholly capable of being clearer when he wants to be. If we give the benefit of the doubt to the supposition that *al-Tawḥīd* is the way al-Ṣadūq wants it to be, it becomes evident that these two aspects of clarification and obfuscation work in harmony to further the book's driving apologetic concern. Chapter 8, 'What is Said Concerning Seeing [God]', exhibits some of *al-Tawḥīd*'s more glaring instances of contradictory material. While most of the chapter's reports deliver the unsurprising message that God is far too great to be seen, in one hadith the imam declares that believers will, indeed, see God on the Day of Judgement, and moreover he cautions his listener not to repeat this information! Al-Ṣadūq next introduces a set of reports on the theme that vision with the heart is not like vision with the eyes,[15] before inserting his own discussion of how even in hadiths that do seem to suggest that God can be seen, what is meant is this more theologically palatable sense of an esoteric seeing that is quite unlike physical seeing. Read in sequence, then, the chapter first denies that God can be seen, then suddenly suggests that he actually can be, before mollifying this contradiction by clarifying that some types of 'seeing' are not like others. Al-Ṣadūq has taken the reader through a process of disturbance and disambiguation. His material in sequence asserts a doctrine, contradicts it and then shows how these seeming contradictions can be reconciled, and in so doing communicates a vital message: however strange or troubling a single report from the imams may seem, the reader should always be certain that there exists either another report or the discerning power of a scholar that will explain such problems away.

We are again reminded here that al-Ṣadūq's goal is not to enunciate doctrine but to defend the imams' hadiths themselves. This project is threatened by the potential accusation that however many hadiths he may assemble, he excludes many others that might not have been so agreeable. Al-Ṣadūq does not respond to this threat by defending his selection qualitatively with a discussion of narrators and *asānīd*;[16] rather, he takes steps to make his sample in *al-Tawḥīd* look representative, even to function as a metonym for the entire corpus. We see this in the sheer volume of the work, sometimes adducing tens of proof-texts for a single doctrine (sometimes with a note from al-Ṣadūq saying that he would have included more were it not for his wish for brevity),[17] but also in gestures like these, where al-Ṣadūq purports to show his own reading process as a compiler. He includes not just the clearest reports but also the ambiguous ones that they serve to explain, giving not only the finished product of a neat summary of doctrine but also the disparate diversity of texts from which such doctrines are constructed. In so doing, he attempts to gain a hold on readers' perception of whatever they may hear reported from the imams in the future, suggesting that just as the unwieldy plurality of *al-Tawḥīd*'s contents yields to orthodox readings, so too will other unlikely- or contradictory-looking hadiths about universe-sized eggs. The whole corpus is here justified by means of a part of it, as al-Ṣadūq extends the apologetic reach of *al-Tawḥīd* far beyond its covers.

2 *ʿAẓama*

Thus far, *al-Tawḥīd* has been driven by apology. Section 1 sees al-Ṣadūq attempting to present a theology that is acceptable to the prevailing intellectual forces of his early Buwayhid context, and simultaneously to represent the entire corpus of the imams' hadith as similarly sound. This studiedly apologetic tone, however, dissipates around the middle of the book, and the present reading identifies this change in register as the start of section 2. We are now confronted with a set of chapters that transport the reader to somewhere a great deal more mysterious than encountered thus far, material that not only shows little interest in apologetic but threatens to undermine it. *Al-Tawḥīd* starts to address such matters as the meanings of the letters of the alphabet, the meanings of God's many names and the fact that the heavens are balanced on the back of a rooster, which stands on top of an enormous rock which, in turn, rests on the back of an enormous fish. What, we may ask, is al-Ṣadūq trying to do?

The change in mood, and with it section 2, begins with chapter 29, 'God's Names and the Difference Between their Meanings and the Meanings of the Names of Created Beings'. Thus advertised, the chapter purports to address another stock question of *tashbīh*, but it soon lapses into a twenty-odd-page exegetical odyssey in which al-Ṣadūq, declaring it necessary to understand the meanings (sg. *maʿnā*) of God's names, sets out to explain them one by one, drawing on an eclectic mix of tradition, speculation and lexicography. For some names, he offers a simple synonym, such as with *khabīr* ('knowing;' 'aware'), which he equates to *ʿālim* (which, indeed, means much the same thing); others have lengthier discussions citing various proof-texts to establish their semantic field, while other names require careful conceptual clarification (while *ḥayy* means 'alive', this does not entail that God may die). We are still in broadly conventional theological territory (there is not a rooster in sight), but al-Ṣadūq has embarked upon a new direction that will escalate steeply over the next few chapters.

In a string of similar chapters, first the *basmala* (chapter 31), then the letters of the alphabet (chapters 32 and 33) and the phrases of the call to prayer (chapter 34) are given similarly lengthy interpretations, although this time these are delivered as hadiths from the imams. The effect of these vistas of interpretation is a potent illustration of the profundity of the imams' knowledge. The explanation of God's names was a cautious introduction, with al-Ṣadūq providing the explanations and these being thoroughly uncontroversial, grounded in theological reasoning and lexicographical evidence and supported by frequent citations. The subsequent chapters, however, shift back to the imams' hadith, even as their topics become distinctly more ambitious. The letters, in particular, signal a move to far more esoteric territory: the assertion of an intrinsic link between the Last Judgement and the nineteenth through 22nd letters of the alphabet is clearly a step or two up from adducing exemplars for the lexicographical difference between *al-Raḥmān* and *al-Raḥīm*.[18] Al-Ṣadūq is gradually building an image of the inspired and inimitable scale of the imams' understanding. In chapter 34, in which the call to prayer is interpreted, every phrase is expanded into an elaborate set of theological truths. We are beyond reason here, as the imams' interpretations assert meanings that no dialectic can confirm or deny, resting only on their God-given authority and so implicitly asserting it. The choice of subject is as apt as can be; the imams' knowledge, al-Ṣadūq shows his reader, plumbs the depths of language, speech and interpretation, bringing the very letters of the alphabet alive with hidden meaning and enchanting the whole of speech and text in a vast web of signification, one before which any lesser interpreter must be humbled.[19]

A pivotal moment of this new section is chapter 30, 'The Nature of the Qur'an'. It begins with the following narration:

> I asked al-Riḍā, 'O son of God's Messenger, tell me of the Qur'an, is it Creator or creation?' He replied,
>
> 'It is neither Creator nor creation, rather it is the speech of God, exalted and mighty is he.'[20]

This is brave new territory for *al-Tawḥīd*. Confronting no less a question than that which fuelled the debacle of al-Ma'mūn's inquisition a century before, and which was still hotly contested, he opens his chapter with an unmistakeable attack both on the teachings of dominant groups and the very premise over which they differ.[21] This once apologetic book, al-Ṣadūq announces, is now taking the fight to its opponents in this strange and radical hadith of the imam.

This is not the start of a sustained theological argument, however. The notion of a middle ground between a created and an uncreated Qur'an is not elaborated upon in the hadiths that follow, rather the idea developed is that the Qur'an, as the speech of God, is quite above such arbitrary speculation as to its nature or its meanings. The eye-catching doctrinal challenge of the first hadith is now rendered secondary, and is instead made to fuel a staunch traditionist rebuttal of all theological debate in this arena. A subsequent hadith restates the matter to this effect:

> I said to Abū al-Ḥasan Mūsā b. Ja'far, 'O son of God's messenger, what say you of the Qur'an? For there is disagreement among us in this matter, some saying that it is created and others that it is not created.' Said he,
>
> 'I do not say as they do in this matter. Rather I say that it is the speech of God.'[22]

Al-Ṣadūq intervenes to underpin this disavowal of speculation with a discussion of the unreliability of language itself. Statements regarding the Qur'an's createdness or otherwise, while possibly carrying legitimate meanings, also risk heretical ones. Crucially, he says, the Arabic word for 'created', *makhlūq*, can also mean 'falsified'. The Mu'tazilī viewpoint that the Qur'an is created thus carries a sacrilegious double meaning, while an Imāmī hadith stating that it is uncreated, inasmuch as it may in fact mean unfalsified, cannot be condemned even by the most ardent rationalist.

These arguments may carry echoes of al-Ṣadūq's earlier apologetics, but this should not distract us from the new and powerful ideas that he now introduces. This attack on theological disputation itself, buoyed up by arguments about the labyrinthine nature of meaning, builds directly upon the previous chapters' depictions of just how far these webs of signification can reach and of how their true understanding is the sole prerogative of the imams. The alternative to unseemly disputes, al-Ṣadūq implies with increasing volume, is submission to their knowledge.

The extent of this shift becomes fully apparent with chapter 38, 'Recounting God's Majesty (*'aẓama*)'. The chapter's assembled hadiths set out to illustrate the vastness of the divine, and illustrate it does, with all the potential conflict with anti-*tashbīh* transcendentalism that the word implies. It brims over with accounts of vast cosmological distances such as those between the curtains of smoke, light and fire that veil the Almighty, angels whose wings are covered in many-mouthed faces which forever voice the praises of the creator, other angels wondrously assembled of intermingled ice and fire[23] and, of course, the sea of shadows in which swims the fish upon whose back is balanced the rock on which stands the colossal rooster upon whose back the very heavens are placed. In keeping with the title of the chapter, the appropriately formidable dimensions involved, such as angels' necks the length of which would take a bird a half-millennium to fly,[24] are relayed in detail. God, the chapter tells us, is certainly great.

The change in register that these chapters enact is quite unmissable. We have already learned that God is great in the first section, but this was a greatness beyond understanding, beyond *tashbīh*, not to be described. The metaphysical circus of chapter 38 not only seems to conflict with the theological details of the first section but resoundingly throws down the gauntlet to Muʿtazilī models of knowledge (including their Imāmī adherents), wherein the universe was mapped according to reasoned processes, and accounts of burning angels and gigantic fish were firmly dismissed.[25] These hadiths take *al-Tawḥīd* much closer to al-Ṣadūq's Ḥanbalī contemporaries, departing abruptly from the cautious accommodations of earlier chapters to present accounts of the cosmos that admit no explanation or justification except the inspired speech of God's vicegerents.[26] Until now al-Ṣadūq has been seeking to demonstrate that his hadith corpus is in conformity with theological norms, but the words of the imams, he now shows his reader, are not all so benignly knowable.

Following these cosmological fireworks, in chapter 41 they are condensed to a simple theological point: 'That [God] Can Only Be Known Through Himself'. Al-Ṣadūq now denies knowledge of God to the hitherto unmentioned entity of reason (*ʿaql*).[27] He contemplates the 'Ḥayy b. Yaqẓān' scenario of the man who grows up in complete isolation and infers the central truths of religion from reasoned observation of nature,[28] and declares that this is impossible (unless that man receives divine inspiration). Reason is flawed and limited, al-Ṣadūq declares, and the only way to God is through divine guidance, guidance that is embodied, of course, in the hadith of the imams.

Sections 1 and 2 thus leave the reader with two quite distinct messages. Section 1 demonstrates that the imams' words are in conformity with the teachings of rationalist theologians, while section 2 presents the imams' words as containing truths that are unimpeachably beyond those theologians' reach. Recent views of al-Ṣadūq and of *al-Tawḥīd* have tended to ignore this contrast, focussing on section 1 to characterize the whole book as a work of rapprochement with Muʿtazilī ideas.[29] Due attention to section 2 can only complicate such a partial and simplistic verdict. It would be a leap of faith indeed to write off these chapters' sustained, coherent and combative account of the imams' knowledge, including the potential challenge it represents to the apologies of section 1, as the product of mere accident or indecision. Once again, these apparent contradictions make better sense if we understand them as working in tandem and by design. Section 2 lays down a dramatic challenge, one upon which al-Ṣadūq will build in what follows, but he gains much by delaying this challenge until the middle of a book that started with transparent theology. Section 1 has provided insurance, hammering home to the reader the imams' capacity to give sound, intelligible answers to important questions, and repressing any attempt to tar them with anthropomorphism, be it by Shīʿīs or non-Shīʿīs. Al-Ṣadūq shows first that his rationalist interlocutors have nothing to offer that the imams' hadith cannot supply, before going on to show that the hadith can offer a good deal more.

3 *Jabr*

Al-Ṣadūq has now nailed his traditionist colours firmly to the mast, but it is a mark of *al-Tawḥīd*'s complexity that we are still only in the middle of the book. More specifically, at this point there remains to be dealt with the second of the two doctrines that he began by disavowing: the excess of predestinationism (*jabr*), which occupies the book's third section. As he turns to confront the problem of *jabr*, however, al-Ṣadūq does not return to the style with which he treated the problem of *tashbīh*; rather, we again see something different. Indeed, *al-Tawḥīd*'s third section builds on the revelations of the second, demonstrating how one should be guided by the imams' hadith in the face both of difficult theological questions and of these texts' own numinous strangeness.

Hard problems

As noted earlier, while anthropomorphism can be faced down with total denial, the same is not true of the question of free will and predestination; rather, any account must negotiate some kind of path between the two. Al-Ṣadūq notes that the Imāmīya had been condemned for erring on the side of predestination, a standard criticism of traditionist groups levelled by the Muʿtazilīs, who emphasized free will, but even the most enthusiastic assertion of free will must still reckon with God's omniscience and omnipotence. This third section, then, takes up by far the harder of the two theological problems to which *al-Tawḥīd* is addressed.[30]

Section 3 and its discussion of *jabr* begin at chapter 53, but the daunting nature of the subject becomes more apparent with chapter 54, '*Badāʾ*'. One of the most troublesome theological bogeymen facing the Imāmīya in this period, *badāʾ* most commonly refers to the idea that God can change his mind, an idea that met with horror and ridicule among theologians of almost every stripe and especially among Muʿtazilīs.[31] While later narratives associating this doctrine with moments in early Shīʿī history – specifically the career of the early revolutionary al-Mukhtār and the succession crisis of Jaʿfar al-Ṣādiq – are hard to verify, by al-Ṣadūq's time the doctrine was firmly associated with the Imāmīya. This association is reflected in the quantity of hadiths in which the imams discuss *badāʾ*, a corpus that thus presents a serious hurdle to al-Ṣadūq's efforts to defend Imāmī hadith. Far from the relative ease with which he was able to put *tashbīh*-related concerns to rest, al-Ṣadūq now faces a highly contentious doctrine which risks serious damage to the credibility of the Imāmīya and their traditions, and thus demands a response.[32]

To juxtapose so troublesome a theological topic with the previous section's assault on theological argument can only be a provocative gesture. Having offered a hymn to the limits of dialectic, al-Ṣadūq now jumps into what looks like an urgent need for it. This is not a retreat, however; rather, this most controversial issue serves precisely to demonstrate how the supremacy of tradition over argument works in practice, a demonstration that al-Ṣadūq executes through the compiler's arts of selection and arrangement.[33] To understand this, we must proceed through his chapter on *badāʾ* in some detail.

Al-Ṣadūq begins chapter 54 with a pair of hadiths declaring that God 'has never before been worshipped/glorified with something like *badāʾ*'. In so doing, he brings the subject to the table with some very useful ambiguities. *Badāʾ*, we learn, is unique, mysterious, an unprecedented phenomenon concerning which we rush to judgement at our peril. Moreover, while the stronger implication of the traditions is an affirmation of *badāʾ*, inasmuch as God is worshipped therewith now (and certainly settles on that meaning in light of what follows), it could at this stage also constitute a disavowal of the concept. All we know for certain at this point is that the imams understand *badāʾ* and we don't; we read on.

In the next two traditions (hadith nos. 3 and 4), the word *badāʾ* itself is absent. What they each affirm is that God can alter his creation, postponing and hastening, confirming and erasing, the second tradition shoring up this inoffensive truth with a Qurʾanic verse. The implication, though left implicit, is clear: that it is to this divine capacity to instigate change that *badāʾ* refers. This sets the scene for the fifth and sixth reports in which *badāʾ* is fully instated as indispensable creed. No prophet, they state, has neglected to preach this doctrine, standing as it does alongside such foundational notions as the prohibition of wine and prostration to God.

'If people only knew', preaches the next report (hadith no. 7), 'The rewards of affirming *badāʾ*, they would not shrink from attesting to it'. Again, if the reader is perturbed by preceding endorsements of *badāʾ*, she is reminded that this is down to flawed understanding. A key blow is then struck in the eighth tradition, which denies unequivocally that there can be any deficiency of God's knowledge of unfolding events. Nothing can surprise him, for he knows totally the past, the present and the future. The heretical implications of the doctrine's Shīʿī loci classici, that the defeats of al-Mukhtār or the death of al-Ṣādiq's son Ismāʿīl were somehow unanticipated by God or unplanned, are now firmly disavowed.[34] The ninth report serves to sum up, affirming with a long taxonomy the two principal claims that al-Ṣadūq has now conveyed: first, that *badāʾ*, far from denigrating God's knowledge, concerns the complete extent to which that knowledge and power subsumes the ever-changing face of creation; secondly, that *badāʾ* is an obscure and difficult concept, the understanding of which we should therefore defer to those who know.

Al-Ṣadūq now steps in to contribute his own summary. Unlike the largely cosmetic summaries of the first section, here al-Ṣadūq adds to the message received from the hadiths with a highly focussed discussion of a specific issue: a worrying hadith in which the imam al-Ṣādiq appears to evoke *badāʾ* with regard to his son Ismāʿīl's death. The most widely reported core of the hadith reports the imam saying, 'Never was there unto God an instance of *badāʾ* as there was regarding Ismāʿīl'.[35] The text is particularly difficult as it seems to describe *badāʾ* as something of which God is on the receiving end. Al-Ṣadūq's response is to unleash what is in his extant writings an almost uniquely concentrated effort to suppress these problematic implications. In just a few lines he blasts the problem-text with potential different (less troublesome) versions, mitigating context (e.g., the suggestion that al-Ṣādiq was talking about his forefather Ismāʿīl the son of Abraham) and lexicographical acrobatics.

This chapter is very unusual in *al-Tawḥīd*, ordering each of its hadith with meticulous industry to deliver a precise, nuanced message. There is no doubt that *badāʾ* is an especially hazardous topic, requiring a firm hand to put it to rest, and its treatment here provides both a robust apology to critics and a corrective to any wayward Imāmīs. Located at the juncture between sections 2 and 3, however, and their intensifying message that readers should suspend any desire to subject the imams' hadith to human reason, this chapter delivers a firm and meaningfully placed warning against presumptuous misunderstanding. Al-Ṣadūq signals the perilous theological road that his readers now tread, and by pulling acceptability even out of so infamous a group of reports, he shows them just how faulty their initial interpretations can be. 'If people only knew the rewards of affirming *badāʾ*, they would not shrink from attesting to it'.[36]

'Something between the two'

Following *badāʾ*, section 3 continues into a run of chapters addressing various aspects of the relationship between God's power and human agency and culpability. These chapters address central, often technical topics connected to the question of *jabr*, such as will (*irāda*), intention (*mashīʾa*) and capacity (*istiṭāʿa*). Though at first glance they resemble the subdivided structure of section 1, these chapters resemble neither that section's treatment of *tashbīh* nor the chapter on *badāʾ* that they immediately follow. In pronounced contrast to the first section, here there is a near-total absence of any overt apology for the imams' teachings. Signature Muʿtazilī positions are often overtly contradicted, including by a whole chapter (63) devoted to affirming that God may forgive major sins (despite his pledge to punish them) and that the Prophet may intercede with God on behalf of the faithful on the Day of Judgement. Al-Ṣadūq here ignores didactic concerns that exercise him considerably elsewhere when he addresses his fellow Imāmīs, such as how the catastrophic death of al-Ḥusayn may be reconciled with God's intentions.[37] Meanwhile, the chapters include a great deal of ambiguous material that we would have expected to find clarified and sanitized by al-Ṣadūq's glosses had it appeared in section 1. Such hadiths as those in which ʿAlī refuses help in battle from his retainer Qanbar because his defence is a matter for God to decide, or in which one of the imams incautiously admits entry to an Umayyad agent, declaring that he can only do what God allows, are easily open to radically fatalistic interpretations, but al-Ṣadūq does nothing to dispel such readings.[38]

Not only are these chapters disinterested in encouraging a Muʿtazilī-friendly reading, but they seem designed to resist any reduction to a closed doctrinal formulation. They do contain hadiths enunciating very specific, technical positions, such as that God's will is accident and that it is among his attributes of action,[39] but these are not expanded upon; rather, they are crowded out by the majority of texts which assert more general assumed truths such as that nothing happens that is not according God's will, or that nothing is demanded of God's servants beyond what they are capable of. Nor are the compiled hadiths free of contradictions: in chapter 55, we read that both wretchedness (*shaqāwa*) and felicity (*saʿāda*) are from God,[40] but in another hadith we conversely read that 'Whatever good befalls you is from God, and whatever ill befalls you is from yourself'.[41] Al-Ṣadūq's summaries, however, are gone, and readers are left alone with the imams' utterances to make of them what they will regarding these vexing questions.

A notable feature of many chapters in the third section is a return to the kerygmatic style of hadith that we saw in *al-Tawḥīd*'s second chapter; indeed, we encounter many texts which identify themselves as sermons (*khuṭba*), preachings (*waʿẓ*) and testaments (*waṣīya*). Some reports even contain passages of poetry. The imams' words are no longer to be subdivided; rather, speculation is to be rendered subordinate to the unrestrained majesty of their speech. The following is reported from ʿAlī in chapter 60:

> *Qadar* is a mystery amidst God's own mystery, a veil amidst God's own veil, a sanctuary amidst God's own sanctuary, raised up in God's own hiddenness and concealed from his creation. It is sealed with God's seal and preeminent in his knowledge. God has placed his servants far from the knowledge of it, raising it up beyond their sight and the limits of their reason, for they do not grasp it with the reality of sovereignty nor with the power of eternity, not with the majesty of radiance nor the splendour of unicity. It is a vast ocean which belongs to God alone and whose depth is the distance between heaven and earth, whose width is the distance between east and west, black as gloaming night, filled with fish and serpents, at times rising and at others subsiding. At its bottom is a glowing sun, which none must approach save God, the one, the unique. Whosoever approaches it has challenged God, majestic and exalted, in his command, and vied with him for his power, clutching at his veil and his secret. He will come to face God's wrath, and his fate will be Hell, most wretched of ends.

The principle behind this new emphasis on rhetorical force over subdivided precision becomes explicit in chapter 59, 'The Denial of Free Will and Predestination'. Twelve hadiths unanimously assert that this infamous dichotomy is a false one, and that one can affirm both God's omnipotence and humanity's capacity for culpable choice. Unlike the previous chapters, where potential conflicts and paradoxes are passed mutely by, here the paradox is identified and sanctified. To deny either of these twin truths of divine power and human choice, the hadiths repeatedly state, is unbelief, while the truth is 'something in between'.

What we see here is still not doctrinal resolution, rather it is a continuation and intensification of the previous section's message of submission to text. Not only does the chapter not offer a way to reconcile these two principles, but it actively discourages any attempt to do so. The answer, we learn, is 'More vast than the space between heaven and earth',[42] and in another hadith al-Ṣādiq tells a disciple who presses him on the matter, 'If I answered your question you would turn to unbelief!'[43] We are being asked to take the imams' word for it, submitting to their superior knowledge, just as we were asked to in the second section when they informed us about the hidden meanings of the alphabet. The difference is that now this reverence for the imams' hadith is being applied not to curiosities but to a sustained theological problem – 'A deep sea; approach it not!'[44]

It is in the middle of chapter 60 that al-Ṣadūq steps in, after a long absence, to lend this traditionist agnosticism a systematic dimension. What he presents is a more ambitious version of the tactic we saw deployed earlier regarding the (non-)

createdness of the Qur'an: an absolutist textualism based on a hermeneutic of radical ambiguity. Focussing on the term for God's decree, *qaḍāʾ*, al-Ṣadūq states that some scholars name as many as ten meanings for it, which he lists, focussing, however, on the assertion that as well as 'to decree' the verb can also mean 'to know'. A text that appears to express the maximalist, fatalist position that all human action and choice is decreed by God could therefore, in fact, carry the less controversial meaning that God is all-aware of such things. An almost identical manoeuvre is executed with *qadar*, a term commonly used to denote preordainment but here again potentially reduced to knowledge. Through this assembly of alternative meanings, al-Ṣadūq is able to declare that the statement 'All things are by God's *qaḍāʾ* and *qadar*' (a common sentiment in the hadiths) cannot be censured, since these terms' combined polyvalence more than suffices to ensure that such a statement is always potentially true.[45]

Here, then, is the final trump card in this defence of the imams' hadith. The exegetical, apologetic constraining of meaning found in section 1 is turned on its head, as meaning is thrown wide open in this declaration of consuming, paradigmatic uncertainty. The twist is reminiscent of al-Ṣadūq's treatment of medical hadiths in *al-Iʿtiqādāt* – there, too, he lists all the reasons why a hadith might be infallible, imamic speech but still useless as medical advice, while his father declares that the imams' inscrutable habit of saying what they do not mean is an essential component of revelation, even if it hinders hadith's capacity to provide guidance. In *al-Tawḥīd*, too, al-Ṣadūq is now restricting his texts' capacity to produce instructive meaning, again for the same purpose of defending their supreme status as holy writ. This time, however, he has more to say about how the faithful should respond to these limits of instruction. After *qaḍāʾ*, al-Ṣadūq supplies another list of ten meanings, this time for the word *fitna*, usually rendered 'test', 'sedition' or 'civil strife'. This at first seems a little removed from deep theology, but al-Ṣadūq's meaning soon becomes clear enough: the mysteries of destiny and the ambiguities of the imams' words are not to be met with speculation or disputation – that way, among other things, lie 'killing', 'violence' and 'unbelief'. Uncertainty is there for a reason, and we should meet it by piously abstaining from discussion.

Theology and practice

This could be the conclusion of *al-Tawḥīd*, and it certainly points towards the vigorous condemnation of theological speculation that forms the book's last chapter. At the very least al-Ṣadūq has now answered, albeit in very different ways, both of the charges that he set out to address in his introduction. He presses on however, apparently aware that however ingenious his defence of the imams' hadith, and however grim his warnings of *fitna*, they do raise questions that need answering. If the faithful cannot hope to understand what the imams are saying, might this not lead to a hermeneutic paralysis whereby the hadiths, however sacred they may be, stop being useful? Al-Ṣadūq does not directly acknowledge this potential hazard, but he seems to pre-empt it. As *al-Tawḥīd* closes, he noticeably shifts his emphasis towards more practical matters, recognizing the pressure to demonstrate that his assertions of uncertainty lead not to doubt-stricken paralysis but to faithful, virtuous action.

Chapter 60, in the middle of which al-Ṣadūq supplies his ten meanings of *qaḍā'*, has a more idiosyncratic title than its predecessors. While earlier chapters tend to be named after a particular aspect of the predestination problem, chapter 60 is entitled '[God's] Decree (*qaḍā'*), Preordainment (*qadar*), Sedition (*fitna*), Bounties, Prices and Rewards'. The fourth and fifth components, in particular, are of dubious relevance to the discussion thus far, and they are quite absent until the chapter's very end. Only then, after the meanings of *qaḍā'* and *fitna*, does al-Ṣadūq move somewhat precipitously to a set of hadiths forbidding the monopolization of goods and the manipulation of prices. 'Prices are God's concern; he raises them as he wills and lowers them as he wills.'[46] Carefully arranged, the opening hadiths are clarified and expanded upon by later ones, increasingly engaging with specifics of market etiquette. As for the purpose of this sudden burst of *fiqh*, it is precisely to demonstrate the link between how a believer should conduct herself and the preceding message of unquestioning trust in a mysterious God. Al-Ṣadūq makes this objective explicit in his concluding remarks:

> When [an increase in prices] is as a result of acts of God then it should be met with submission and contentment, as it should be in cases where it is a result of scarcity of resources or income. Acts of people and acts of God alike are known first to God, just as is the making of all creation, in accordance with his decree and foreordainment, as I have explained regarding the meanings of *qaḍā'* and *qadar*.[47]

Al-Ṣadūq has deftly swept *al-Tawḥīd*'s theological vagaries back into the real world. The topic is, of course, ideal; what better than market forces to stand for the labyrinthine interface between human action and unknowable provenance? This is not an allegory; however, this is *sharī'a*. Al-Ṣadūq has just collapsed the preceding 200-page conundrum of divine will and human agency into the realm of the unknowable, and the appearance now of the known rules of the law is ringingly emblematic of the message of the whole book. Obey God's law and submit to his will, al-Ṣadūq tells his reader. The rest is commentary.

This message is played out in a variety of ways across *al-Tawḥīd*'s concluding chapters. Sometimes there is a specific focus, such as chapter 61's exploration of how God's infinite justice relates to the death of infants. Here, too, submission to God and the imams' teachings is paramount – no reasoning can make much of a dent in the trauma of infant mortality, only the inspired counsel of God's *ḥujja* that their souls will be given due opportunity to demonstrate their worth, whereupon the virtuous will enter paradise under the care of no less heavenly a nurse than Fāṭima herself.[48] More common, however, are texts within chapters with an apparently abstract focus that direct the reader away from doctrine towards more pious, even ethical concerns, in a way not dissimilar to what we find in al-Ṣadūq's *adabī* writings. For example, in among chapter 60's material on preordainment we read from ʿAlī: 'All the world is ignorance save where there is knowledge, all knowledge is a condemning witness save that which is acted upon, all action is vanity save that which is sincere, and sincerity is imperilled so long as the servant does not ponder the fate that awaits him';[49] 'The generous man is he who attends to what God has ordained', declares another hadith, 'While the miser is he who begrudges what God has ordained'.[50] No pretence is made here of unravelling the deeper workings of fate and destiny; rather, the emphasis is now firmly on how the reader should behave. Righteous conduct is presented as the correct response to the mysteries of existence and the antidote to fruitless speculation. Elsewhere the texts strike a still more pietistic register: 'Lord, dishevelled, dust-covered and with tattered garments, turned away from door after door, if I only swear by God I shall remain faithful.'[51]

In chapters 64 and 67 (the intervening chapters will be addressed presently), al-Ṣadūq offers his belligerent conclusion, delivered in both chapters with the systematic unanimity that previous chapters have so often lacked. Chapter 64, 'Teaching, Demonstration, Proof and Guidance' presents seventeen hadiths affirming that knowledge comes from God alone, and that it is humanity's duty only to acknowledge divine guidance and to act thereupon with humble righteousness; 'Whosoever acts in accordance with what he knows, he has no need of what he does not know.' Three chapters later, the sermon builds into the last chapter, 'The Prohibition of Dialectic, Disputation and Self-Aggrandizement Regarding God'. Amassing 35 hadiths, none of them more than a few lines in length, al-Ṣadūq presents narration after narration delivering outright condemnation of dialectic theology (which is tellingly merged with self-aggrandizement). When a hadith appears in multiple versions, they are now grouped together. The simple, ordered, unanimous, repetitive clarity delivered here is unparalleled in *al-Tawḥīd*'s text, while the chapter's message is seamlessly wedded to the whole section's accumulated discourse of piety, humility and the contrasting hubris of idle speculation; 'Command your fellows to spare their tongues, to put aside squabbling over religion, and to exert themselves in worshiping God.'[52]

In isolation, this final chapter might be read (and often is) as a typical polemic against dialectic theology, but placed at the climax of *al-Tawḥīd* it presents a number of powerful, carefully interwoven assertions. It fuses the epistemological objection to reason's encroachment on the role of revelation with the pietistic command to suspend such idle speculation and focus on godly conduct. This, in turn, is merged with al-Ṣadūq's justification of the imams' hadith. Just as readers are exhorted to adopt a pious agnosticism towards the divine mysteries and complex theological questions, they are urged to meet the imams' traditions with a similar attitude. The words of God's *ḥujaj* are the only true guide to God's will, but like their subject matter they, too, can be mysterious and confusing, even dangerous if improperly approached. Just as the reader should act and endure with the conviction that God knows best, she should read the imams' hadith with the reverent conviction that they contain the truth, however baffling they may appear. *Al-Tawḥīd* sets out over its course a vision of traditionism as an ethical, hermeneutical, theological and epistemological paradigm, a way of living, of thinking and of reading with the Imāmī hadith corpus enthroned at its heart.

Arguing with the imam

Reverence for the imams' words cannot but entail reverence for the imams themselves. Indeed, the potential rupture between the two, brought about by the occultation, is, as we have seen, a driving force behind al-Ṣadūq's anxiety to uphold the status of the hadith. Before *al-Tawḥīd*'s final polemic, it is this connection between the imam's words and the imam's person that al-Ṣadūq addresses in chapters 65 and 66. Each consists of a single long narrative, each describing a council (*majlis*) of al-Riḍā at the court of al-Maʾmūn. As we saw in Chapter 3, there are a great many more of these in *ʿUyūn*, but here al-Ṣadūq selects just two, which narrate different iterations of the same scenario discussed previously: the jealous caliph plans to discredit the imam by having him publicly defeated by skilled disputants whom he has summoned, but al-Riḍā, of course, roundly defeats all who oppose him.

We are clearly in a stylistic space very different to that which we have occupied thus far. These reports, in their length, their drama, their narrative detail and the extent to which their religious discussions are only one component of what is being portrayed, stand far apart from the usual building blocks of *al-Tawḥīd*. This difference, moreover, is evidently recognized in al-Ṣadūq's cordoning them off into two separate and prominently placed chapters; though these and other *majlis* narratives contain much that is relevant to *al-Tawḥīd*'s earlier concerns, there has been no sign of them until now.

The first of these councils falls into two distinct parts. In the first part, al-Riḍā debates with representatives of the Christians, the Jews and the Zoroastrians, while in the second part he confronts ʿImrān the Sabean, identified as a dialectic theologian (*mutakallim*). The debate with the religions of the book is a comforting triumphalism; a fantastical, indeed mythic vision of the traditionist ideal. Al-Riḍā begins by conceding to his non-Muslim opponents that he will debate with them using only their own religious texts, which he proceeds to do with devastating success. The Catholicos and the Exiliarch are dumbfounded as the imam cites at them line after line from the Torah and the Gospels in which the coming of Muḥammad is foretold (many of which are entirely fictional), the Jew and the Christian conceding every time that their texts are just as al-Riḍā says. He also knows the interpretation of passages that they do not, such as the identity of the foretold camel rider, bathed in light. He even knows the textual history of the Gospels, explaining to the Catholicos, who is quite open about his ignorance on the subject, how they were lost after Jesus's illusory crucifixion and only rediscovered by Matthew, Mark, Luke and John a century later.

This is *al-Tawḥīd*'s vision of traditionism distilled and writ large. Knowledge of scripture, of its words, meanings and origins, is all, granting total victory and total ownership of knowledge itself. Coming at the close of a work that has engaged extensively with *kalām*, the utter absence of argument from this 'debate' rings unmistakeably polemical, a monument to the omnipotence of correct knowledge of scripture. This, we are told, is how things should be.[53] The non-Muslim antagonists, with their stark, uncomplicated alterity and looser demands for realism, allow this paradigm to be cast in more absolute a mould than would Muslim interlocutors. The imam's intellectual ideal stands in damning contrast with the tortuous negotiations of theologians, and more than once his traditionist arguments are direct echoes of al-Ṣadūq's own.[54]

The debate changes in tone when the defeated people of the book retire and ʿImrān the Sabean takes the floor. In addition to his non-Muslim, scripture-bereft identity, ʿImrān is described as a theologian and debater who has out-talked all the scholars of Kufa, Basra, Syria and Arabia. Neither a Muslim nor even one of the People of the Book, he can ask questions and be answered concerning the very fundamentals of the nature of God, but despite this potential subversion the debate goes very smoothly. ʿImrān does not retort, does not argue with al-Riḍā to any notable extent, rather he poses successive questions which act effectively as foils to which the imam responds with kerygmatic speech of the sort encountered in chapter 2 and elsewhere. The imam finishes a particular explanation, asks ʿImrān if he understands, to which the latter will give a humble affirmative before politely asking: 'Master, tell me more.' The scene is not a debate but an education, which accordingly culminates in ʿImrān not only accepting Islam but becoming a loyal disciple of al-Riḍā.

The picture painted of traditionism has evolved here. This being a debate with few scriptural references, the imam no longer figures as the ideal traditionist; rather, he himself becomes scripture. The figure of ʿImrān is the obedient object of the imam's inspired, guiding speech. We now see those stirring sermons with which al-Ṣadūq began *al-Tawḥīd* represented as he has sustainedly contended that they should be, as scripture to be heeded without question, that it might bring the misguided into the fold.

The mood changes as we move to the next chapter and a new council on a new occasion. The debate here is also with a *mutakallim*, but is profoundly different in tone from that with ʿImrān. The interlocutor, Sulaymān al-Marwazī's religious affiliation is not dwelt upon, but his character as a disputant is established with a great degree of verisimilitude. Unlike ʿImrān, al-Marwazī argues, retorting, protesting and persisting in his opposition to the positions explained by al-Riḍā. The strategy is not a happy one. Al-Marwazī is made to squirm, contorting and contradicting himself until he finally cracks, and beyond the arguments themselves the atmosphere here is quite different to that of the previous debates. Reverence was consistently in the air as the imam spoke to ʿImrān, to the point where halfway through they paused and those assembled retired to pray. ʿImrān was always polite, and al-Maʾmūn, too, stepped in to question the imam with similar deference. Conversely, this second council has a savage tone to it, as al-Maʾmūn mocks al-Marwazī from the sidelines with increasing derision. It is, of course, in the caliph's interests for al-Marwazī to prevail, but once he realizes that he has backed the wrong horse, he turns on his pawn, begging him sarcastically to desist in good grace, and himself pointing out the contradictions in al-Marwazī's arguments, even as his onlooking courtiers laugh. Having seen the imam as the ideal traditionist and then as scripture itself in the previous chapter, what we now see is a brutal warning of the humiliation awaiting those who contest the imam and thus, in al-Ṣadūq's era of occultation, those who contest the imams' narrated words.

Al-Ṣadūq concludes the second council with a note to the effect that this happened every time al-Maʾmūn tested al-Riḍā, since God ensures that his *ḥujja* will always triumph, even as he ensures that the true followers of his *ḥujja* will triumph, too. It is, nevertheless, difficult to read these accounts only as images of truth victorious. The first council concludes with a thorough redemption of ʿImrān, detailing his subsequent fealty to al-Riḍā following his conversion at the end of the debate. On the other hand, there lurks al-Maʾmūn. The subtext of the caliph's defeat is shunted loudly into text as one of the onlookers muses, 'I fear for the imam, lest this caliph come to envy him, perhaps poisoning him or doing him some other harm.'[55] The second debate, meanwhile, has no such conclusion, and the narrative ends abruptly when al-Marwazī at last concedes defeat. Al-Marwazī is not offered the redemption afforded to ʿImrān, a fact in keeping with the raucous, irreverent tone of the debate.

Though the imam triumphs, all is not well here. Not only is the murderous conclusion of al-Maʾmūn's designs made explicit at the end of the first *majlis*, but the comparative lack of resolution at the close of the second is also troubling. Given the irreverent tone of the discussion, it adds to the suggestion that something sordid has taken place. We feel that the imam, mighty as he is, has been dragged somewhere he is not meant to be, his refutations of al-Marwazī forming a jarring chorus with the crowing of al-Maʾmūn and his courtiers. Al-Riḍā's appointment by al-Maʾmūn was a tarnishing one for the Imāmīya, such that al-Ṣadūq, nearly two centuries after the event, is still anxious to absolve the imam of any complicity in *ʿUyūn*.[56] There is something of Karbala here; something of the perverse, violent resistance to the divine which killed al-Riḍā as it killed al-Ḥusayn and, as al-Ṣadūq writes, has forced the imam's indefinite absence upon his followers.[57] As *al-Tawḥīd* closes, these two chapters reimagine its ideal of adherence to textual authority as loyalty to the living, resplendent teacher, but in so doing they also show the true, sullying cost of disrespecting the imam and his teachings, of forcing them into the unnecessary hubris of debate against which al-Ṣadūq fulminates in his final chapter.

Conclusion

The principal goal of this chapter, as the first of two sustained readings of two of al-Ṣadūq's compendia, has been to put fully into practice the method of reading hadith compilations set out in this book's introduction. I have attempted to show conclusively that the hadiths in *al-Tawḥīd* cannot be reliably read in isolation as individual statements of al-Ṣadūq's own views, but must be understood in relation to the broader objectives of the book in which they are compiled. Furthermore, with the acknowledgement that *al-Tawḥīd*'s internal structures are conscious decisions of the compiler, the hadiths that it contains must also be read in relation to those structures, with attention paid to how an individual hadith's meaning is conditioned by its location among the other hadiths, chapters and sections that make up the work as a whole. The resultant reading describes a work in which al-Ṣadūq is working above all to defend the Imāmī hadith corpus, portraying the imams' words as a source both of clear answers to fundamental questions and of endless, unknowable mysteries. Accordingly, al-Ṣadūq is energetically concerned to shape how readers approach the hadith he presents, inviting different ways of reading in each of *al-Tawḥīd*'s three sections: the hadiths of the first section are to be read as confirmation that the imams' speech affirms the transcendence of God; those of the second section are to be met with a spirit of self-effacing awe, acknowledging that their contents are beyond uninspired human understanding; those of the third section are to be heeded in their generalities – that God is truly omnipotent, but that we remain culpable for our actions – but not subject to overzealous inquiry. The overall effect is a distinctive, traditionist hermeneutic theology, rooted in the compiler's aspiration to control how his collected texts are read, one that seeks to balance reverence for the imams and their teachings with functional guidance in matters of belief.

This reading of *al-Tawḥīd* departs from most recent assessments of the work in the greater emphasis that it places upon al-Ṣadūq's resistance to dialectic theology, above all to the Muʿtazila. Though the book does contain hadiths that echo Muʿtazilī ideas (and do so more closely than some chapters of *al-Iʿtiqādāt*), in the context of the broader work these do not present as discrete statements of doctrine, let alone as part of a broader strategy of rapprochement or an overall shift in al-Ṣadūq's views. They are, instead, clearly governed by parts of the book in which a more definitive message is delivered, including the last chapter's relentless denunciation of *kalām*, the dressing-down of independent reason delivered in chapter 41 ('That God Cannot Be Known Save Through Himself'), and even the weird uranographies of the middle section. Though this conclusion regarding al-Ṣadūq's attitude to Muʿtazilism is an important one for the assessment of his work, the more important conclusion of these observations is their methodological aspect: that consulting a book like *al-Tawḥīd* without due attention to the dynamics of its compilation risks an incomplete, distorting assessment of what part of it appears to say.[58]

I began this chapter by noting that *al-Tawḥīd* is not primarily intended as a theological encyclopaedia. The study that followed has repeatedly reaffirmed this, showing that al-Ṣadūq's focus is on his stated objective of defending the hadith corpus itself, and that he is not especially interested in giving a final answer regarding whether God can, in fact, fit the universe into an egg without changing the size of either, or in a technical definition of *istiṭāʿa*. He is certainly concerned that his readers accept the transcendence of God and the corresponding falsehood of anthropomorphism, but he is at least equally concerned to convince them that the imams teach the truth of such doctrines more perfectly than anyone else. Furthermore, when it comes to more intractable questions of free will, al-Ṣadūq categorically places reverence for the imams' words above any exhaustive answer. There is no suggestion that he includes hadiths the contents of which he considers inherently problematic, but he actively discourages the reader from reaching hasty conclusions regarding what these texts actually mean. A complaint that this reading of *al-Tawḥīd* might well invite is that it has not greatly advanced our understanding of the details of al-Ṣadūq's theological views. The fact remains that *al-Tawḥīd* contains a far greater volume of hadiths concerning fundamental questions such as God's transcendence, attributes and essence than do al-Ṣadūq's brief treatments of these topics in his creeds. Notwithstanding the fact that their use in *al-Tawḥīd* is very different, al-Ṣadūq's narration of these texts cannot but have a bearing on his views regarding these matters, and students of Imāmī theology may be justifiably frustrated that I have not devoted more attention to this avenue of inquiry. My defence must be that the inquiries pursued above addressed fundamental questions of a different sort, questions that had to come first. *Al-Tawḥīd* is undoubtedly a valuable resource for reconstructing a more detailed theology, but to be effectively used as such we first need to know what al-Ṣadūq is trying to say and how he is trying to say it. Thus conceived, this chapter is not offered as a replacement for more strictly theological studies of this work, but is suggested as their starting point.

5

Kamāl al-dīn wa tamām al-niʿma

Looking for the imam

Introduction

In all of the preceding chapters, we have found al-Ṣadūq's pre-eminent concern to be the exhortation of reverence for the hadith of the imams. *Al-Tawḥīd* conveys with especial eloquence the ideal of the imams' words as the single, sufficient source of guidance towards true understanding of the Qurʾan and of Islam. In Chapter 2, however, we explored how this preoccupation with the imams' hadith is inseparable from the Hidden Imam's ongoing absence; since the imam can no longer be consulted in person, new pressures are placed upon the hadith corpus' promise to represent the imams and their teachings in text. *Kamāl al-dīn wa tamām al-niʿma* ('The Perfection of Religion and the Completion of Grace') is al-Ṣadūq's only surviving stand-alone work on the occultation, and is thus his most extended engagement with this question that lies at the core of his engagement with hadith.[1]

Out of the scores of treatises about the occultation said to have been written in the first century after al-ʿAskarī's death, *Kamāl al-dīn* is among the oldest to have survived. The *al-Ghayba* of Muḥammad Ibn Abī Zaynab al-Nuʿmānī (d. 345/956 or 360/971) is almost certainly older, while the first extant substantial Imāmī treatment of the topic is in *al-Kāfī*, only a generation before al-Ṣadūq.[2] *Kamāl al-dīn* is thus of great historical value as a document of this doctrine's development among the Imāmīya, and it contains many texts and ideas for which we have no prior exemplar and some for which we have no other exemplar at all. Yet *Kamāl al-dīn* is also a curious work, in the context both of other Imāmī literature on the subject and of al-Ṣadūq's other writings. As he addresses this most fundamental question of early Imāmī traditionist thought, al-Ṣadūq pursues a unique interrogation of how the whole edifice of proof by text can operate. Like *al-Tawḥīd*, this is a book that revolves around questions regarding the status and nature of the imams' traditions. It is another book of hadith that is also a book about hadith, one to which al-Ṣadūq brings his full ingenuity as a compiler to make *Kamāl al-dīn* his most fascinating and complex work.

As observed, *Kamāl al-dīn* was neither al-Ṣadūq's first nor his only book on the occultation. As he tells us in the introduction, when the Hidden Imam commanded him to write the work in a dreaming visitation, al-Ṣadūq objected that he had already given the subject ample discussion. What he had yet to do, however, the imam pointed out, was illustrate how the occultation had been prefigured in the careers of earlier prophets – how the imam's current absence from his community was part of a long-standing pattern in God's ongoing revelation of his will, observable in the careers of many prophets past, rather than constituting a disturbing rupture of any kind. Accordingly, al-Ṣadūq explains, it is this particular aspect of the occultation that he now seeks to address.[3]

Like the opening sentiments of *al-Tawḥīd*, this little origin story tells us much about what *Kamāl al-dīn* is and what it is not. Al-Ṣadūq has told us that *Kamāl al-dīn* does not set out to give a definitive creed of occultation for the faithful, nor to systematically defend the doctrine against the polemics of others. Indeed, al-Ṣadūq remarks in his introduction that someone who has not already accepted the basic premises of the imamate has no business with this book's subsidiary questions regarding who the imam is.[4] Such groundwork had already been set out in other books, sadly lost to us. This, then, is no more a straightforward account of al-Ṣadūq's beliefs about occultation than *al-Tawḥīd* is a straightforward account of his beliefs about God's justice and unity. In *Kamāl al-dīn*, al-Ṣadūq instead builds on the pre-existing arguments of more straightforwardly didactic works in order to create something that is more ambiguous and more ambitious.[5]

The structure of *Kamāl al-dīn*

Kamāl al-dīn is both a longer and a more structurally complex work than *al-Tawḥīd*. Like *al-Tawḥīd*, al-Ṣadūq does not divide it into separate books (the common division of editions into two volumes being a consideration of size alone). There are, however, four easily identifiable sections, each dominated by a distinct group of texts, preceded by a long introduction. Section 1 (chapters 1–20) concerns stories of previous prophets and related figures; section 2 (chapters 22–38) contains statements of the Prophet and the imams prophesying the occultation of the *qāʾim*; section 3 (chapters 41–6) presents direct testimony of the Hidden Imam's existence, in the form both of letters from him and of recounted meetings with him; section 4 (chapters 47–55) is dominated by accounts, most of them not hadiths, of those who, like the Hidden Imam, have lived a very long time.

As these sections make apparent, *Kamāl al-dīn* is organized not around particular theological issues but around different proof-corpora; each section is distinguished as much by the type of texts it includes as by the arguments it deploys. This is in keeping with the fact that *Kamāl al-dīn* does not announce itself as a general theological guide to the occultation. Nonetheless, al-Ṣadūq does not ignore the key theological arguments entirely; some of these are addressed in the book's introduction, while others are covered in occasional, individual chapters that punctuate the banks of proof-texts that make up the bulk of the work. Thus, between the first and second sections is chapter 21, 'The Reason Wherefore an Imam is Required', and between sections 2 and 3 is chapter 40, 'That the Imamate is Never Possessed by Two Brothers Except for the Two Ḥasans (al-Ḥasan and al-Ḥusayn)'. Not unusually, *Kamāl al-dīn* also has a concluding miscellany (*nawādir*), in which a number of adjunct issues are discussed without being structured into chapters. A complete translated table of contents for *Kamāl al-dīn*, including annotation of the main divisions, is supplied in Appendix II.

This outline of *Kamāl al-dīn* and its contents already indicates two important elements of the work's character. First, three out of four of its sections are dominated by narrative texts (the exception being section 2's foretellings), a predominance that sets it stylistically apart from al-Ṣadūq's other writings (even *ʿUyūn* devotes a good deal less space to al-Riḍā's biography relative to the amount allotted to his teachings). Second, all four sections are organized around a particular kind of proof-text and, correspondingly, a particular kind of proof. Even more so than in *al-Tawḥīd*, each section reads very differently to the others, offering very different kinds of hadiths (and sometimes texts that are not hadiths at all) to different effects. What unites them is the concern to argue the truth of the Hidden Imam and his occultation, with each of these four bodies of proof-texts offering different possibilities for this task.

The burden of proof

The introduction to *Kamāl al-dīn* is an important text in its own right, constituting not only by far the longest surviving piece of dialectic prose from al-Ṣadūq but also one of the earliest such pieces of substantial length to survive from any

Imāmī author. While the introductions to al-Ṣadūq's other compendia extend to a couple of pages at most, *Kamāl al-dīn*'s introduction reaches up to 150 pages in printed editions, and is thus an invaluable resource for the study of al-Ṣadūq and for the study of the Imāmīya in the fourth/tenth century. Furthermore, its long introduction makes *Kamāl al-dīn*, of all al-Ṣadūq's works, the text within which we have a real opportunity to measure his compiled material (of which the body text is composed) against a detailed opening discussion of what he aims to achieve with its compilation.

The concern that this introduction sets out is, above all, the question of proof – of how the twelfth imam's occultation and, by extension, his legitimacy as the last successor to Muḥammad who will return at the end of time, are to be established as fact. Al-Ṣadūq announces at the outset that this new book on the occultation will deal in particular with the evidence of earlier prophets' lives and exploits. How that evidence is to be used is far from straightforward, however. *Kamāl al-dīn* does not merely undertake to present such stories of previous prophets as may support the Imāmī view on occultation; the book is an extended experiment in how these stories can function as proof and how, as such, they may interact with the broad range of other probative strategies used by al-Ṣadūq, his fellow Imāmīs and others.

Proof 1: *Tawātur*

Much of the introduction is concerned with shoring up certain core theological proofs of the imamate in general, preparing the ground for the more specific concerns that dominate the rest of the book. Foremost among these is the contention that only God himself can nominate the *ḥujja* who will guide humanity, a discussion that begins with Q 2:30, 'And God said to the angels, "I shall place a vicegerent (*khalīfa*) upon the earth"', referring to Adam, the first prophet and therefore the first *ḥujja*. Al-Ṣadūq delves into this verse to considerable depth, affirming that this divine nomination of Adam is identical with the Imāmī doctrine of the imamate, and that it invalidates categorically any suggestion that the community may choose their own imam, an egregious folly exemplified in Abū Bakr's accession to the caliphate.[6] He also allots some space to a handful of technical questions, such as the legitimacy of an imam who conceals his own imamate,[7] and to brisk refutations of rival Shīʿī groups, such as the Kaysānīya and the various strands of the Wāqifīya.[8] Though *Kamāl al-dīn* clearly has a variety of types of reader in mind, not least fellow Imāmīs, these opening polemics express a dominant concern with Muʿtazilī-leaning, Zaydī Shīʿī antagonists –

people who do not deny the cause of an ʿAlid imamate outright, but who accept neither the occultation nor many of the imamological ideas behind it, and who are particularly cynical of the textual proofs for such doctrines.[9]

It is, accordingly, not long before the introduction arrives at the axial question of how one identifies the hidden son of al-ʿAskarī as the imam, and, indeed, how one justifies his imamate in the face of his unusual hiddenness. Al-Ṣadūq's approach is, predictably, emphatically text-based, throwing his efforts behind the concept of *tawātur* – a density of textual evidence too formidable to dismiss as forgery. He contends vigorously and repeatedly, including lengthy citations from earlier Imāmī authorities,[10] that it is by this most solidly textual of means that the truth of the Hidden Imam and his occultation is proven, regardless of the stubbornness of the majority who ignore these massed narrations' irrefutable evidence. This is an assertion not only that the hadiths confirming the occultation are, indeed, *mutawātir* (possessed of *tawātur*) but also that such text-based probative methods have real value in this context. Al-Ṣadūq cites opponents of the Imāmīya who mock the so-called inevitablists (*lābuddīya*), a group of Imāmīs who claimed that the Hidden Imam's existence was proven from first principles by logical necessity, a view close to what we find expressed by later figures such as al-Ṭūsī.[11] Against these other Imāmīs and their opponents, al-Ṣadūq maintains that hadith offers all the proof he needs.

We observed in Chapter 2 how rare it is to find al-Ṣadūq delving into the technicalities of hadiths and *asānīd*. In some ways, then, this extended insistence on *tawātur* might appear to be a change of heart. As well as being the longest single example of al-Ṣadūq's prose, *Kamāl al-dīn*'s introduction also contains, in its discussions of *tawātur*, the longest single example of al-Ṣadūq discussing matters of authenticity. It is not, however, in the *isnād*-based details of *tawātur* that al-Ṣadūq concentrates his arguments; indeed, the identity and quality of transmitters are not discussed at all. The *tawātur* that al-Ṣadūq presents is a concern purely of volume, not of reports' quality but of their number.[12] Even here he prefers to be vague, only once entering discussion of just how many sources are needed to constitute *tawātur*, which he names (rather modestly) as three.[13] Rather than battling through such details, al-Ṣadūq keeps his justification for proof by *tawātur* on the conceptual level, focussing on the point that the need for textual proofs is embedded within the very fabric of religion itself. We cannot reject texts, for it is only by texts that we know of Muḥammad and his miracles, only by texts that we can know his teachings, and on this basis al-Ṣadūq boldly asserts that his opponents cannot reject his textual proofs without implicitly denying the validity of all textual proofs, textual proofs without which Islam could not exist. He thus asserts that the *tawātur* of the texts proving the existence, legitimacy and occultation of the twelfth imam is fundamentally equivalent to the *tawātur* that underpins the key texts of Islam, and thus that one must either accept their probative force or join the undesirable company of the Brahmins (*barāhima*), that is to say those outside Islam who do not accept any Abrahamic sacred texts and so reject all of God's prophets.[14]

This is an audacious declaration of textual strength, and one that responds to anxieties at the heart of Imāmī hadith scholarship. Al-Ṣadūq asserts probative equivalence, claiming for the Imāmī hadith corpus as much validity as any other, and thus struggles directly against the ostracization of Imāmī hadith that was so widely practiced by non-Imāmīs. We began this book by noting the importance of the Imāmī hadith corpus as a principal distinguishing feature of the Imāmīya, an essential by-product of which was that Imāmīs could not easily draw upon their own books of hadith to argue with other groups, especially non-Shīʿīs, who did not regard them as authoritative. We shall see later how many Imāmīs attempted to circumvent this problem through recourse to other source-corpora, and al-Ṣadūq himself does briefly acknowledge the difficulty.[15] Nevertheless, with these opening claims to *tawātur* he meets such reservations head-on, declaring his hadiths to be binding proof whether others acknowledge them or not.

Proof 2: From the impossible to the possible

Even as al-Ṣadūq labours to assert the unimpeachability of the occultation's textual proofs, as the introduction progresses he introduces a second avenue of proof that works along different lines. This is the objective 'to move [the occultation of the twelfth imam] from the realm of the impossible to the realm of the possible (*min ḥadd al-maḥāla ilā ḥadd al-jawāz*)'.[16] It is this endeavour that underpins *Kamāl al-dīn*'s stated raison d'être as commanded by the imam to al-Ṣadūq in his dream: narrating the occultations of earlier prophets. If Moses can be hidden from his *shīʿa* (followers),[17] so, too, can the twelfth imam. If Noah can live for a thousand years, so too can the twelfth imam. The sacred precedent of prophetic history proves that Imāmī claims about their Hidden Imam are, at least, possible.

This is a probative strategy quite distinct from the aspirations to *tawātur* just outlined, not to mention a much more modest one. Al-Ṣadūq has regressed from proof to possibility, from declaring the Hidden Imam a textually indisputable fact to the mere aspiration of convincing the reader that it could have happened.

What brings the two strategies closer is al-Ṣadūq's citation of a group of hadiths in which Muḥammad declares, 'Whatsoever has befallen previous communities will befall my community also.'[18] This, al-Ṣadūq points out, lends these stories of earlier prophets a greater significance than merely making the occultation of the imam possible. If, as the Prophet says, the experiences of previous communities must be repeated, then to learn of the occultations that occurred in former times is to be compelled to accept that such a thing is bound to occur in the age of Islam. Not only can something that has happened before happen again, but in the case of prophetic history what has happened before must happen again.

These two proofs are functionally linked in important ways. If events in the past are to prefigure the present, it must surely be established whether or not they happened, a task for which *tawātur* is a useful tool. Conversely, the admission of this second line of argument somewhat gives the lie to the confidence of al-Ṣadūq's previous claims of *tawātur*. If the narrated accounts of the imam's existence do, indeed, prove his existence beyond any doubt, there would scarcely be a need to look for further proof in exemplars from the distant past. These two modes of proof conflict at least as much as they complement, a relationship that we shall see played out over the course of *Kamāl al-dīn*'s many pages.

A key, immediate consequence of al-Ṣadūq's plurality of proofs is that these different kinds of argument offer the reader a range of ways to read the many texts that will pass before him over the course of the book, as well as a corresponding range of expectations from those texts. Sometimes there will be clear indicators of what a particular text is for. The first section of the book is a collection of stories of earlier prophets, texts that the introduction has just specifically tied to the 'whatsoever has befallen' line of argument, and which al-Ṣadūq accompanies with frequent commentary asserting their value in these terms. Similarly, elsewhere there are groups of texts that clearly undertake to represent *tawātur*. In many places, however, things are not so clear, and it is left up to the reader to decide whether a text is meant to be read as an inviolable fact, the disputation of which is tantamount to disputation of the reality of the mission of Muḥammad himself, or as a precedent of the prophetic past that must find an echo in the present, or as some combination of the two.

Changing history

Though how al-Ṣadūq develops these strategies in what follows is highly unusual, his founding concern with how best to prove the truth of the Hidden Imam and, in particular, the role of texts in that process, is entirely in keeping with wider trends in Imāmī writing in the early decades of the greater occultation. Where al-Ṣadūq stands out, however, is that while he doubles down on textual proofs for the Hidden Imam, exploring new ways to make them effective, his fellow Imāmīs are usually to be found doing the opposite, seeking alternative avenues of proof that reduce the need for hadiths. Al-Mufīd, for instance, includes eyewitness accounts of the Hidden Imam's birth in his *al-Irshād*, but prefaces these with the insistence that they are not a necessary proof of his existence; instead, certainty in this matter is to be attained through rational theology.[19] The earlier al-Nuʿmānī, meanwhile, is more of a traditionist and does not make recourse to pure reason, but this only makes his avoidance of texts bearing direct witness to the Hidden Imam even more pronounced: he relies entirely on hadiths containing earlier Imams' predictions of the Hidden Imam's existence, thereby totally excluding the corpora of accounts of meetings with the imam, of letters from him, and even of reports of al-ʿAskarī designating his son as his successor (even though his teacher al-Kulaynī, from whom he usually narrates in abundance, includes all three).

Both al-Mufīd and al-Nuʿmānī thus express a striking lack of confidence in the corpus of hadiths about the Hidden Imam. This is even clearer when we compare al-Mufīd's approach here with the usual pattern of his disagreements with al-Ṣadūq. Normally in *Taṣḥīḥ*, part of al-Mufīd's criticism is that al-Ṣadūq's proffered hadiths are unreliable, a problem to which al-Mufīd responds by producing what he deems to be more reliable hadiths. In this instance, however, while al-Ṣadūq declares his narrated proofs for occultation to be *mutawātir*, al-Mufīd denies altogether the utility of such texts as proof. The anomaly is all the more conspicuous for its being based upon a deceptive hyperbole. Al-Mufīd's reasoning runs as follows: we know that there has to be an imam who meets certain criteria, and we know that nobody alive whom we can see meets those criteria; therefore, this imam must be hidden, and therefore the claims that it is the hidden son of al-ʿAskarī must be true.[20] He clearly still needs texts to establish at the very least that those claims regarding the son of al-ʿAskarī have been made, let alone to dispute the claims of various Ismāʿīlī and Wāqifī groups who posited different hidden figures as the imam; when pressed, he admits as much in other writings on the subject.[21] Not only, then, is al-Mufīd distancing himself from textual evidence with unusual vigour, but he is doing so disingenuously, seeking to deny the extent to which he still relies on this corpus.

Al-Nuʿmānī's approach, meanwhile, is part of an important trend that points us towards why the Imāmī accounts of the Hidden Imam were found to be so problematic by Imāmī scholars. Though al-Nuʿmānī uses Imāmī hadith extensively and is clearly engaging an (at least partly) Imāmī audience, he also adduces a large volume of what he identifies as hadiths narrated by Sunnīs, which he is keen to assert are sufficient to prove his claims.[22] This approach is pursued more concentratedly by two of al-Ṣadūq's own students, ʿAlī b. Muḥammad al-Khazzāz (d. circa 420/1030) and Aḥmad b. ʿAyyāsh al-Jawharī (d. 401/1012), both of whom wrote books in which they set out to prove the doctrine of the Hidden Imam using only Sunnī hadith.[23] The clear implications of this approach and its popularity – that Imāmī narrations alone were insufficiently persuasive in these matters – reflect an established dynamic of Shīʿī historical polemics in this period. Though such disputes hinged on competing accounts of the past, arguments were largely structured not around radically different versions of events but around competing interpretations of events that were acknowledged by all parties. A prominent example was the Prophet's sermon at Ghadīr Khumm: Shīʿīs and Sunnīs agreed that the Prophet had described ʿAlī as the *mawlā* ('master' and/or 'friend') of the community, but disagreed over the statement's meaning. Imāmīs possessed no dearth of narrations in which matters were less ambiguous, such as accounts of how the Prophet's ghost visited Abū Bakr and demanded that he relinquish the caliphate to ʿAlī, but such texts were of little use if others would not accept their veracity; the consensus around these histories was too strong.[24]

When it came to the twelfth imam, however, Imāmī scholars' modus operandi was seriously challenged. They now had to assert the truth of several miraculous events from the recent past, events which non-Imāmīs, let alone non-Shīʿīs, had no reason to acknowledge had ever happened: that al-ʿAskarī, widely believed to have died childless, had indeed had a son, and that this son was now supernaturally concealed and protected from ageing or death, even while Ismāʿīlī and Zaydī Shīʿīs had imams who were entirely visible. An immense burden of proof thus fell upon Imāmī arguments for the occultation. Specific elements of the narrations on the subject might have discouraged their use by some scholars,[25] but in many Imāmīs' total exclusion of the entire corpus in favour of other proofs, rational or textual, we see the deeper anxiety arising from the exceptionally difficult nature of the task before them. Al-Ṣadūq stands alongside his contemporaries in his acknowledgement of this difficulty – that the occultation is an unusual kind of problem, and that justifying this doctrine requires something beyond the usual mechanisms of demonstration through text and *isnād*. This acknowledgement is already visible in his introduction in the 'whatsoever befell' strategy of proof, and its implicit undermining of the certainty with which al-Ṣadūq claims *tawātur*. On the other hand, he departs radically from his fellows and, indeed, his students, in that his response to these difficulties is an embrace of an expanded corpus of textual proofs, one that retains at its core the testaments of those who encountered the imam and a conviction that such testaments can be persuasive.

1 Tales of the prophets

Section 1 of *Kamāl al-dīn* begins with the motion from the impossible to the possible, embarking in earnest on al-Ṣadūq's stated goal of demonstrating that the current occultation of the imam is part of a comfortably established pattern in the history of God's revelations to humankind. To this end, he presents a large body of reports over the first twenty chapters giving a select history of the occultation of prophets since the beginning of time. We read story after story of God's chosen and their adventures in a wonderful corpus of *qiṣaṣ al-anbiyā*ʾ ('stories of the prophets'), hereafter referred to as '*qiṣaṣ* texts'. Al-Ṣadūq presents a range of Qurʾanic prophets in chronological order, each allotted their own chapter, starting with Idrīs (identified as a son of Adam), and proceeding through Noah (Nūḥ), Ṣāliḥ, Abraham (Ibrāhīm), Joseph (Yūsuf), Moses (Mūsā) and Jesus (ʿĪsā) up to Muḥammad himself. Though their protagonists are familiar, as often as not the events described are less so: we read about Noah's flood and about Joseph's longing to be reunited with his father Jacob, but we also read about Abraham's encounter in the desert with the mysterious old man from beyond the sea and about the hidden island on which Jesus's loyal followers were secreted to safeguard his religion. The narratives are filled with the dramatic unfolding of the divine will, with marvels and wonders and with suspense and vindication.

Al-Ṣadūq's stories of the prophets are thoroughly subjected in substance and presentation to his objectives. No story passes in which it is not clear to the reader how the prophet protagonist underwent some form of concealment that is portentously analogous to the present occultation of the imam. The care with which al-Ṣadūq has selected his corpus is very clear. He does not tell the prophets' stories from beginning to end, instead presenting a highly focussed anthology of all the episodes of occultation occurring in each prophet's career. Some prophets were hidden from their followers on more than one occasion, in which case the separate episodes will be presented with no attempt to link them together. Sometimes al-Ṣadūq introduces a prophet's story with a brief, instructive summary, but for the most part the stories are made up of narrations, transmitted from a stock of teachers familiar from his other compendia.

The stories are emphatically diverse, and exactly what may constitute an occultation varies considerably from text to text. A prophet may be hidden, like the twelfth imam, for fear of persecution, such as when the infant Abraham is hidden from the depredations of Nimrod, who has heard tell of a child to be born who will spell his downfall.[26] In other instances, more benign episodes in a prophet's life will be appropriated for the occultation paradigm, such as Moses's adoption by Pharaoh's daughter (and thus his subsequent absence from his mother and the Israelites), Joseph's years in Egypt apart from his grieving father and even Solomon's remaining closeted with his new wife.[27] Al-Ṣadūq adds commentary when parallels are less obvious, while the diction of the accounts themselves sets them firmly within *Kamāl al-dīn*'s desired frame of reference. The word *ghayba* and its cognates are a recurrent presence in the stories, as are the stock Imāmī terms of *rujūʿ* ('returning'), *khurūj* ('emergence') and *ẓuhūr* ('reappearance') as descriptors of the different protagonists returning from their occultations. Moreover, the occultations themselves are regularly enriched with further details which can only resonate deafeningly with the Imāmī reader. Prophets will console their followers with the promise of a future *qāʾim*, who will one day come to relieve them (this being neatly identified with the next prophet in the sequence of chapters: Idrīs foretells the appearance of Noah, Noah tells of Hūd and so on); the expected figure will often be identified as a young man (*ghulām*) like the *mahdī* himself; many a loyal *shīʿa* accompanies prophets and awaits (*intiẓār*) their return from occultation, even while their faith and resilience are sorely tested; we hear how when prophets do return many people lack the purity of heart to recognize them; sometimes there is a *faqīh* to whom they may turn for guidance in the prophet's absence; prophets leave trustees (sg. *waṣī*) after them; those who seek a sign of the hidden *ḥujja* will always be granted one if they persevere.

The corpus is a remarkable one, and it is regrettable that we can know little about its sources without earlier texts coming to light. Nonetheless, its sheer size and the pervasive presence of Shīʿī motifs within the individual hadiths indicates a number of important things about this group of texts and al-Ṣadūq's use thereof. Excluding the highly unlikely event of large-scale forgery on al-Ṣadūq's part, it shows that in the mid-fourth/tenth century there already existed a prodigious array of *qiṣaṣ* texts that were steeped in Shīʿī and Imāmī concepts and language, including but by no means limited to those directly pertaining to the Hidden Imam. This tells us, in turn, that by this time there was an established interest among Imāmīs in identifying and imagining precedent for the current soteriological status quo in the vast literature of *qiṣaṣ al-anbiyāʾ*. This, in turn, makes it very unlikely that *Kamāl al-dīn*'s stated objective of recounting the Hidden Imam's precursors among the prophets constituted an entirely new venture.[28] Such a conclusion fits the complexity already apparent in *Kamāl al-dīn*'s introduction and indicates that simply illustrating these imamic-prophetic correspondences is not the sum of al-Ṣadūq's objectives in this book. Rather, al-Ṣadūq is drawing on a pre-existing Imāmī supply of *qiṣaṣ* texts to explore how these marvellous stories of hidden infants and disappearing prophets can be of use in the broader contests over proof that suffused discussions of the occultation.

2–3 Finding the imam

The impression that al-Ṣadūq's aims are not confined to the *qiṣaṣ* texts is strengthened by the fact that when these tales of earlier occulted prophets finish at the end of section 1, we are still not far beyond the first third of the book. This extraordinary corpus has resoundingly and very entertainingly accomplished al-Ṣadūq's professed aim to show the long-standing pedigree of the occultation, but as the curtain falls on the last of the prophets, Muḥammad (whose presence among the Arabs prior to his mission is rendered analogous to the twelfth imam's unrecognized presence among the believers[29]), it is clear that our author has more to offer. What follows in *Kamāl al-dīn*'s next two sections is the next stage of the story: that of Muḥammad's successors and the twelfth imam himself. Section 3 takes us into the details of the Hidden Imam's life, but before that section 2 presents the all-important corpus relating how his significance, disappearance and final return were foretold in the utterances of his predecessors.

Foretelling

As al-Ṣadūq arrives at texts directly dealing with the Hidden Imam himself, the shape of *Kamāl al-dīn* changes radically. Though it narrates few events, section 2 is considerably longer than section 1, due to the fact that it tells us the same thing again and again. The hadiths in its seventeen chapters (22–38) together serve only two functions: foretelling the key details of the twelfth imam's career – that he will be the last imam, the *qāʾim*, who will vanish and then return – and recording his formal investiture (*naṣṣ*) as imam, an essential component of Imāmī imamology.[30] Al-Ṣadūq adduces an enormous set of hadiths to deliver these few pieces of information, hereafter referred to as '*naṣṣ* texts', with separate chapters delivering texts attributed respectively to each of the earlier imams, Fāṭima, Muḥammad and God.

With these chapters we have thus moved decisively to al-Ṣadūq's other mechanism of proof, to *tawātur*. This is a volume of narrations that is designed to impress, far more extensive than the *qiṣaṣ* texts, with 57 predictions attributed to Jaʿfar al-Ṣādiq alone. In all its diversity, section 1 contained not a single report supported by multiple narrations, but in section 2 repetition is the order of the day, with many texts differing little or not at all except for their chains of transmission. Emphasis is further placed on the texts' *asānīd* by the division of chapters according to the sources of the hadiths therein, rather than their subject matter.[31] Meanwhile, the minimum of narrative detail that the *naṣṣ* texts supply regarding the imam's life reduces any potential to draw correspondences between these hadiths and those of section 1, marginalizing the 'whatsoever befell' line of argument. These first two sections thus embody quite separately al-Ṣadūq's two strategies of proof, pursuing them in two separate groups of chapters with two very different bodies of hadith that are communicated to the reader in two very different ways.

Signs

Section 2's predictions of the Hidden Imam are followed by chapters describing the actual events of his preternaturally long life, starting with his birth and infancy and then exploring his shadowy relationship with the faithful who seek his guidance. These chapters have a strong commonality of subject matter with those of section 2, but there are also pronounced differences in form, content and presentation, as well as in their relation to the other sections; accordingly, they are here considered a separate, third section. Section 3 confronts us with the twelfth imam himself, the figure whose existence the preceding *naṣṣ* texts have guaranteed and the figure whose exploits the *qiṣaṣ* texts have prefigured. This, then, is the shared object whereat al-Ṣadūq's two proof-corpora and their respective probative logics meet. As they do so, the Hidden Imam may appear all the more real for having been proven twice over, but this convergence of *Kamāl al-dīn*'s different mechanisms also threatens to release the tensions between them.

The texts that al-Ṣadūq now presents – texts whose primary subject matter is the twelfth imam and his occultation, which we will call 'occultation texts' – are concentrated in five chapters: a brief chapter concerning the imam's mother (chapter 41), two giving stories of his birth (chapters 42 and 43) and then two very long chapters, the first (chapter 44) collecting accounts of people seeing the imam in person and even speaking with him, and the second (chapter 46) giving accounts and copies of the many letters that the imam sent to the faithful through the medium of his emissaries during the nearly seventy years of the minor occultation. Here, therefore, is the locus for parallels to be drawn between these accounts of the twelfth imam's life and the *qiṣaṣ* texts presented earlier. These parallels as they now appear are too numerous and varied to list in full, though we have alluded to many already and will discuss several more in what follows. As for *tawātur*, al-Ṣadūq's collected occultation texts exhibit a number of the devices that he employs in the *naṣṣ* texts. Volume once again plays a powerful role, with 24 reports being supplied for eyewitness accounts of the imam and 42 records of letters received from him. Multiple *asānīd* are supplied for some of the traditions, and al-Ṣadūq also gives a separate list of all those who saw the imam, giving 65 names in total.[32] Recalling al-Ṣadūq's pronouncement that as few as three corroborating reports constitute *tawātur*, the goal here is to present a truly formidable body of evidence, one that cannot be rejected except alongside a total rejection of textual evidence and thus of the foundation of all religion.

A central component of these chapters' proof-building is the concept of the *dalāla* (pl. *dalāʾil*) – the 'sign' or 'proof'.[33] The term *dalāla* is widely used in Muslim contexts to denote a miraculous sign that proves Muḥammad's prophetic status, and in the late fourth/tenth and early fifth/eleventh centuries there proliferated a literature of 'signs of prophecy' (*dalāʾil al-nubuwwa*) devoted to documenting these prophetic miracles.[34] In Imāmī discourses, meanwhile, a *dalāla* could also be a sign proving an imam's imamate, and by al-Ṣadūq's time there already existed an established Imāmī literature chronicling the *dalāʾil* of the imams, including those of the Hidden Imam, for whom these signs of legitimacy merged with signs of his very existence.[35] The concept appears in abundance in *Kamāl al-dīn*'s occultation texts, where the term *dalāla* is used with a self-conscious specificity. Many of al-Ṣadūq's narrators preface their accounts of wondrous encounters with the imam with descriptions of how they had been searching for a *dalāla* to strengthen their faith, while al-Ṣadūq himself occasionally intervenes to explain to the reader what constituted the *dalāla* in a given report.[36]

The centrality of *dalāʾil* to these occultation texts thus embodies al-Ṣadūq's concern with proof, but such *dalāʾil* are also exactly the sort of proof that al-Ṣadūq's Imāmī contemporaries were so wary of. These are the same materials that al-Nuʿmānī excludes entirely and to which al-Mufīd denies any probative value. Outside the Imāmīya, many groups, not least the Muʿtazilīs, did not accept that anyone after the Prophet could perform miracles, and the compiled *dalāʾil* of the imams therefore risk being read as accounts of the impossible, damaging the credibility of al-Ṣadūq's enterprise, *tawātur* or no *tawātur*.[37] On the other hand, if al-Ṣadūq manages to realize his claims that these accounts' textual credentials really are unassailable, leaving the reader no choice but to believe what they describe, these occultation texts become a powerful challenge to the Imāmīs' opponents. The stakes in these chapters' address, then, are high.

It is, therefore, extremely surprising that al-Ṣadūq's attempts to present *tawātur* here are accompanied by a great many self-evident weaknesses in these chapters' narrations. We may recall that in *al-Tawḥīd* al-Ṣadūq pares his hadiths down to a core of his favoured sources, the better to mount that book's defence of the corpus. By contrast, the collective state of these chapters' *asānīd* is lamentable, riddled as they are with defects that would be just as apparent to an unschooled reader as to one learned in hadith. Whatever the status of the named narrators (a number of whom are quite unknown beyond their names), many of the reports in these chapters are transmitted from unnamed sources, sometimes identified generically (e.g., 'an Iraqi') and in other instances only as 'a man'.[38] The result is that in these crucial eyewitness testaments to the twelfth imam's existence, the witnesses themselves are not always identified. In other instances, the occultation texts' sources show less conventional abnormalities, such as the following opening of an encounter with the Hidden Imam:

> We heard the following from a shaykh from amongst the followers of hadith called Aḥmad b. Fāris al-Adīb: 'Once in Hamadān I heard a tale, which I told as I heard it to one of my brethren, who asked that I set it down for him in writing. Finding no objection to this I did so, placing liability for the tale with the one who told it. I heard that in Hamadān there are a people called the Banū Rāshid, all of whom are Shīʿīs, their creed that of the followers of imamate. I asked the reason why they, of all the people of Hamadān, had become Shīʿī. An old man among them who seemed righteous and upright told me the following:
>
> "The reason for this is that our forefather from whom we trace our descent once set out for the Ḥajj..."'[39]

The story of encountering the imam that finally follows is clearly a far cry from the credibility promised by a conventional *isnād*, its opening having cast it somewhere between anecdote and legend. This sort of material plainly ill-fits any notion of *tawātur*, and furthermore such source-related abnormalities are not the only apparent flaws that al-Ṣadūq admits here. The reader must also contend with overt internal contradictions in content, regarding such details as the imam's age or his physical appearance,[40] and even significant ruptures with established imamological doctrine, such as in texts claiming that the

Hidden Imam has a brother called Mūsā who shares his occultation with him, or even that al-Ḥusayn designated not his son ʿAlī but his sister Zaynab as his successor.[41]

More generally, the miracles – the *dalāʾil* – claimed in *Kamāl al-dīn*'s occultation texts often have a conspicuously sensational quality. While it is true that al-Ṣadūq faced many readers, Imāmīs and not, who denied that the imams had any miraculous powers, the question of how far to push this point remained an important one, as can be seen in his varying approach across his writings. When it suits him, he will admit hadiths in which imams resurrect the dead and command the sun to reverse its course, but elsewhere, as we have seen, al-Ṣadūq offers a picture of the imams' *dalāʾil* that is clearly sanitized, restricting their powers to precognitive knowledge (*ibtidāʾ*) or even knowledge transmitted from Muḥammad, the better to ingratiate sceptical readers;[42] this exact same restriction to *ibtidāʾ* is applied by al-Mufīd when assembling his own *dalāʾil* of the Hidden Imam.[43] *Kamāl al-dīn*'s occultation texts, however, show little sign of such circumspection. While miraculous foreknowledge is the dominant *dalāla* in many accounts, especially those in which the imam sends letters,[44] narrations concerning direct contact with the imam present a far broader spectrum of wonders: we read of fantastical lost cities, letters rewriting themselves, the Hidden Imam walking concealed among the people and, in one report, tormenting his usurping uncle Jaʿfar the liar by appearing out of thin air at distressing moments.[45] Not only does al-Ṣadūq's inclusion of these texts invite greater opposition from those to whom such marvels were inherently anathema, it also casts the very existence of the twelfth imam as infused with the miraculous, leaving the reader who objects to such miracles little choice but to reject the imam as well.

In short, al-Ṣadūq's occultation texts, the centre of *Kamāl al-dīn* and the basis upon which its proof of the Hidden Imam must stand or fall, appear needlessly, even flippantly hazardous. Non-Imāmīs of the period were condemning Imāmī accounts of the Hidden imam as ridiculous, a problem to which other Imāmī authors responded with a variety of alternative, less miracle-strewn strategies of proof.[46] Conversely, and in tenacious contrast to the extant writings of his contemporaries, al-Ṣadūq is uniquely willing to court controversy, admitting sources that are diversely miraculous, obscurely sourced and contradictory to core tenets of the Imāmīya's own beliefs. As happened towards the middle of *al-Tawḥīd*, we here find him making clear efforts towards one objective – here the assertion of *tawātur* – but at the same time including material that just as clearly undermines those efforts. While one might be tempted to attribute this anomaly to the state of al-Ṣadūq's available sources, such a hypothesis founders both upon other Imāmīs' repeated capacity to produce less troublesome occultation corpora and upon al-Ṣadūq's own ability to vet his material, as demonstrated thoroughly in his other writings. As in *al-Tawḥīd*, the most consistent explanation is to attribute this puzzle to al-Ṣadūq's authorial intentions, and then to ask what he aims to achieve by it.

Echoes

The answer to this question can only be that the advantages accrued by this textually and doctrinally problematic material outweigh the risks. Such a trade-off brings us back to the twofold proof at the heart of *Kamāl al-dīn*, for while the eccentricities of the occultation texts may threaten al-Ṣadūq's assertions of *tawātur*, these same features greatly enhance the 'whatsoever befell' mode of proof, increasing the range of correspondences between the occultation texts of section 3 and the *qiṣaṣ* texts of section 1. The way in which this works is not immediately obvious. After all, if we start from the first principles of al-Ṣadūq's plan of action, 'from the impossible to the possible', the essential elements of the twelfth imam's occultation that need to be proved possible are few and simple: God's *ḥujja* needs to be hidden and he needs to live a long time. Both of these phenomena are already in generous evidence in al-Ṣadūq's *qiṣaṣ* texts, and as far the occultation texts are concerned, he need only adduce reports in which these elements are illustrated; this, too, he has evidently done in abundance. Thus far, then, there is no apparent need for all the troublesome material; there are plenty of narrations available with which al-Ṣadūq could affirm these two core components of the Hidden Imam, including their resonance with the *qiṣaṣ* texts, without deviating from the more stable-looking corpora supplied by al-Kulaynī or even al-Mufīd.[47]

We imagine here a far simpler *Kamāl al-dīn*, but simple *Kamāl al-dīn* is not. We should recall the dictum that underpins al-Ṣadūq's use of the *qiṣaṣ*: that whatsoever has befallen previous communities shall befall Muḥammad's community. The 'whatsoever' component opens up a far broader range of possibilities than merely confirming essential details, instead suggesting that whatever the *qiṣaṣ* texts contain can potentially constitute guiding precedent. Al-Ṣadūq readily has the texts to anchor the bare essentials of the occultation in the prophetic past, but these same texts offer a richer, denser field of resonance between their narratives and the imamic present. In 'whatsoever has befallen', al-Ṣadūq finds a paradigm that embraces the *qiṣaṣ al-anbiyāʾ* with all their wonders, their jellyfish being ridden by bees and little furry people with asymmetrical ears, enjoining the reader to absorb all of this as a potential blueprint for the current reality of the imam's occultation. If he is to take such a paradigm to its logical conclusion, he requires a more colourful Hidden Imam, and this he duly produces by assembling an appropriately wonder-filled set of occultation texts. In so doing, he turns what might have been a brief point of theology into a potentially endless intertextual web of resonance and signification.

The exchange of images that this strategy engenders between different texts and corpora is nowhere more intense than in the subgroup of occultation texts that we may term 'encounter narratives', texts recounting how select believers continue to be granted a meeting with the Hidden Imam despite his occultation. Pious Shīʿīs tirelessly seeking a sign from their vanished imam are beckoned by a mysterious messenger in the night, attracted by a light at a solitary window or even confronted by an astonishing, glittering city in the desert, eventually leading them to their hidden master. These narratives are precisely the kind of material that sets *Kamāl al-dīn* apart from other Imāmī works of the period; not only do they teem with loudly miraculous elements, but their very suggestion that meeting the imam is still possible is highly controversial, and is expressly condemned by al-Nuʿmānī.[48] It is this possibility, however, that al-Ṣadūq undertakes to illustrate in glorious technicolour, finding in these encounter narratives a wellspring of resonances with the *qiṣaṣ* texts. The most likely place to find the Hidden Imam (on the advice of *Kamāl al-dīn*) is at Mecca, where every year he attends the Ḥajj among the faithful, and where, as many narrations affirm, 'He sees them and yet they do not see him'.[49] This evocative image of the imam walking unrecognized among the people is prefigured in the earlier chapter on Joseph: just as God kept Joseph's brothers from recognizing him as they stood before him in Egypt, so he can hide his imam in plain sight among the pilgrims around the Kaʿba. However, as al-Ṣadūq's reader knows, Joseph was hidden neither entirely nor forever. His wicked brothers did not recognize him, but his righteous brother did, and al-Ṣadūq even goes out of his way to argue that his father Jacob knew that he was alive, though he could not see him.[50] So it is that we find the imam, too, revealing himself to deserving pilgrims. The emissary al-ʿAmrī saw him at Mecca, clinging to the Kaʿba's cover and crying, 'O God, avenge me upon my enemies!'[51]

These parallels between corpora continue to expand the longer one looks for them. In the example just cited, the line between past and present is explicitly drawn by al-Ṣadūq in his commentary, but the vast majority of such similarities are left implicit. A recurring figure in the encounter narratives is that of 'the seeker' – the pious Shīʿī wandering at a loss at the story's opening, searching for al-ʿAskarī's successor, news of the house of Muḥammad or even just 'a sign' (*dalāla*).[52] One such figure is Abū Saʿīd Ghānim al-Hindī ('the Indian'). Inspired by reading the Torah at the court of the king of India, Abū Saʿīd journeys across Asia in search of God's last prophet. On encountering Sunnī Muslims in Kabul, he makes the mistake of informing them that the Prophet whom he seeks was rightfully succeeded by ʿAlī b. Abī Ṭālib, and the resulting antagonism nearly costs him his life. After a narrow escape, he gains access to a prudently secretive Shīʿī who informs him of the truth, including that the imamate is now held by Muḥammad's *waṣī*, the twelfth imam, whom Abū Saʿīd in turn successfully seeks out and at last meets.[53]

This account is strikingly similar to the story of Salmān the Persian given in the *qiṣaṣ* section. Salmān, too, begins his story in distant lands of unbelief, but is compelled to set out in search of God's messenger following an encounter with a hidden text. Like Abū Saʿīd, Salmān's quest involves much trial and error, and he, too, must negotiate a mixture of many hostile unbelievers and a few secretive custodians of the truth. He follows a succession of reclusive Christian teachers before the Prophet, at last, passes by the pillar in the desert upon which he sits, and his stylitic patience and devotion are rewarded. Nor is Salmān alone in pursuing such a quest; al-Ṣadūq identifies the Prophet's own status before his mission as analogous to the occultation, and he tells the stories of a number of less-known figures like King Tubbaʿ and Saṭīḥ the soothsayer,[54] who also set out, guided by scripture, inspiration and provenance, to seek news of God's last messenger, to await him and even to find him. In the more distant past, Solomon appears in a narrative of mysterious meetings that presents a remarkable fusion of Shīʿī motifs of occultation and the night-time wanderings of Harūn al-Rashīd in the Thousand and One Nights. Secluded from his *shīʿa* with his new bride, Solomon is compelled to walk the city in disguise and run a series of errands at his beloved's bequest. On one occasion, he meets a fisherman who gives him a pair of fish without ever discovering that he is God's representative. On another occasion, he brings his parents-in-law to dinner, and only once they have eaten their fill does he reveal his true identity as king and prophet with a display of magical power.[55] A little later in his encounter narratives, al-Ṣadūq supplies many testimonies to the effect that his readers, too, can never be sure that an unsolicited invitation might not bring them before their imam. 'He sees them though they do not see him.'[56]

Al-Ṣadūq is not merely adjusting one of his corpora the better to fit the other here; rather, he has enhanced and expanded both the occultation texts and the *qiṣaṣ* texts with potentially awkward material to create between them as rich a field of correspondence as possible. If we look back to the *qiṣaṣ* texts, there are plenty of instances where al-Ṣadūq has evidently sacrificed individual points of theological coherence to this more pressing objective. For example, elsewhere al-Ṣadūq is a vigorous defender of the staple Imāmī doctrine of prophetic infallibility, but many of *Kamāl al-dīn*'s prophets look decidedly imperfect. Idrīs was angry with his community for rejecting his message, and therefore refused to ask God to send them rain in a disastrous drought, only relenting when God rebuked him for this unnecessary spite.[57] Such a fallible prophet would usually be intolerable for an Imāmī author,[58] but here the image of the prophet in his cave, delaying the people's final salvation for wrath at their sins, is a valuable echo of the Hidden Imam, indefinitely absent and supremely wronged. Another anomalous concession is al-Ṣadūq's negotiation of the concept of a 'hiatus' (*fatra*) between prophets. God, the good Imāmī may be absolutely assured, never leaves his creation without *ḥujja*,[59] but in *Kamāl al-dīn* we read that the world endured without one for a whole week after the death of the prophet Ṣāliḥ,[60] while Salmān and many others inhabit the centuries-long gap between Jesus and Muḥammad.[61] Such characters are the perfect simulacrum of the Shīʿī awaiting the twelfth imam, but this *ḥujja*-devoid hiatus breaks the very core Imāmī tenet that necessitates the idea of occultation in the first place. Al-Ṣadūq does, eventually, give a hefty denial of the possibility of such a *fatra*, specifically addressing the time between Jesus and Muḥammad, but this is postponed to the very end of *Kamāl al-dīn*, not allotted a distinct chapter but buried in the book's concluding miscellany (*nawādir*),[62] and there is no attempt to reconcile the direct contradictions between the accounts of Salmān given in this final correction with those in the *qiṣaṣ* texts in section 1. This physical separation of the necessary theology and productive narratives is only a particularly vivid instance of what al-Ṣadūq is doing constantly between his stories of prophets and of the Hidden Imam. Cautions of source criticism and theological rectitude are pushed to the margins, for what is required here is the proliferation and cross-pollination of motifs, as al-Ṣadūq works to create as many links as possible between past and present.

There is more to this endeavour than simple allegory. Prophets may mirror the Hidden Imam, seeker figures like Salmān may mirror the Shīʿa, but such correspondences shift and transmute between stories, sometimes with improbable results. Salmān is one of many ascetic wanderer figures who are an easy model for the awaiting Imāmīya. As often as not, however, these wanderers mirror the hidden *ḥujja* himself rather than those seeking him. Jesus's days in the desert, for instance, become both a monastic seclusion and an occultation, while Joseph's ten years of concealment from his people also takes on an ascetic colour, celibate and unanointed with oil or kohl. The imam's absence from his people becomes a sojourn in the wilderness, his trials merging with theirs as stories and images overlap.[63] Seeker and imam meet inextricably in the figure of Alexander, ('the Horned One'); Alexander is a king who would leave his royal duties to seek adventure, a desire which his subjects fruitlessly entreat him not to indulge. They are left unmistakeably in the guise of the bewildered Shīʿa robbed of their imam, but Alexander meanwhile appears less as a messiah waiting to return than as one seeking enlightenment himself:

> Alexander was once journeying through the world when he came upon an old man who was examining the skulls of the dead. He bade his soldiers halt and called out, 'Old man! Why are you examining these skulls?'
>
> 'I am trying to tell,' replied the old man, 'Which of them belonged to eminent persons and which to the lowly. Yet I cannot tell, though I have been examining them these twenty years!'
>
> Alexander took his leave and journeyed on. 'It was for me and none other that he meant those words,' said he as he went.[64]

Alexander has left his subjects waiting, but we still see in him the hubristic conqueror, whose experiences as he journeys will ultimately win him wisdom. *Kamāl al-dīn* makes of him both an imam who remains apart from his followers and a Shīʿī searching for the hidden truth. No less a figure than Abraham is found in a similar mould. Following his more conventional encounter with Nimrod, where he is, like Moses and like the imam, hidden from a tyrant as a child, al-Ṣadūq tells us that Abraham also had a second occultation 'in which he wandered the world alone that he might reflect'. On the edge of the sea he encounters an old man praying, praying, as it turns out, for God to let him see his great prophet Abraham, and he is duly pleased to learn that his prayer has been granted. Abraham, it seems, has been hidden from one *shīʿa* only to appear to another, but he is clearly as bewildered as anyone else by the experience. Prophet again merges with seeker, discovering the old man from beyond the sea in an image older than both Alexander and Abraham.[65]

By opening up *Kamāl al-dīn*'s different proof-corpora even to the most questionable material, the content of which he has to surreptitiously disavow later in the book, al-Ṣadūq is pouring energy into a mechanism of proof that relies on facilitating as many parallels across these corpora as possible. As he does so, the 'whatsoever befell' maxim becomes less about proving specific historical moments than about creating a fertile intertext of wonders, wherein his readers are encouraged to see everywhere elements of the Hidden Imam and of their own reality as his Shīʿa. The more they read of *Kamāl al-dīn*, the more they absorb the occultation as a set of leitmotifs which have a reality beyond any one textual exemplar or historical event.[66]

4 The plausible and the implausible

For all its potency, readers of *Kamāl al-dīn*'s beguiling feast of images retain the capacity to ask how much of this is true. We can see reasons why al-Ṣadūq's undermining of his own claims to *tawātur* serves his purpose, but the fact remains that if his readers decide that these stories never happed then his attempts at proof are done for. The 'whatsoever befell' paradigm requires things to have befallen, and no less outlandish a tale than that of Abū Saʿīd the Indian is still presented with a prodigious body of *asānīd*.[67]

Al-Ṣadūq is quite aware of this difficulty, and we find him maintaining through *Kamāl al-dīn* a strong interrogative voice, a voice that bids the reader ask what is or is not plausible. Through the *qiṣaṣ* texts and the occultation texts alike, al-Ṣadūq's commentary sporadically frames reports with the complaint that detractors of the Imāmīya believe such stories as this (al-Khiḍr and the fountain of youth, for instance) but scorn to accept the true miracle of the occultation.[68] This question of what is believable is certainly a courageous one to raise in a book that includes jellyfish-riding bees,[69] but it is highly significant in that it takes us beyond the two avenues of proof with which al-Ṣadūq frames *Kamāl al-dīn* in his introduction. With the arrival of a new metric of plausibility, the validity of these texts ceases to be solely about *tawātur* or mythic correspondence; rather, it becomes about what could (or could not) have happened, regardless of who says so.

Living longer

It is in the last, fourth section of *Kamāl al-dīn*, after the *qiṣaṣ* texts, the *naṣṣ* texts and the occultation texts, that this line of discourse takes centre stage. Concluding his long run of testimonies to the Hidden Imam's existence, al-Ṣadūq begins an extensive treatment of the problem of his unusual longevity, and specifically whether it is believable that he really will live on in hiding until the end of the world. This is a noticeably anomalous step. The question has already been addressed, along with other contested aspects of the imam's nature, in earlier sections, especially in the *qiṣaṣ* texts. We have already seen Noah live for 900 years! Why does al-Ṣadūq now return, after laying out his assembled proof texts, to this question in particular? Though the problem is comparatively new, it does not feature prominently among the extended polemics of *Kamāl al-dīn*'s introduction, and numbers as only one among the many miraculous elements of the occultation described by al-Ṣadūq thus far.[70]

This shift in focus is all the more conspicuous for being accompanied by a new corpus of texts. These are ostensibly compiled as stories of miraculous long life that are more outlandish than that of the twelfth imam, but unlike *Kamāl al-dīn*'s preceding corpora, they are not drawn from the Imāmī hadith corpus. We are no longer contemplating the history of revelation with stories of previous prophets, nor the more recent careers of the imams; rather, al-Ṣadūq's exemplars of the extremely old (*muʿammarūn*), hereafter '*muʿammarūn* texts', are for the most part culled from Arab lore – stories purporting to date back to before Muḥammad that are recounted in histories, genealogical literature and *adab* compendia. Spread across nine chapters (47–55), *Kamāl al-dīn*'s *muʿammarūn* texts include such figures Naṣr b. Duhmān, who lived 190 years until his body and mind were utterly decrepit, only to have them restored following the prayers of his tribe, and ʿUmar b. ʿĀmir, who was restored by rainfall and lived for over 800 years.[71] Often their stories are accompanied by gobbets of poetry, be it to transmit the wisdom they have gained in their long lives or to bemoan the world's futility, only intensified by their so lingering in it.[72]

It is not hard to see the utility of these texts' content for al-Ṣadūq's goals. Here is an abundant source of precedents for the imam's longevity, one that could amount to a valuable proof via the 'whatsoever befell' paradigm. Nevertheless, the change in genre remains significant. Al-Ṣadūq is taking his reader still further away from the corpora of proofs upon which authors of legal and theological literature were usually accustomed to rely – most of these *muʿammarūn* texts do not even have an *isnād*. We earlier saw al-Ṣadūq in works like *al-Khiṣāl* combining a hadith compendium's limited sources with an *adab* compendium's form and subject matter; here al-Ṣadūq seems to do the opposite, confronting serious polemics of doctrine (polemics at the heart of which exist disputes over the authenticity of materials) by way of texts that are traditionally the prerogative of *adab* and its comparative disinterest in source-verification.

Despite these *muʿammarūn* texts' clear utility for al-Ṣadūq's project as further precedent for the Hidden Imam's longevity, he does not introduce them as such. Instead, they are framed by the complaint that the opponents of the Imāmīya believe these accounts and those like them, but then have the gall to reject belief in the Hidden Imam as implausible.[73] These stories of the *muʿammarūn* are thus presented not as proof-texts but as anti-proof-texts, examples of the inferior standards of proof and plausibility to which other groups, in their hypocrisy, subscribe. The proof-texts presented in *Kamāl al-dīn*'s earlier chapters, al-Ṣadūq states, should be compared to these and confirmed as superior (or at least less absurd).

Al-Ṣadūq is keen to identify these narrations as enemy property. Most, as noted, are supplied without *asānīd*, one text purporting to have been found written on a rock near Alexandria and another even being quoted from a damaged text such that the story breaks off mid-narrative (disappointingly, just before a talking snake is about to reveal the crucial difference between two types of jinn).[74] This can only serve to cast al-Ṣadūq's preceding images of *tawātur* in a favourable light. In those instances where the *muʿammarūn* texts' sources are discussed, it is often stressed that they are narrated by non-Imāmīs from non-Imāmī sources.[75] When telling the story of King Shaddād, who lived for 900 years and built the city of Iram, al-Ṣadūq tells how no less a non-Shīʿī than Muʿāwiya b. Abī Sufyān learns of this magical city, summons the man who claims to have seen it and seeks corroboration of his account from Kaʿb al-Aḥbār, a narrator whom al-Ṣadūq elsewhere castigates as blamefully unreliable.[76] Discussing 'The Old Man of the Maghrib' Abū al-Dunyā, al-Ṣadūq notes that 'It is not even now confirmed among them that he has died',[77] identifying the story as the concern of an altericized 'them', rather than something on which al-Ṣadūq or his fellow Imāmīs might take a view. Over and above these distinctions, al-Ṣadūq repeatedly evokes the comparative sacrality of these and his earlier sources, asking how people can believe such things from mere men with pens, but then reject confirmations of the occultation uttered by the imams or the Prophet himself.[78]

These polemics of origin are accompanied by commentary ridiculing the fantastic quality of the *muʿammarūn* texts. 'They believe', al-Ṣadūq objects in one instance, 'that this gazelle's dung endured in excess of 500 years, unchanged by either rain or wind, or by the passing of days, nights and years, yet they do not believe that the *qāʾim* from Muḥammad's house will endure until he rides out with the sword!'[79] Regarding the magical city of Iram, he strays into hyperbole, decrying his detractors' telling 'of a place like unto Paradise itself', hidden somewhere on earth, a comparison that the reports he cites do not quite make.[80]

With this hostile othering of the *muʿammarūn* texts and their sources, al-Ṣadūq erects rhetorical barriers between these texts and his previous corpora; between proofs and anti-proofs. In practice, however, things are not so clear-cut, whatever al-Ṣadūq's protestations, and we do not have to look hard to see elements in these stories that have more to offer *Kamāl al-dīn*'s objectives than their ostensive function as exemplars of what others believe. Many times al-Ṣadūq will point to illustrative truths in accounts even as he derides them as implausible, and many more times the core messages of *Kamāl al-dīn* will appear unannounced in material that he labels as unworthy or incidental. The story of Iram, for example, in which a jewel-encrusted city in the middle of the desert is stumbled upon by the narrator as he searches for his lost camel, bears uncanny similarity to one of al-Ṣadūq's encounter narratives, the story of the shaykh of the Banū Rāshid. This tells how the shaykh, having become stranded from his caravan on the way to Mecca, put his trust in God and wandered on foot, eventually finding himself in a green oasis, in the midst of which was a shining citadel rising resplendently out of the grass. Entering, he was told by attending servants that God intended a blessing for him, and was led behind a veil to where there sat a young man above whose head was suspended a sword. The man announced himself as the *qāʾim* of the house of Muḥammad, who would rise up with this sword at the end of time to fill the world with justice. The lost pilgrim from Hamadān fell on his face in reverence, but the imam kindly raised him up, and sent him home with a purse full of gold.[81]

In another *muʿammarūn* text, Khumarawayh[82] b. Aḥmad b. Ṭūlūn seeks to plunder the treasure of the pyramids, whereupon he encounters an inscription in Greek that none can read. He is advised by a wise man that the only person with the knowledge to decode the text is a 300-year-old bishop who lives in Ethiopia. The bishop is too old to make the journey north, and so the king resorts to an exchange of letters. Eventually, the bishop reveals that the inscription instructs that none will be able to open the pyramid's treasury until the *qāʾim* from the house of Muḥammad comes to claim it.[83] Besides the plainly occultation-affirming climax of the story, the necessity to seek knowledge from an absent, age-old authority and the epistolary means of doing so have clear resonances with al-Ṣadūq's *qiṣaṣ* and occultation texts.

It is apparent that there is far more than parody at work here. Although al-Ṣadūq expressly distances his arguments from having any stake in the truth of these reports, and makes polemical capital from the intimation that they might not be true, this procession of stories of the long-lived steadily expands his readers' reservoir of images wherein they are by now thoroughly drilled to see the reality of *ghayba*. For all the improbable details, the talking wolves and the exploding dung,[84] there is an ongoing attempt at *tawātur* here. By the time the names of almost fifty such prolonged men and women (alongside one or two vultures) have passed before them, only the most relentlessly cynical readers can have resisted the idea of such longevity becoming a little more plausible, regardless of whose books attest to it.

Al-Ṣadūq seems here to be having his cake and eating it. He is shoring up the credibility of his earlier corpora of sources by favourably contrasting them with less reliable material, even as he uses this same dubious material to expand and develop his image of *ghayba* as a perennial reality. What he is also doing as a result is destabilizing the relationship between his different strategies of proof. In sections 1 and 2, this relationship was clearly demarcated, with different corpora in different sections serving different strategies. With the *muʿammarūn* texts, conversely, *Kamāl al-dīn*'s readers are confronted with narrations that are both explicitly labelled as unreliable, that is to say lacking in *tawātur*, and vivid examples of occultation as an ever-present phenomenon, and must therefore be unsure how they are supposed to read them.

Bilawhar and Yūdhāsaf

This blurring of readerly expectations only intensifies as we move to the last and most improbable of *Kamāl al-dīn*'s diverse proof-corpora. Following a final *muʿammarūn* text, chapter 55 presents an extremely lengthy set of semi-linked stories centred around an Indian prince named Yūdhāsaf, better recognized as the Buddha.[85] At the end of a short *isnād* of mostly unknown sources,[86] the text begins thus:

> I have heard that there was once a king amongst the kings of India. His soldiers were many, his kingdom was large, he was held in dread by his people and was victorious over his enemies. But he was also possessed of great hunger for the pleasures of this world, its delights and its diversions, and so was ruled and swayed by his passions. For him the most beloved and trusted of men was one who flattered him and lauded his opinions, while the most despised and doubted was one who neglected his commands and bade him do otherwise than he wished.[87]

We have moved even further away from the usual stuff of legal and theological truth-claims here. The characters of these stories are not Arabs to whom are attributed familiar poems and to whom tribes and acquaintances trace their genealogies, named and categorized in known sources. Instead, this opening places us squarely in the land of once upon a time and far, far away.

Reading on, we learn how this impious king is confronted by a lone sage who seeks to correct his wicked ways, and who tells him the story of Yūdhāsaf with that aim. This story, in turn, is that of the young, sheltered prince Yūdhāsaf, the son of another, more graphically impious king; this king has banished all men of religion from his kingdom on pain of death, a pogrom in which so many were burned to death that the land of India remained ablaze for an entire year. Prince Yūdhāsaf, meanwhile, undergoes the transformative realization of change and mortality familiar from Buddhist literature, stealing out of the palace into the real world, where he sees before him the shocking realities of decay and death from which he had been protected. Cast into doubt, he seeks the means of answering his mortal dilemma, and learns of the men of religion who once filled the land but whom the king has driven into hiding, and whom now he dearly wishes to find and to consult. The wise man of God Bilawhar, who lives in safety far away, hears of the prince's plight, and travels in disguise to find him and to teach him. They meet in secret and begin Yūdhāsaf's education, an education which consists largely of Bilawhar telling the prince improving stories, some of which contain characters who tell stories in turn.

As we have by now come to expect, this change in sources occasions a corresponding change in rationale for including them.[88] At the end of this long set of tales, hereafter the 'Yūdhāsaf texts', al-Ṣadūq declares that he has only included material like this in order to lure curious readers, hoping that once attracted by these tales of magic and derring-do, they will read the rest of the book and so learn about the Hidden Imam. As is the case with the *muʿammarūn* texts, however, there is much to suggest that al-Ṣadūq is investing more in the persuasive power of these stories than he wants to admit. The Yūdhāsaf texts brim over with the same set of motifs that pervade the *muʿammarūn* texts, the *qiṣaṣ* texts and the occultation texts. Men of God are forever struggling to spread the faith in the face of despotic, idolatrous rulers, whose depredations often compel the pious to do their work in secret, described all the while with typical Imāmī vocabulary such as '*imām*', '*khurūj*' and, of course, '*ghayba*'.

Thus far, al-Ṣadūq's use of the Yūdhāsaf texts is not dissimilar to what he does with the *muʿammarūn* texts: disavowing any probative commitment to the material while still carefully selecting it to reinforce *Kamāl al-dīn*'s driving narratives. There is, nonetheless, an important difference between these two corpora, one that shines a light on what al-Ṣadūq achieves by including them. This is the change in register offered by these new, unfamiliar stories from India, one that opens up al-Ṣadūq's images of the imam to new imaginative possibilities. As well as being free from any category of regulated sources, the Yūdhāsaf texts, in the utterly distant and non-Abrahamic context of India, are unmoored from constraints of verisimilitude, and this allows the images of the occultation they contain to take on a mythic, archetypal quality.[89] The wicked tyrants here are not just ʿAbbāsids but raw idolaters, not merely rejecting the messages of lone prophets but condemning entire religions to be burned to death; the persecuted sages do not teach obscure theology but essential truths of God's oneness and power and of man's frailty. While this allows a scaling up of some aspects of the drama – equating the ʿAbbāsids with the genocidal tyrant, and the imams with the universal sage – just as important are the elements of the occultation that these stories render a little less cosmic, a little more familiar. The men of God hide for fear of persecution, not as a result of some inscrutable divine act. They are not miraculously concealed, only hidden in another country, and if they are needed they can return.[90]

Secrets

A central theme of the Yūdhāsaf stories is wisdom. Yūdhāsaf addresses his teacher as *al-ḥakīm*, 'the wise man', and his teachings are fittingly replete with maxims (*ḥikam*) along such generic lines as 'the worst of deeds is disobeying God', 'Foolishness is to be content with the world and to neglect what is permanent and lasting'[91] and so on. Wisdom (*ḥikma*) has a tenacious and multifarious presence in *Kamāl al-dīn*. Beyond the Yūdhāsaf stories, the *muʿammarūn* texts are full of wise aphorisms from Luqmān-like, long-lived sages, and it is also a pivotal term in the earlier texts about the prophets and the Hidden Imam, though in these earlier chapters it is wisdom of a different sort, focussed on the problem at hand. Al-Ṣadūq acknowledges a number of potential reasons for the occultation in *Kamāl al-dīn*, but his preferred response is expressed in the answer of Jaʿfar al-Ṣādiq to the disciple Ibn al-Faḍl:

> The meaning of the wisdom (*ḥikma*) behind his occultation is the meaning of the wisdom behind the occultations of those of God's *ḥujaj* who have gone before him, and the meaning of the wisdom therein will not be revealed until his reappearance, just as the meaning of the wisdom of what al-Khiḍr did when he scuppered the boat, killed the boy and rebuilt the wall was not revealed to Moses until the time of their parting. O Ibn al-Faḍl, this matter is one of God's matters, a secret among God's secrets, something unseen among the unseen things of God. We know that God, blessed and exalted, is wise, and so we believe that all of his actions are wisdom, even if their meaning is not revealed.[92]

Kamāl al-dīn, of course, sets itself the task not of explaining the occultation but only of proving that it happened. In the Yūdhāsaf stories, though, it becomes ever clearer that these two objectives can overlap. Al-Ṣadūq's endless stream of exemplars of occultation are framed as proving the truth of the Hidden Imam, but they also make it more familiar. He tells us firmly that we cannot know the wisdom behind the imam's vanishing, but he is constantly showing us how that wisdom works, and also, perhaps, that the transgression of seeking answers is forgivable. An important reference point in *Kamāl al-dīn* is the Qurʾanic example of Abraham, who asks God to show him his power to bring the dead to life. 'Do you not believe?' chides the Almighty, to which Abraham responds, 'Only let my heart be set at rest.'[93] God indulges his request by elaborately returning four dead birds to life, breaking the rules to set a believer's heart at rest in a way full of resonance for al-Ṣadūq's readers.

Another figure emblematic of how to relate to divine mystery is that of al-Khiḍr. Evoked earlier in his locus classicus in *al-Kahf*, al-Khiḍr appears precisely as a curious blurring between human and divine wisdom, and also of the creative tension between theological principle and instructive narrative; 'One among our servants to whom we grated some mercy, and taught some of our knowledge',[94] whose inerrant foreknowledge of things to come frustrates and baffles his would-be disciple Moses. Al-Khiḍr's appearances in *Kamāl al-dīn* span the full range of the book's shifting motifs. He starts life as a seeker, adventuring in the service of the *ḥujja* Alexander, an adventure which leads to his drinking from the Water of Life, whereupon he takes on not only *qāʾim*-like longevity but also the ability to remain hidden in plain sight. He comes to give authoritative counsel to Muḥammad al-Bāqir, but elsewhere appears, Shīʿī-like, lamenting the deaths of the Prophet, ʿAlī and al-Ḥusayn. He attends the Ḥajj unseen like the Hidden Imam, whose companion he is in their shared longevity. In his wanderings, transformations and sporadic presences, this elusive, myth-filled figure thus embodies the possibilities that *Kamāl al-dīn* offers the believer, foremost among them the possibility that the wisdom of God's divine plan will eventually yield up a final, cathartic explanation.[95]

For now, nonetheless, the imam remains hidden. In Chapter 2, we met al-Ṣadūq's father's doctrine that occultation is part of a pervasive necessity of secrecy in revelation, and there are nods to such an idea in *Kamāl al-dīn*. On a doctrinal level, it appears most clearly in the question of whether or not it is permitted to reveal the Hidden Imam's name. The short answer is that this is absolutely forbidden; numerous hadiths throughout the book condemn naming the imam, and at the very end al-Ṣadūq gives a chapter (57) dedicated to affirming the prohibition.[96] These injunctions, however, are only half the story, for *Kamāl al-dīn* is all the while replete with texts that do name the Hidden Imam.[97] Long before we reach the direct prohibition in chapter 57, we are in no doubt that the imam's name is Muḥammad and that a great many people have said so, because al-Ṣadūq himself has told us. In a manoeuvre similar to al-Ṣadūq's treatment of the inter-prophetic *fatra* discussed earlier, here again we see him intervening at his work's close to give a ruling that he has himself repeatedly violated in the main body of the text. Just as is the case with the *fatra*, this apparent contradiction plays a valuable role, allowing al-Ṣadūq to enrich his narratives with unorthodox material that he can later disavow once it has served its purpose.[98]

In his somewhat half-hearted prohibition of naming the imam, al-Ṣadūq is negotiating a theme of secrecy that pervades *Kamāl al-dīn*. The need for secrecy and hiddenness is, of course, integral to the narratives of occultation that the book tells and retells. The *ḥujja* is hidden from persecution, the king leaves his people to wander the earth alone, the faithful lie low until guidance returns, the one who seeks the truth must remain silent lest the unenlightened masses take offence. Salmān's parents cast him into a well when he resolves to leave idol-worship and seek God's messenger, while Abū Saʿīd the Indian nearly meets his death at the hands of angry Sunnīs in Kabul when he ill-advisedly confesses his devotion to ʿAlī.[99] And yet, inextricable from this need for secrecy is the limit of secrecy. *Kamāl al-dīn* is not just about the hiddenness of the imam but about the fact that he is not hidden forever, nor, perhaps, from everyone. When prophets vanish, they first foretell their return or the coming of the next prophet. The faithful do not know where the imam is, but they do know that he is somewhere, walking among them, seeing them though they do not see him. Hidden though it is, the truth may still appear to the wanderer in the desert, and one day the imam will return. Secrecy is essential, but it is also partial.

More specifically, the power of the written word to reveal secrets is never far away in *Kamāl al-dīn*. At its centre are the assembled epistles of the Hidden Imam, commanding secrecy even as they reveal the imam's power to their recipients.[100] The stories of encounters with the imam, too, often conclude with the imam commanding the lucky disciple never to speak of what he has seen,[101] yet what these good Shīʿīs saw is now set down in writing for the reader of *Kamāl al-dīn* to peruse at leisure! In this way, al-Ṣadūq's book itself becomes a potent testament to the unseen, initiating the reader into the company of those who know of the imam's disclosure, revealing in text that which, paradoxically, must not be uttered aloud. At the beginning of the book, we are told that al-Ṣadūq was commanded to write it by the Hidden Imam himself in a dream. The inspirational dream is not an uncommon opening motif in literature of the era, but the deeper significance here is plain: al-Ṣadūq joins the company of those whose stories he tells, guided by a nightly vision of the imam just as they were.[102] Later on in the work, near the end of the chapter concerning those who received letters from the twelfth imam, our author tells us that one such message was received by his own father, who had written to the imam asking that he might be blessed with a son. The imam's answer came that he would, and that son was, of course, Muḥammad b. ʿAlī – al-Shaykh al-Ṣadūq himself.[103] *Kamāl al-dīn*, then, is not just another book of hadith, narrated by a discerning compiler, but is something much more like the many letters and signs of God's occulted *ḥujja* that it contains. A secret document for the privileged few, this book and even its author are direct consequences of the will of the Hidden Imam, offering its reader a much more immediate experience of truth than the long transmission of *tawātur*.

Conclusion

The occultation is, by any account, a difficult theological problem. God can never leave his creation without a *ḥujja*, and what use is an imam whom the believers can neither consult nor even see? Al-Ṣadūq echoes many of his fellow scholars when he bemoans the dismay and confusion (*ḥayra*) that afflicts the Imāmīya with regard to this question.[104] These difficulties, moreover, are lodged in the very bones of Imāmī traditionism in al-Ṣadūq's era, the imam's vanishing inseparable from the need to substitute living authority with text, an endeavour that we have seen al-Ṣadūq under chronic pressure to justify. More worryingly still, many of al-Ṣadūq's contemporaries saw the occultation as unusually inimical to being proven by means of hadith. If *al-Tawḥīd* ends with the defiant insistence that the imams' words should be proof enough, *Kamāl al-dīn* confronts a worry that, when it comes to this most intractable dilemma of the imam's absent presence, they might not be.

Al-Ṣadūq's response to these challenges in *Kamāl al-dīn* is simultaneously to embrace proof by text with new determination and to subject it to new levels of interrogation. The work is unique in al-Ṣadūq's surviving writings in the volume of texts it includes that are not the imams' hadith, but quite unlike his fellows' recourse to Sunnī hadith, these other texts are not performing a task that the imams' hadith cannot; rather, they allow al-Ṣadūq to use the imams' hadith in a different way. Though he does begin by pronouncing his hadiths' certain *tawātur*, al-Ṣadūq evidently recognizes that his occultation texts' *asānīd* are not enough to carry the day. What he also recognizes, though, is that they may persuade in other ways: through the sheer drama and mythic fertility of the narratives they create, through their resonances with millennia of storytelling, through their penchant for the curious and the magical. The very features that drive other Imāmī authors away from these occultation accounts – their far-fetched stories and internal contradictions – are identified by al-Ṣadūq as a potent resource. Instead of narrowing his corpus down to a canonical account, he exploits precisely all that is blurred and unstable in the occultation literature to transcend problems of authenticity and create a seething feast of images, driven by plurality and mutability, in which the Hidden Imam can come alive to the reader.[105]

Al-Ṣadūq's mode of instruction in *Kamāl al-dīn* is inseparable from the particular nature of compilation. It thrives on the distance between the author and the texts he presents, the ambiguity allowed over where these texts are from, what they are and what they might mean. On a matter so sensitive as the occultation, this enables al-Ṣadūq to sidestep difficulties of exact definition and orthodoxy. The construction of the Hidden Imam in this book is achieved not primarily through direct statements by the author, but through suggestions that co-opt the imagination of the reader. The Shīʿa are told not only to wait patiently for the imam's return but also that he walks unseen among us, perhaps that he pines for us as we do for him, that we might even meet him at the end of an extraordinary adventure. As the text becomes more suggestive, there are hints that at the end of our search for the imam we could become like him, like a wandering king, like a prince rescuing maidens from towers, or some combination of all three.[106] These solutions to the trauma of the imam's absence are far too heterodox to be enunciated outright; rather, the reader is made to do the work, extrapolating from the meeting points between assembled texts, as al-Ṣadūq employs the allusive capacity of compilation to achieve what brute dialectic cannot.[107]

Conclusion

Hadith literature and Twelver Shīʿism

Presence and absence

Shīʿī groups of the ʿAbbāsid period and beyond wrote about their differences principally in terms of the nature of the true imam – his qualifications, his identity and the expectations that accompanied his presence. Shīʿī discourses of the era were accordingly peopled by a diverse crowd of imamologies and imams, with some of the latter leaving their own significant political and intellectual legacies. Just as important, however, and almost always more enduring in the life of Shīʿī communities, were the institutions and social dynamics that developed from and around these theories and personalities. These faces of Shīʿism were just as various as the Shīʿīs' many imams, with different communities becoming structured variously around initiatic hierarchies, armed revolution, apolitical quietism and empire. Since before the time when al-Ṣadūq was writing, Twelver Shīʿism has become increasingly distinguished among Shīʿī groups by its consistent investment in the *fuqahāʾ*, *fiqh* and the school of law as the principal authority and epistemic centre of the community. These institutions are just as integral to Twelver Shīʿism over the last millennium as the occulted twelfth imam for whom the group is so named. It is, in turn, through these institutions that hadith literature occupies a central, definitive place in Twelver thought. Over the broad sweep of history, the place of hadith within Twelver Shīʿism is not dramatically dissimilar from its place within the many iterations of Sunnism. It is, perhaps, partly as a result of this that this branch of Shīʿism, with its *fuqahāʾ* and debates around dietary laws, is sometimes cast as altogether less radical, even less authentically Shīʿī than those 'redder' Shīʿisms in which the imams' charisma appears less completely, even bureaucratically routinized.

This study of al-Ṣadūq has concentrated upon his use of hadith, and in so doing it has repeatedly illustrated how deeply early Twelver hadith scholarship was imbued with the distinct concerns of Twelver Shīʿism, as it wrestled with its foundational imamological conundrum – the presence and absence of the Hidden Imam. The development of a full-fledged hadith literature by Imāmīs as the imam faded from view occasioned manifold interrogations not only of the teachings of the imams and the doctrine of the imamate but also of the very foundations of the representation of authority through text. This is a strangely self-aware emergence of a scriptural corpus, confronting head-on the problems of authority's absence, its consequent need for recollection and the danger that such recollections will only underscore the absence that motivated them. Al-Ṣadūq strives with a fierce epistemological urgency to assert the viability of his hadith corpus as scripture, as access to God's *ḥujja* on earth, walking a tightrope between the insistence upon that *ḥujja*'s total inerrancy and the transmitter-compiler's prerogative to mediate and evaluate his texts. The idealism that he negotiates is coupled with a vigorous readiness to experiment, approaching different audiences and exploring different sorts of textual proof, testing the ways in which his corpus may produce knowledge and authority. He sets out the imams' hadith as the font of all wisdom, not only in matters of law and theology but across the expanding intellectual horizons of his era. The meeting point between this idealism and experimentation is al-Ṣadūq's continued, multifarious aspiration to let his readers meet the imam, delivering to them the salvific combination of divine guidance and deep, numinous bewilderment that is coming face to face with the conduit of God's perfect truth.

Traditionism

In publishing a book dedicated to the thought of a single, hitherto underexamined Muslim author, I am aware that I risk antagonizing the growing number of my colleagues who call for an expansion of the scholarly imagination beyond the 'The Man and His Works' paradigm of monograph-production. One reason for pressing ahead regardless is that the author in question is an author of compilations, and therefore the very contention that his works can yield an intellectual portrait worth painting is, as I have argued throughout this book, a contention that deserves to be made. My abiding concern has been to illuminate the authorial agency of al-Ṣadūq and thus of compilers like him, and with it the rich expressive capacity of compiled material. Part II, in particular, has sought to test the limits of this approach, forestalling decisive, detailed accounts of al-Ṣadūq's theology for the sake of paying as much attention as possible to the nuances of his writing – how he presents hadiths, how he wants them to be read, what he wants them to mean and, indeed, what he thinks they are. Whatever readers may dispute in my conclusions regarding al-Ṣadūq's thought, I hope that this book will encourage more such experiments with other compilers and other kinds of compendia.

Al-Ṣadūq was not just a compiler but a compiler of hadith, and to finish I would like to set out what I see as the implications of the compilation criticism practised in this book for the study of hadith literature and, in particular, literature produced by traditionists – Muslims like al-Ṣadūq who place especial emphasis upon the authority of hadith, and who accordingly prioritize hadith compilation at the expense of other kinds of writing. This study has retained the vocabulary of 'rationalists' and 'traditionists', recognizing the great importance that Muslim authors like al-Ṣadūq accorded to the relative embrace of independent reasoning – at the expense, as they saw it, of deference to the letter of scripture – as a variable between different thinkers and groups. Nonetheless, the ingenuity with which we have seen al-Ṣadūq presenting his narrated traditions must impose a degree of caution upon such vocabulary, or at least some of its potential conclusions. Not only does al-Ṣadūq exert copious intellectual energy, indeed reason, in his acts of compilation, but compilation and transmission are utterly enmeshed within his ways of reasoning and writing. Across the compendia explored in the preceding chapters, al-Ṣadūq has shown an exacting sensitivity to the mimetic possibilities of compiled hadith, quite beyond what is accounted for in schemata of authenticity and thresholds of proof.

Beyond dispelling any notion that traditionism can be considered 'unreasonable', these observations can and should affect how and where we locate what it is that traditionists think. By one metric, al-Ṣadūq's views on central questions may be found in *al-Iʿtiqādāt*, his traditionist character surely represented in his care to support his given views with textual (rather than rational) proofs. But we have also seen a far more expansive account of his views, especially in *al-Tawḥīd* and *Kamāl al-dīn*, an account that is not easily distilled to a set of abstract doctrines. If we are to take seriously the proposition that compilations can be complex acts of representation rather than just being amassed proof-texts, then we have to take seriously the notion that these works might not merely be expressing neat doctrines at greater length. Just as the dialectic theologian or philosopher may elaborate upon simple statements of creed with lengthily and intricately argued discussions that defy easy summary, so in these compilations al-Ṣadūq expands upon and develops his basic convictions. To a very real extent, *Kamāl al-dīn*'s rhapsody of motif and myth *is* al-Ṣadūq's view of the Hidden Imam; *al-Tawḥīd*'s shifting landscape of instruction and ambiguation *is* al-Ṣadūq's understanding of the proper relation between text and reason. A literary view of compilation that deems it a worthy recipient of criticism bids us consider a correspondingly discursive view of the discourses that traditionists enunciate in their compilations, discourses that are embedded within the negotiations between compilers, their readers and their texts.

Appendix I

Table of contents for *al-Tawḥīd*

Page numbers differ between editions, and are supplied only for scale.

Introduction

1. The Reward of Those Who Know and Declare God's Oneness
2. The Oneness of God and the Prohibition Against Likening Him to Created Things (*tashbīh*)
3. The Meanings of God's Oneness, the Declaration Thereof and the Person Who Declares It
4. Exegesis of 'Say he is God the One' (Q 112:1)
5. The Meaning of Divine Oneness and Justice (*ʿadl*)
6. That He is Neither a Body Nor a Form
7. That He is a Thing
8. What is Said Concerning Seeing [God]
9. [God's] Power
10. [God's] Knowledge
11. The Attributes of Essence and the Attributes of Action
12. Exegesis of God's Words, 'All things perish but his face' (Q 28:88)
13. Exegesis of God's Words, 'Oh Iblīs, what prevents you from prostrating to what I have made with my hand?' (Q 38:75)
14. Exegesis of God's Words, 'A day when a shin is uncovered, and they are called upon to prostrate . . .' (Q 68:42)
15. Exegesis of God's Words, 'God is the light of the heavens and the earth.' (Q 24:35)

Section 1 – Affirming God's transcendence (chapters 1–28, ~180 pp.)

In this first section, the chapters all assert different aspects of the basic notion that God is unlike any created thing. Three main types of chapter are included: those affirming his transcendence in broad terms, those upholding a particular theological concept and those disambiguating Qurʾanic verses that might imply God's similitude to creation (*tashbīh*).

16. Exegesis of God's Words, 'They have forgotten God, and he has forgotten them.' (Q 9:67)
17. Exegesis of God's Words, 'On the day of resurrection the whole earth is in his fist, the heavens folded into his right hand.' (Q 39:67)
18. Exegesis of God's Words, 'No! On that day they shall indeed be hidden from their Lord!' (Q 83:15)
19. Exegesis of God's Words, 'And there come your Lord and the angels, row upon row' (Q 89:22)
20. Exegesis of God's Words, 'Do they wait only for God to come to them in the shadows of the clouds with the angels?' (Q 2:210)
21. Exegesis of God's Words, 'God despises them.' (Q 9:79), 'God holds them in contempt.' (Q 2:15), 'They scheme and God schemes, and God is the best of schemers.' (Q 3:54), 'They trick God while he tricks them.' (Q 4:142)
22. The Meaning of God's Side
23. The Meaning of [God's] Belt
24. The Meaning of [God's] Eye, [God's] Ear and [God's] Tongue
25. The Meaning of His Words, 'The Jews say that God's hand is withdrawn – bound are their hands, they are accursed for what they say, and His hands are spread wide' (Q 5:64)
26. The Meaning of His Pleasure and His Anger
27. The Meaning of His Words, 'And I breathed my spirit into him.' (Q 15:29)
28. The Inapplicability of Place, Time, Rest, Movement, Descent, Ascent and Locomotion to God
29. God's Names and the Difference Between Their Meanings and the Meanings of the Names of Created Beings
30. The Nature of the Qur'an
31. The Meaning of, 'In the Name of God, the Most Compassionate, the Most Merciful'
32. Exegesis of the Letters of the Alphabet
33. Exegesis of the Letters of the Abjad
34. Exegesis of the Letters of the Calls to Prayer
35. Exegesis of Guidance, Delusion, Providence and Debasement from God
36. Refutation of the Dualists and Zindīqs

Section 2 – The mysteries of God's majesty (chapters 29–52, ~160 pp.)

The exact nature of this section is not immediately obvious (much of its transformative nature is in the content of its chapters, and is not much signposted by their headings). Its departure from section 1 is marked at the point where chapters cease to be about matters that concern God's transcendence and enter into more obscure topics: the meanings of names and so on.

37. Refutation of Those Who Say that God is the Third of Three, Amounting to a Single Deity
38. Recounting God's Majesty (*ʿAẓama*)
39. God's Subtlety
40. The Minimum Permissible Level of Knowledge of God's Oneness
41. That He Can Only Be Known Through Himself
42. Proof of the Impermanence of the World
43. The Hadith of Dhiʿlib
44. The Hadith of Subbukht the Jew
45. The Meaning of 'God be Exalted' (*subḥān Allāh*)
46. The Meaning of 'God is Greatest' (*Allāhu akbar*)
47. The Meaning of 'The First and the Last' (Q 57:3)
48. The Meaning of God's Words, 'The Most Compassionate is seated on the throne' (Q 20:5)
49. The Meaning of His Words, 'And his throne was on the water.' (Q 11:7)
50. The Throne and Its Attributes
51. That the Throne Was the Fourth Creation
52. The Meaning of God's Words, 'His seat encompasses the heavens and the earth.' (Q 2:255)
53. God's Predisposition of his Creation Towards the Declaration of His Oneness
54. *Badāʾ*
55. Will and Intention
56. Capacity
57. Tribulation and Experience
58. Happiness and Wretchedness
59. The Denial of Free Will and Predestination
60. Decree, Preordainment, Sedition, Bounties, Prices and Rewards
61. Infants and God's Justice with Regard to Them
62. That God Deals with His Servants Only According to Their Best Interests
63. Command, Prohibition, the Promise and the Threat
64. Teaching, Demonstration, Proof and Guidance

Section 3 – Free will and predestination (chapters 53–67, ~140 pp.)

This third section returns to conventional theology, at least in terms of its subject matter. The second of al-Ṣadūq's opening concerns, that of free will and predestination, is now addressed. Many of the chapters, like those in section 1, address particular concepts within this area. Towards the end, the section's subject matter gradually shifts towards a general discussion of theology and hadith.

65. Record of the Council of al-Riḍā ʿAlī b. Mūsā with the Scholars of Different Religions and Confessions, Such as the Catholicos, the Exiliarch, the Leaders of the Sabeans, and the Chief Magus, and What He Told ʿImrān the Sabean Regarding God's Oneness in the Presence of al-Maʾmūn
66. Record of the Council of al-Riḍā with Sulaymān al-Marwazī, the Disputant of Khurāsān, in the Presence of al-Maʾmūn
67. The Prohibition of Dialectic, Disputation and Self-Aggrandizement Regarding God

(**Chapters 65–6** – The councils of al-Riḍā)

These two chapters are, formally speaking, a striking departure from what precedes, constituting long narratives of the imam al-Riḍā's debates with various interlocutors. Thematically, however, they are integral to the third section.

Appendix II

Table of contents for *Kamāl al-dīn wa tamām al-ni ʿma*

Page numbers differ between editions, and are supplied only for scale.

Introduction

1. On the Occultation of Idrīs
2. Recording Noah's Appearance as a Prophet
3. On the Occultation of Ṣāliḥ
4. On the Occultation of Abraham
5. On the Occultation of Joseph
6. On the Occultation of Moses
7. Moses' Passing and the Onset of Occultation Amongst the Trustees (sg. *waṣī*)
8. The Foretelling of the Prophet Muḥammad al-Muṣṭafā by Jesus, Mary's Son
9. The Account of Salmān the Persian Regarding the Subject of the Previous Chapter
10. On the Account of Quss b. Sā ʿida al-Ayādī
11. On the Account of Tubba ʿ
12. On the Account of ʿAbd al-Muṭṭalib and Abū Ṭālib
13. On the Account of Sayf b. Dhī Yazn
14. On the Account of Baḥīrā the Monk
15. The Story of the Leader of the Monks on the Route to Syria and his Knowledge of the Matter of the Prophet
16. On the Account of Abū al-Muwayhib the Monk
17. On the Account of Saṭīḥ the Soothsayer
18. The Account of Yūsuf the Jew Regarding the Prophet
19. The Account of Dawwās b. Ḥawwāsh, Who Came from Syria

Section 1 – Stories of the prophets (chapters 1–20, ~70 pp.)

In this group of chapters, as their headings illustrate, al-Ṣadūq sets out instances of occultation observable in a diverse corpus of stories of the prophets.

20. The Account of Zayd b. ʿAmr b. Nufayl
21. The Reason Wherefore an Imam is Necessary
22. The Continuation of the Trusteeship (*waṣīya*) from Adam Onwards
23. God's Investiture of the *Qāʾim*
24. The Prophet's Investiture of the *Qāʾim*
25. What the Prophet Related Concerning the Coming of the Occultation
26. What the Prince of Believers (ʿAlī) Related Concerning the Coming of the Occultation
27. What is Narrated from the Noblest of Women (Fāṭima) About the Matter of the *Qāʾim*
28. The Account of the Tablet
29. What al-Ḥasan b. ʿAlī Related Concerning the Coming of the Occultation
30. What al-Ḥusayn b. ʿAlī Related Concerning the Coming of the Occultation
31. What ʿAlī b. al-Ḥusayn Related Concerning the Coming of the Occultation
32. What al-Bāqir Related Concerning the Coming of the Occultation
33. What al-Ṣādiq Related Concerning the Coming of the Occultation
34. What al-Kāẓim Related Concerning the Coming of the Occultation
35. What al-Riḍā Related Concerning the Coming of the Occultation
36. What al-Jawād Related Concerning the Coming of the Occultation
37. What al-Hādī Related Concerning the Coming of the Occultation
38. What al-ʿAskarī Related Concerning the Coming of the Occultation
    i. What is Narrated from the Hadith of al-Khiḍr
    ii. What is Narrated from the Hadith of the Horned One (Alexander)
    iii. Returning to What is Narrated from Imam al-ʿAskarī
39. Regarding One Who Denies the *Qāʾim*
40. That the Imamate is Never Possessed by Two Brothers Except for the Two Ḥasans (al-Ḥasan and al-Ḥusayn)
41. What is Narrated Regarding Narjis, Mother of the *Qāʾim*
42. What is Narrated Regarding the Birth of the *Qāʾim*
43. Those Who Congratulated Abū Muḥammad al-ʿAskarī on the Birth of the *Qāʾim*

Section 2 – Foretellings of the imams (chapters 22–38, ~150 pp.)

Here al-Ṣadūq collects reports from the eleven earlier imams, Muḥammad and Fāṭima, prophesying the occultation of the twelfth imam.

44. Those Who Witnessed the *Qā ʾim*, Saw Him and Spoke with Him
45. The Reasons for the Occultation
46. Record of the Letters [Sent by the *Qā ʾim*]
    i. The Supplication to be Uttered During the *Qā ʾim*'s Occultation
    ii. Returning to the Letters
47. What Has Reached Us Regarding Exceptional Longevity
48. The Hadith of the *Dajjāl*
49. Jesus and the Gazelle in the Country of Nineveh
50. The Hadith of Ḥabāba al-Wālibīya
51. The Hadith of Mu ʿammar al-Maghribī, Abū al-Dunyā
52. The Hadith of ʿAbīd b. Sharya
53. The Hadith of al-Rabīʿ b. al-Ḍabʿ al-Fazārī
54. The Hadith of Shaqq the Soothsayer
55. The Hadith of Shaddād and his Garden
    i. Record of the Extraordinarily Long-Lived (*mu ʿammarūn*)
    ii. Discourses from the Author of this Book
    iii. The Story of Bilawhar and Yūdhāsaf
    iv. The Meaning of Such Stories' Inclusion in This Book
56. What is Narrated Regarding the Reward of Those Who Await Deliverance
57. The Prohibition Against Naming the *Qā ʾim*
58. The Signs of the *Qā ʾim*'s Emergence
59. Miscellanies of the Book, and the Author's Clarification Regarding the Meaning of the 'Hiatus' (*fatra*)

Section 3 – Accounts of the Hidden Imam (chapters 41–6, ~100 pp.)

Here al-Ṣadūq presents the core proof-texts of the Hidden Imam: eyewitness testimonies, alongside the many documents reported to have been written by him. Though comparatively few chapters make up this section, it is of comparable size to the previous two, chapters 44 and 46 both being of considerable length.

Section 4 – The *Mu ʿammarūn* (chapters 47–55, ~120 pp.)

This is the last substantial group of chapters, which focusses on those possessed of unusually long life. The role of the long story of Yūdhāsaf within the section is not immediately obvious.

Notes

Introduction

1 This canon was only fixed much later, around the turn of the eighth/fourteenth century.

2 Though his beliefs in the hidden, twelfth imam render him solidly a part of what we now call Twelver (*Ithnā ʾ ʿasharī*) Shīʿism, the tradition to whose canon he belongs, al-Ṣadūq refers to himself as an Imāmī Shīʿī. 'Imāmī' is an older term than Twelver, being a label that had been attached to Shīʿī groups since the second/eighth century. The second/eighth-century Imāmīya were the group out of which emerged a number of distinct Shīʿī groups, including the Twelvers as well as the Nuṣayrīya and (further back) the Ismāʿīlīya. While a distinct Twelver Shīʿism clearly owes its origins to the point where a group of Imāmīs fixed the number of imams at twelve, something that had already happened several decades before al-Ṣadūq, the term 'Twelver' was not yet regularly used by Imāmīs themselves, and those like al-Ṣadūq, who believed in the occultation of the son of al-ʿAskarī, simply saw themselves as the 'true' Imāmīs (see al-Nawbakhtī, *Firaq al-shīʿa* [Istanbul: Jamīʿat Mustashriqīn Almānīya, 1931], 90–3), though doubtless other, differently inclined Imāmīs believed the same about themselves. However, it is clear that writers like al-Ṣadūq still saw Imāmīs who held other beliefs as being their fellows in some sense. We read, for example, in the works on the question of the twelfth imam written by al-Ṣadūq and his father that the Imāmī faithful were 'confused' about this matter, clearly indicating an impulse among Imāmī scholars to solidify a homogenous orthodoxy on this point among a still-heterogenous Imāmīya (see Muḥammad b. ʿAlī al-Shaykh al-Ṣadūq [Ibn Bābawayh], *Kamāl al-dīn wa tamām al-niʿma*, ed. ʿAlī Akbar Ghaffārī [Qum: Muʾassasat al-Nashr al-Islāmī, 1429 h.], 31–4; Ibn Bābawayh the Elder, *al-Imama wa'l-tabṣira min al-ḥayra* [Qum: Madrasat al-Imam al-Mahdī, 1985], 7–9). Accordingly, in what follows we refer to al-Ṣadūq and his earlier and contemporary co-religionists as Imāmīs, while the term Twelver will be used only when it is necessary to specifically differentiate those Imāmīs who believed in the hidden, twelfth imam and when we are discussing the later Twelver tradition. For discussion of the transition between these two names, see Etan Kohlberg, 'From Imamiyya to Ithnā-'Ashariyya,' *BSOAS* 39/3 (1976): 521–34; Hassan Ansari, *L'imamat et l'Occultation selon l'imamisme* (Leiden: Brill, 2017), xix.

3 Sunnī, like Imāmī, is still a contentious label in al-Ṣadūq's period. There were certainly Muslims calling themselves *ahl al-sunna* ('the people of the *sunna*'), but

the point when and the extent to which this became an exclusive marker of identity that included all the groups whom it has subsequently come to include is subject to debate. Ashʿarīs, Shāfiʿīs, Muʿtazilīs and others, who would all subsequently be treated as types of Sunnī, still had significant, sometimes violent differences, and correspondingly often lacked a sense of shared affiliation. Nonetheless, from a Shīʿī perspective there already existed in the fourth/tenth century a majority of Muslims who agreed on certain matters which differentiated them sharply and consciously from most – certainly Imāmī – Shīʿīs. This majority accepted the first three caliphs and the reigning ʿAbbāsid caliphs as legitimate, and also vested authority in a notion of the consensus (*ijmāʿ*) of the Muslim community as a whole. The range of views regarding the importance of prophetic hadith – the source of the *sunna* – was broader than it would become, but a consensus that it was an essential source was increasingly established among this majority, as was the institutionalized authority of a religious scholarly class who based a significant part of their authority in their understanding of prophetic hadith. Al-Ṣadūq and his contemporaries usually referred to these Muslims as the *ʿāmma* or *ʿawāmm* – 'the masses' – but in what follows they will be referred to as Sunnīs. Accordingly, Sunnī hadith literature, which only recognized prophetic hadith as authoritative, will be differentiated from Shīʿī hadith literature and its distinctive recognition of the imams' hadith. For a recent survey of scholarship on the emergence of Sunnīs as a distinct identity, see Christine D. Baker, *Medieval Islamic Sectarianism* (Leeds: Arc Humanities Press, 2019), 17–25.

4 See, for example, Mohammad Ali Amir-Moezzi, 'Remarques sur les critères d'authenticité du hadîth et l'autorité du juriste dans le shi'isme imâmite', *Studia Islamica* 85 (1997): 5–39, at 5.

5 For a discussion of the reasons for this seemingly radical loss, see Hassan Ansari, 'Uṣūl-i riwāyī (4): āthār-i mafqūd-i Shaykh-i Ṣadūq, chirā wa chigūnah?' http://ansari.kateban.com/post/1735, posted 11 February 2011, accessed 30 July 2016. As well as the usual suspects of violence and persecution, Ansari also points out that many of these 'lost' works may well have been subsumed into those that survive. Similarly, we may owe the vanishing of almost all of Ibn Bābawayh the Elder's works to al-Ṣadūq's subsequent prolific transmission of his father's traditions.

6 The Arabic *ḥadīth* (pl. *aḥādīth*) can function as a collective noun in the singular, a function that usage of 'hadith' in English has come to follow. Thus, 'the imams' hadith' refers to their utterances in general, and 'a book of hadith' is a book containing many hadiths.

7 Despite his prominent, indeed canonical position in the earlier history of Imāmī Shīʿism, al-Ṣadūq has received little scholarly attention. There is as yet no monograph devoted to the study of his work, nor even do we see him as the primary subject of article-length studies. Rather, he remains a component of studies whose focus lies elsewhere (an exception to this is Marcinkowski, who has written a brief introduction to al-Ṣadūq). The most complete survey of his works

to date is that supplied by Newman. See Muhammad Marcinkowski, 'Twelver Shî'ite Scholarship and Bûyid Domination: A Glance on the Life and Times of Ibn Bâbawayh Al-Shaikh Al-Sadûq (d.381/991)', *Islamic Culture* 76/1 (2002): 69–99; Andrew Newman, *Twelver Shiism: Unity and Diversity in the Life of Islam* (Edinburgh: Edinburgh University Press, 2013), 62–72.

8 Ismāʿīlī thought has tended to place significantly less emphasis upon hadith than Imāmīs, Zaydīs and indeed Sunnīs. Nevertheless, the most important early Ismāʿīlī scholar of hadith, al-Qāḍī al-Nuʿmān (d. 363/974), was a contemporary of al-Ṣadūq. Zaydī Shīʿism, meanwhile, has an ancient and independent tradition of hadith scholarship that remains regrettably understudied. For a brief introduction to both traditions' approaches and relevant scholarship, see Farhad Daftary and Gurdofarid Miskinzoda (eds), *The Study of Shiʿi Islam: History, Theology and Law* (London: I. B. Tauris, 2014), 177–9.

9 Scholarship regarding Sunnī thought in this period now constitutes a populous and vigorous field of substantial studies regarding the formation of institutional schools of law, the conceptualization of the value of hadith and the compilation and canonization of hadith compendia. We have a vivid (though by no means uncontested) picture of the intellectual context in which hadith compendia like those of al-Bukhārī and al-Tirmidhī were written, read and consulted as sources of doctrine and law. This cannot yet be said for analogous stages in the development of Shīʿī hadith literature. For overviews see Wael Hallaq, *The Origins and Evolution of Islamic Law* (Cambridge; New York: Cambridge University Press, 2004); Jonathan Brown, *The Canonization of Al-Bukhārī and Muslim: The Formation and Function of the Sunnī Ḥadīth Canon* (Leiden: Brill, 2007), 8–15, 47–206.

10 One of the best overviews of Shīʿī hadith as a discrete topic remains the single chapter in Jonathan Brown, *Hadith: Muhammad's Legacy in the Medieval and Modern World* (Oxford: Oneworld, 2009), ch. 6.

11 See note 1 to this chapter.

12 See Christopher Melchert, 'The Imamis Between Rationalism and Traditionalism', in *Shīʿite Heritage: Essays on Classical and Modern Traditions*, ed. L. Clarke (Albany: State University of New York Press, 2001), for a discussion of the viability of this terminology for the early Imāmīya.

13 This is not to deny the gradual process whereby prophetic hadith was accepted as sovereign in what became Sunnī law. See Hallaq, *The Origins and Evolution*, 57–121.

14 It is often said that Imāmīs refer to prophetic hadith as hadith, and narrations from the imams as *akhbār*, but this is misleading. While such a terminology is sometimes used, it is by no means universal, and is not in evidence in al-Ṣadūq's day.

15 For a recent discussion of this process, see Aisha Musa, *Ḥadīth as Scripture: Discussions on the Authority of Prophetic Traditions in Islam* (Basingstoke: Palgrave Macmillan, 2008), 17–80.

16 The history and development of the Twelver doctrine of the Hidden Imam remains contested and obscure in many details. For a recent and authoritative overview, see Ansari, *L'imamat*, 6–13. See also Chapter 1.

17 The imams' words had been written down before in small collections, often by disciples of the imams who recorded what they heard, but it is around the time of al-ʿAskarī's death that we see appearing large, structured collections after the familiar model of a hadith compendium. Some of the authors of these works, prominently al-Ṣaffār (d. 290/903) and al-Barqī (d. 274/887 or 280/893), had been companions of the last imams, but the hadiths they compiled were not restricted to the words of the imams they had met, also including the words of the earlier imams back to ʿAlī and of the Prophet, words that were transmitted by a host of narrators and not by any living imam. See Etan Kohlberg, '*al-Uṣūl al-arbaʿumiʾa*', *Jerusalem Studies in Arabic and Islam* 10 (1987): 128–66.

18 Al-Ṣadūq, *al-Hidāya*, ed. Imam Ḥādī Foundation Editorial Committee (Qum: Muʾassasat al-Imām al-Hādī, 1390 sh.), Introduction, 34–120; Ansari, *L'imamat*, 65–76. See also Aḥmad Pākatchī, *Mawlid-i amīr al-muʾminīn: nuṣūṣ mustakhraja min al-turāth al-islāmī* (Qum: Bunyād-i Nahj al-Balāgha, 1382 Sh.), 55-69.

19 The *asānīd* of the early Shīʿī hadith tradition have yet to receive anything approaching the monumental, systematic attention that figures like Juynboll have applied to the Sunnī hadith corpus. Newman and Haider in particular have made efforts in this direction with careful analyses of select samples of Imāmī *asānīd*, but our picture remains partial, and neither study quite touches al-Ṣadūq, with Newman studying the *asānīd* of earlier collections (al-Kulaynī and his forbears) and Haider studying *asānīd* with a view to reconstructing events in the second/eighth century rather than the circumstances of later compilers. It remains to be seen whether, in the face of a changing field of hadith studies, the will remains in the academy to produce for Shīʿī hadith the kind of reference tools aspired to in the last century for Sunnī hadith. See Andrew Newman, *The Formative Period of Twelver Shīʿism: Ḥadīth as Discourse Between Qum and Baghdad* (Richmond: Curzon Press, 2000); Najam Haider, *The Origins of the Shīʿa: Identity, Ritual, and Sacred Space in Eighth-Century Kūfa* (Cambridge: Cambridge University Press, 2011), 24–53.

The best source of information about al-Ṣadūq's narrators remains the biographical dictionaries that have been exhaustively constructed by Shīʿī scholars, with al-Khūʾī and Ṭihrānī's magisterial encyclopaedias providing essential reference points. Abū al-Qāsim al-Khūʾī, *Muʿjam rijāl al-dīn* (Najaf: Maktabat al-Imām al-Khūʾī, n. d.), 18:339; Āqā Buzurg Ṭihrānī, *Ṭabaqāt aʿlām al-shīʿa* (Beirut: Dār Iḥyāʾ al-Turāth al-ʿArabī, 2009), 1:287–8.

20 Later generations of Imāmī scholars, though not infrequently interested in al-Ṣadūq's intellectual contributions, add very little to the record of these earlier sources. To write a history of al-Ṣadūq's reception in Imāmī thought would require a study at least as long as the present one, though Newman has contributed a part of

that history, examining specifically how medical hadiths in al-Ṣadūq's writings were transmitted into the Safavid period. He observes that al-Ṣadūq's writings seem to have decreased in popularity after the Buwayhid period until the Safavid period, when interest was rekindled. See Andrew Newman, 'The Recovery of the Past: Ibn Babawayh, Baqir al-Majlisi and Safavid Medical Discourse', *Journal of the British Institute for Persian Studies* 50 (2012): 109–27.

21 The year of birth is calculated on the basis that his father is said to have made his request to the Hidden Imam to be granted a son – following which al-Ṣadūq was born – during his visit to Baghdad in 305/917–18. See Ansari, *L'imamat*, 20; al-Ṣadūq, *Kamāl al-dīn*, 529.

22 Al-Khūʾī, *Muʿjam*, 18:58–9, 299–300.

23 Aḥmad b. ʿAlī al-Najāshī, *Rijāl al-Najāshī* (Beirut: Sharikat al-Aʿlamī li'l-Maṭbūʿāt, 2010), 372. Al-Ṭūsī only offers general praise with no more biographical information. See Muḥammad b. al-Ḥasan al-Ṭūsī, *al-Fihrist* (Qum: Maṭbaʿat al-Muḥaqqiq al-Ṭabāṭabāʾ, 1420 sh.), 442.

24 Al-Ṣadūq, *al-Hidāya*, Introduction, 109–10.

25 Al-Ṣadūq's particular reverence for the eighth imam and his shrine in Tus are a notable feature of his writing when compared to his contemporaries, and may reflect his eastern provenance. For instance, other Imāmī discussions of pilgrimage to the imams' shrines from the fourth/tenth and fifth/eleventh centuries invariably place the most emphasis on visitation to al-Ḥusayn's shrine in Karbala, but al-Ṣadūq allots his longest discussion to the virtues of visiting al-Riḍā. See al-Ṣadūq, *Man lā yaḥḍuruhu al-faqīh*, Ed. Ḥusayn al-Aʿlamī (Beirut: Muʾassasat al-Aʿlamī li'l-Maṭbūʿāt, 1986), 2:379–83.

26 Abū Ḥayyān al-Tawḥīdī, *Akhlāq al-wazīrayn* (Damascus: Dār Ṣādir 1965), 166–7.

27 Al-Ṣadūq, *Al-Hidāya*, Introduction, 110–16.

28 See for instance al-Ṣadūq, *ʿIlal al-sharāʾiʿ* (Beirut: Muʾassasat al-Aʿlamī li'l-Maṭbūʿāt, 2007), 34; *ʿUyūn, akhbār al-Riḍā* (Qum: Dhawā al-Qurbā, 1427 h.), 2:92–3.

29 One such instance that has more than once been hypothesized is a perceived conflict between al-Ṣadūq's *al-Iʿtiqādāt* and his *al-Tawḥīd*, based on readings of the latter as conceding to Muʿtazilī doctrines that the former opposes, a hypothesis that has been used in turn to assert that *al-Tawḥīd* represents a later acquiescence. As shall be argued at length in Chapter 4, however, such a reading of *al-Tawḥīd* and therefore the chronology that emerges from it do not stand up to close scrutiny of the work.

30 For the coining of the phrase, see Marshall Hodgson, *The Venture of Islam* (Chicago: Chicago University Press, 1974), 2:36. North Africa, Egypt and later much of the Levant came under the dominion of the Ismāʿīlī Fāṭimids, who established a full-fledged Shīʿī imam-caliphate to rival that of the ʿAbbāsids. In

Syria, meanwhile, the Ḥamdānid dynasty of Aleppo also exhibited strong Shīʿī leanings. While Fāṭimid and Buwayhid Shīʿism is widely studied, Shīʿism under the Ḥamdānids remains an elusive phenomenon. Though the Ḥamdānid rulers' beliefs do not seem to have much impinged upon their statecraft (relations with the ʿAbbāsids remained unexceptional), Aleppo and its environs nonetheless became an important centre of Shīʿī activity, including Imāmīs but also other groups, notably Nuṣayrīs. The authoritative history of the Ḥamdānids remains Maurice Canard, *Histoire de la dynastie des Hamdanides de Jazīra et de Syrie* (Paris: Presses Universitaires de France, 1953), though this work gives little discussion to religion. A brief, more recent assessment is found in Stefan Winter, *A History of the 'Alawis: From Medieval Aleppo to the Turkish Republic* (Princeton: Princeton University Press, 2016), 19–20.

31 The conversation during the century before al-Ṣadūq between a more traditionist Imāmī community in Qum and more rationalist-leaning Imāmīs in Baghdad, including specifically the reflection of these tensions in hadith literature, has been examined in Newman, *Formative Period*. See also Chapter 3.

32 Imāmīs elsewhere in the Shīʿī century were highly motivated to refute the claims of the Ismāʿīlīs and their new imam-caliphate. Both al-Kulaynī and his student al-Nuʿmānī are recorded as having written now-lost refutations of the Ismāʿīlīs. The Ismāʿīlī *daʿwa* in Rayy, however, had suffered some disastrous setbacks in the middle of the century, and al-Ṣadūq is seldom troubled by them. For the Ismāʿīlīs in Rayy during this period, see S. M. Stern, 'The Early Ismāʿīlī Missionaries in North-West Persia and in Khurāsān and Transoxiana', *BSOAS* 23/1 (1960): 79–80; Daniel De Smet, 'From Khalaf (beginning of the 4th/10th century?) to Ḥasan al-Ṣabbāḥ (d. 518 H/1124 CE): Ismailism in Rayy before and under the Seljūqs', *Der Islam* 93/2 (2016): 433—59, at 439–50. See also note 9 to Chapter 5.

33 There are, of course, notable exceptions to this even as far back as Goldziher himself. See Ignaz Goldziher, *Muslim Studies*, trans. S. M. Stern and C. R. Barber (Albany: State University of New York Press, 1971), 2:19–37.

34 Notable works in this respect include Montgomery's study of al-Jāḥiẓ's *al-Ḥayawān*, Kilpatrick's study of al-Iṣfahānī's *al-Aghānī*, Orfali's work on al-Thaʿālibī and Davis's study of Firdowsī's *Shāh nāmah*. In all four the authors seek to radically expand the horizons of meaning offered by these texts, rehabilitating the figure of the compiler-author from that of a faceless tradent to that of a writer who channels a distinctive authorial potency. See James Montgomery, *Al-Jāḥiẓ: In Praise of Books* (Edinburgh: Edinburgh University Press, 2015); Hilary Kilpatrick, *Making the Great Book of Songs: Compilation and the Author's Craft in Abū al-Faraj al-Isḥahānī's Kitāb al-Aghānī* (London: Routledge, 2003); Bilal Orfali, *The Anthologist's Art: Abū Manṣūr al-Thaʿālibī and His* Yatīmat al-Dahr (Leiden: Brill, 2016); Dick Davis, *Epic and Sedition: The Case of Ferdowsi's Shahnameh* (Washington, DC: Mage, 2006).

35 Hilary Kilpatrick, 'Some Late ʿAbbāsid and Mamlūk Books about Women: A Literary Historical Approach', *Arabica* 42/1 (1995): 56–78, at 75.

36 See especially A. Kevin Reinhart, 'Juynbolliana, Gradualism, the Big Bang and Hadith Study in the Twenty-First Century', *Journal of the American Oriental Society* 130/3 (2010): 413–44, at 430–6 and *passim*. Studies to which Reinhart draws attention in this regard that are of particular relevance to al-Ṣadūq are Brown's exploration of the establishment of al-Bukhārī and Muslim's collections as canonical over the fourth/tenth century and Musa's exploration of the mostly third/ninth-century debates regarding the status of the hadith corpus as a whole. See Musa, *Ḥadīth as Scripture*; Brown, *Canonization*. Another important demonstration of the heterogeneity of hadith's scriptural (or not) status in different contexts is Mourad and Lindsay's study of the sixth/twelfth-century scholar Ibn ʿAsākir. See Suleiman Mourad and James Lindsay, *The Intensification and Reorientation of Sunnī Jihad Ideology in the Crusader Period: Ibn ʿAsākir of Damascus (1105-1176) and His Age* (Leiden: Brill, 2013).

37 Al-Bukhārī's *Ṣaḥīḥ* has received a long tradition of Muslim commentators speculating about its formal compilation, specifically al-Bukhārī's often counterintuitive chapter headings, but these are part of a wider tradition of hadith commentary that is receiving increased attention. Recent studies of historical Muslim analyses of al-Bukhārī include Vardit Tokatly, 'The *Aʿlām al-ḥadīth* of al-Khaṭṭābī: A Commentary on al-Bukhārī's *Ṣaḥīḥ* or a Polemical Treatise', *Arabica* 92 (2001): 53–91; Mohammed Fadel, 'Ibn Ḥajar's *Hady al-Sārī*: A Medieval Interpretation of the Structure of al-Bukhārī's *Al-Jāmiʿ al-Ṣaḥīḥ*: Introduction and Translation', *Journal of Near-Eastern Studies* 54 (1995): 161–97; Joel Blecher, *Said the Prophet of God: Hadith Commentary Across a Millennium* (Oakland: University of California Press, 2018), 111–36.

38 See Stephen Burge, 'Reading Between the Lines: The Compilation of *Ḥadīṯ* and the Authorial Voice', *Arabica* 58/3–4 (2011): 167–97; 'Jalāl al-Dīn al-Suyūṭī, the *Muʿawwidhatān* and the Modes of Exegesis', in *Aims, Methods and Contexts of Qur'anic Exegesis (2nd/8th-9th/15th C.)*, ed. Karen Bauer (London: Oxford University Press, 2013), 277–307; 'Myth, Meaning and the Order of Words: Reading Hadith Collections with Northrop Frye and the Development of Compilation Criticism', *Islam and Christian-Muslim Relations*, 72/2 (2016), 213–28; 'The *Ḥadīth* Literature: What is it? And Where is it?', *Arabica* 65:1–2 (2018): 64–83.

39 Some approaches that have been applied productively in other studies of hadith compendia, such as recourse to manuscript history and authorial biography (for example Mourad and Lindsay, *Intensification and Reorientation*), are of little use to an author like al-Ṣadūq, whose biography is threadbare and the available manuscripts of whose works all date from long after his death (see Newman, 'The Recovery of the Past').

40 Burge suggests that such readings of whole compendia are a natural goal for compilation criticism. See Burge, 'Reading Between the Lines', 174.

To subject compilations to criticism naturally provokes the question of whether or not this defines them as literature. Though the literary possibilities of compilation have been explored in the work of Kilpatrick, Montgomery and others in their study of undisputed artists like al-Jāḥiẓ, hadiths compiled as such are seldom considered as literary. Of the studies of the art of compilation discussed earlier, only Burge asserts that what he is doing amounts to treating these compilations as literature. This he qualifies to mean that they are discursive such that they can be elucidated by literary criticism (Burge, 'Myth, Meaning and the Order of Words', 215, 226). In an earlier article, meanwhile, he states that though these compilations may be productively subjected to literary readings, they are nonetheless 'not literary in the full sense' (Burge, 'Reading Between the Lines', 196). This question could be interrogated at greater length, indeed a far greater length than the present study, and the answer would hinge not least on the troubled applicability of Western notions of the literary to premodern Arabic contexts in general. My purpose in naming it here is to affirm that the extent to which al-Ṣadūq's works are literary will be kept open as we set out to read them. For a valuable overview of these problems, see Micheal Allen, 'How *Adab* Became Literary: Formalism, Orientalism and the Institutions of World Literature', *Journal of Arabic Literature* 43 (2012).

41 The encyclopaedic approach has become the common assumed reading strategy for hadith compendia, but there is evidence to suggest that some compilers at least had in mind a partially linear reading, intending the reader to start with the first chapter and more generally to read chapters in their compiled sequence. See Burge, 'Reading Between the Lines', 187, 190; 'Jalāl al-Dīn al-Suyūṭī', 295–6.

42 See Tokatly, 'The *A'lām al-ḥadīth* of al-Khaṭṭābī', 60, 87; Burge, 'Jalāl al-Dīn al-Suyūṭī', 299. Mourad and Lindsay in particular have explored this obfuscating capacity of the compilation in their study of the forty hadith on the virtues of *jihād* by Ibn ʿAsākir al-Dimashqī (d. 571/1176). Ibn ʿAsākir's task was to provide a manifesto authorizing the diverse counter-crusading campaigns of his patron, a difficult task for a conventional *fiqhī* discussion of *jihād*, containing as it must all the exacting conditions, caveats and prohibitions concerning when the faithful should march to war. By contrast, he could in good faith present (without commentary) forty hadiths that contained no such inhibiting detail. See Mourad and Lindsay, *Intensification and Reorientation*, 56–8, 70.

43 Hodgson, for instance, describes such strategies in detail in al-Ṭabarī. See Hodgson, *The Venture of Islam*, 1:353–8.

44 Such an approach is regularly of use to scholars examining hadith compendia. See Burge, 'Reading Between the Lines', 187; 'Jalāl al-Dīn al-Suyūṭī', 285; Fadel, 'Ibn Ḥajar's *Hady al-Sārī*', 163–4. It is also integral to the approach of premodern

Muslim commentators on al-Bukhārī's structure. If, for instance, al-Bukhārī supposedly wishes to inform readers about the subject outlined in his chapter title, commentators will ask why he includes material that seems to have little to do therewith, or indeed excludes material that would seem to have been pertinent. See Tokatly, 'The *A'lām al-ḥadīth* of al-Khaṭṭābī', 55–7.

45 Paul Ricoeur, *The Symbolism of Evil*, trans. Emerson Buchanan (Boston: Beacon Press, 1969), 347–57, esp. 355.

46 For seminal early contentions of this approach see Suzanne Pinckney Stetkevych, *The Mute Immortals Speak: Pre-Islamic Poetry and the Poetics of Ritual* (Ithaca: Cornell University Press, 1993), 1–86; Stefan Sperl, *Mannerism in Arabic Poetry: A Structural Analysis of Selected Texts (3rd Century AH/9th Century AD – 5th Century AH/11th Century AD)* (Cambridge: Cambridge University Press, 1989), 1–7 and *passim.*

47 Burge draws productive parallels between this approach and what in biblical scholarship is termed 'canonical criticism'; this approach, too, examines how the texts in a given collection are presented, the order in which they are placed, how they are grouped and so on. See Burge, 'Reading Between the Lines', 171–7; 'Myth, Meaning and the Order of Words', 215.

48 Burge draws methodologically upon Eco, Greimas and especially Frye, extrapolating a framework from the latter's readings of the biblical text. Frye models a word's meaning as a conversation between an individual usage, its use across the larger work in which that usage occurs, its dictionary definition and its meaning in others' usage thereof, and Burge explores how a hadith in a compilation may be conceived as operating along the same quadripartite lines – possessing meaning in terms of its individual usage and its usage elsewhere in the same compilation, as well as in terms of how it is used by other compilers and, for some hadiths, also a 'dictionary meaning', a long-standing, conventional understanding of a hadith and what it is about. Thus conceived, compilation becomes an active process of adaptation and reappropriation, setting hadiths in conversation with the pre-existing range of ways they have been compiled and read, prompting them to speak in ways that are slightly or even radically different. See Burge, 'Myth, Meaning and the Order of Words', 215–21 and *passim.*

49 Numerous studies have explored how the selection of hadiths reflect the priorities of a given compiler. See Eric E. F. Bishop, 'Form-Criticism and the Forty-Two Traditions of an-Nawawi', *The Muslim World* 30 (1940): 255, 259–60 (an early, often-overlooked example of the approach); Mourad and Lindsay, *Intensification and Reorientation*, 63–81, Fadel, 'Ibn Ḥajar's *Hady al-Sārī*', 165–7; Tokatly, 'The *A'lām al-ḥadīth* of al-Khaṭṭābī'; Louis Pouzet, *Hermeneutique de la tradition islamique: Le commentaire des Arba'ūn al-Nawawīya de Muḥyī al-Dīn al-Nawawī (m. 676/1277): Introduction, texte de arabe, traduction, notes et index du vocabulaire* (Beirut: Dar el-Machreq and Libraire Orientale, 1982).

50 Burge, for instance, finds this approach productive for studying al-Suyūṭī, for whom he has the resource of that prolific author's other works with which any single work may be compared, determining what materials were excluded or included for different projects, as well as their sources. See Burge, 'Jalāl al-Dīn al-Suyūṭī', 280ff. He also acknowledges, however, that with many works of hadith it is not practicable. See Burge, 'Reading Between the Lines', 171–3.
51 See Chapter 2, 52–4.
52 The most significant application of this approach for our purposes is the work of Andrew Newman, who develops it in his *The Formative Period of Twelver Shīʿism.* Newman focusses on al-Ṣadūq's immediate Imāmī predecessors, examining early Imāmī hadith compendia from al-Barqī to al-Kulaynī (thus ending the study around the start of al-Ṣadūq's career) to show how the compilers' selection and arrangement of hadiths with theological content engages the changing circumstances faced by each author and by the Imāmī community. Newman explores both how these changes reflect responses to theological currents (al-Kulaynī, for instance, responding to the more rationalist environment of Baghdad by excluding and dispersing traditions containing doctrines deemed suspect) and also how compendia may reflect the broader experiences of the Imāmī community, with accounts of imams with extraordinary abilities proliferating in context of a Shīʿa still struggling in the aftermath of the occultation.
53 See Burge, 'Reading Between the Lines', 181–2.
54 See Goldziher, *Muslim Studies*, 2:216–18; Burge, 'Reading Between the Lines', 179–88.
55 Disjunctures between a chapter's title and content have often caught the attention of commentators on al-Bukhārī. See Blecher, *Said the Prophet of God*, 111–28; Fadel, 'Ibn Ḥajar's *Hady al-Sārī*'.
56 Burge has demonstrated how al-Bukhārī's *Ṣaḥīḥ* is structured on this level. See Burge, 'Reading Between the Lines', 177–95 and *passim*.
57 See, for example George Warner, 'One Thousand Ḥijaj: Ritualization and the Margins of the Law in Early Twelver Shīʿī *Ziyāra* Literature', *Journal of the American Oriental Society* 2022 (forthcoming).
58 Pouzet, *Herméneutique de la tradition islamique*; Burge, 'Myth, Meaning and the Order of Words', 224.
59 This translation was coined by Fyzee.
60 Al-Ṣadūq, *al-Hidāya*, Introduction, 115.
61 This work is listed under various titles, among them *Iʿtiqādāt al-Imāmīya* and *Risāla fī'l-iʿtiqādāt.*
62 See Michael Cooperson, *Classical Arabic Biography: The Heirs of the Prophets in the Age of Al-Ma'mūn* (Cambridge: Cambridge University Press, 2000), 70–106; David J. Wasserstein, 'The "Majlis of al-Rida": A Religious Debate in the Court of the Caliph

al-Maʾmun as Represented in a Shiʿi Hagiographical Work about the Eighth Imam ʿAli ibn Musa Al-Rida', in Hava Lazarus-Yafeh et al. (eds), *The Majlis: Interreligious Encounters in Medieval Islam* (Wiesbaden: Harrassowitz, 1999), 108–19; Najam Haider, *The Rebel and the Imam in Early Islam: Explorations in Early Muslim Historiography* (Cambridge: Cambridge University Press, 2019), 152–65.

63 The most substantial examination remains Marzoug Alsehail, 'Ḥadīth-Amālī Sessions: Historical Study of a Forgotten Tradition in Classical Islam', PhD Thesis, University of Leeds, 2014. A welcome, recent examination is provided in Roy Vilozny, 'Transmitting Imami Hadith, Preserving Knowledge: Remarks on Three Amālī Works of The Buwayhī Period', *Jerusalem Studies in Arabic and Islam* 50 (2021): 167–83.

64 See Vilozny, 'Transmitting Imami Hadith', 171.

65 See al-Najāshī, *Rijāl*, 373.

66 Al-Ṣadūq, *Kamāl al-dīn*, 117; *ʿUyūn*, 2:312.

67 This is interesting given the stern injunctions against dialectic levelled by al-Ṣadūq in other texts, for example *al-Iʿtiqādāt*, ed. Imam Hādī Foundation Editorial Committee (Qum: Muʾassasat al-Imām al-Hādī, 1389 sh.), 94-7. Nonetheless, it should be noted that a very similar style of mixing text and reason is in evidence in *al-Iʿtiqādāt* itself and in *Kamāl al-dīn*, such that this work does not tell us anything especially new in this regard. It would be interesting to explore whether significant stylistic differences could be detected between these *majālis* and al-Ṣadūq's other more discursive writings.

68 Hassan Ansari, 'Bar rasī-yi matn-i munāẓara-yi Shaykh-i Ṣadūq dar majlis-i Rukn al-Dawla-yi Būyahī', http://ansari.kateban.com/post/1418, posted 28 July 2008, accessed 30 July 2016.

69 Al-Ṭūsī, *Fihrist*, 442–4; al-Najāshī, *Rijāl*, 372–5.

70 See ʿAbd al-Ḥalīm ʿŪḍ al-Ḥillī, *Mā waṣala ilaynā min Kitāb madīnat al-ʿilm li'l-Shaykh al-Ṣadūq Muḥammad b. ʿAlī b. al-Ḥusayn (t. 381 h.)* (Karbala: Dār Makhṭūṭāt al-ʿAtaba al-ʿAbbāsīya al-Muqaddasa, 2016), 27–56; Ansari, 'Uṣūl-i riwāyī'; Hassan Ansari, 'Une Version Incomplète du Kitāb al-Nubuwwa d'al-Ṣadūq', in *Le shīʿisme imāmite quarante ans après: hommage à Etan Kohlberg*, ed. Mohammad Ali Amir-Moezzi and Meir M. Bar-Asher (Turnhout: Brepols, 2009); Pākatchī, *Mawlid-i amīr al-muʾminīn*, 55–80; Fuat Sezgin, *Geschichte des arabischen Schrifttums* (Leiden: Brill, 1967), 1:544–9.

Chapter 1

1 See Ansari, 'Uṣūl-i riwāyī'; Newman, 'The Recovery of the Past'; al-Ḥillī, *Kitāb madīnat al-ʿilm*, 14–57.

2 Newman, 'The Recovery of the Past', 112–17.

3 The authoritative references for the Buwayhid period remain Heribert Busse, *Chalif Und Grosskönig: Die Buyiden Im Iraq (945-1055)* (Würzburg: Ergon-Verlag, 1969); John Donohue, *The Buwayhid Dynasty in Iraq 334H./945 to 403H./1012: Shaping Institutions for the Future* (Leiden: Brill, 2003). For a recent reassessment of the Imāmī experience of Buwayhid rule, see Baker, *Medieval Islamic Sectarianism*, 59–75; for an account of cultural life under the Buwayhids, see Joel L. Kraemer, *Humanism in the Renaissance of Islam: The Cultural Revival during the Buyid Age* (Leiden: Brill, 1986).

4 For an appraisal of the evidence for public Shīʿī ritual under the Buwayhids, see Baker, *Medieval Islamic Sectarianism*, 86–8, also Nassima Neggaz, 'Al-Karkh: The Development of an Imāmī-Shīʿī Stronghold in Early Abbasid and Būyid Baghdad (132-447/750-1055)', *Studia Islamica* 114 (2019): 265–315, at 298–304.

5 The pre-/post-Buwayhid schema is articulated most clearly in Meir Bar-Asher, *Scripture and Exegesis in Early Imāmī Shiism* (Leiden: Brill, 1999), 71–86. The exact extent and nature of this transformation remains debatable, and is closely tied to the question of al-Mufīd's role as a more or less transformative figure. Sander contends that there were strong theological continuities between the Buwayhid Imāmīs and their predecessors, and in terms of some doctrines, particularly the nature of God's justice, he demonstrates this effectively. His theological focus, however, leads to the omission of areas of Imāmī thought where dramatic transitions did take place. While continuity can be observed in questions regarding God's attributes and his justice, great swathes of material from al-Barqī and his contemporaries regarding the extraordinary powers of the imam and his cosmic connection with the Shīʿa find no echo in al-Mufīd, the latter having decisively rejected these aspects of the theology of the earlier Imāmīya. See Mohammad Ali Amir-Moezzi, *The Divine Guide in Early Shi'ism: The Sources of Esotericism in Islam* (Albany: State University of New York Press, 1994); Bar-Asher, *Scripture and Exegesis*; Roy Vilozny, 'A Šīʿī Life Cycle according to Al-Barqī's Kitāb Al-Maḥāsin', *Arabica* 54/3 (2007): 362–96; Paul Sander, *Zwischen Charisma Und Ratio: Entwicklungen in Der Frühen Imāmitischen Theologie* (Berlin: K. Schwarz, 1994), 3–4, 25–7. Moreover, in Sander's astute assertion that the early hadith compendia are valuable sources of theological doctrine, thus facilitating comparison with al-Mufīd's more dialectic texts, he shifts his analysis away from the fact that however similar their doctrines may be, al-Barqī and al-Mufīd differ profoundly in how those doctrines are expressed. Al-Barqī leaves us only hadiths without authorial comment on their content or their provenance, whereas al-Mufīd delivers densely argued positions supported both by rational tools and by hadiths, the sources of which are expressly scrutinized. Sander does not challenge that such a shift takes place, only implying in his conclusions that this change had little effect on some of the Imāmīya's central theological beliefs.

6 See Sabine Schmidtke and Hassan Ansari, 'The Shīʿī Reception of Muʿtazilism (II): Twelver Shīʿīs', in *The Oxford Handbook of Islamic Theology*, ed. Sabine Schmidtke (Oxford: Oxford University Press, 2016) for a recent appraisal of these debates.

7 Devin Stewart, *Islamic Legal Orthodoxy: Twelver Shiite Responses to the Sunni Legal System* (Salt Lake City: The University of Utah Press, 2007), 128–9; Robert Gleave, 'Between Ḥadīth and Fiqh: The "Canonical" Imāmī Collections of Akhbār', Islamic Law and Society 8/3 (2001): 350-82, at 381–2.

8 See Robert Gleave, *Scripturalist Islam: The History and Doctrines of the Akhbārī Shīʿī School* (Leiden: Brill, 2007), 156–7.

9 Martin J. McDermott, *The Theology of Al-Shaikh Al-Mufīd (d. 413/1022)* (Beirut: Dar al-Mashreq, 1978), 324–5.

10 W. Madelung, 'Imamism and Mu'tazilite Theology', in *Le shi'isme imamite*, ed. Robert Brunschvig (Paris: Presses universitaires de france, 1970), 17.

11 Tamima Bayhom-Daou, *Shaykh Al-Mufid* (Oxford: Oneworld, 2005), 94.

12 Melchert, 'The Imamis Between Rationalism and Traditionalism', 277; Ali Adam, *Kitāb Al-Tawḥīd: The Book of Divine Unity of Al-Shaykh Al-Ṣadūq* (Birmingham: AMI Press, 2013), 9; McDermott, *Theology*, 369. Another notable example of this ambiguity is Sander; Sander's chief contention is to demonstrate continuity between the earlier figures and al-Mufīd, and al-Ṣadūq is therefore only of interest to him as a transitional link, but his discussions reveal a similar ambiguity over the nature of al-Ṣadūq's thought, grouping him neither quite as a traditionist with al-Kulaynī and al-Barqī nor as anything else, broadly agreeing with Madelung's earlier assessment on this point. See Sander, *Charisma und Ratio*, 19–24, 165–6 and *passim*. The perception of al-Ṣadūq's quality as a *muḥaddith* in the modern seminary still bears the marks of the Akhbārī-Uṣūlī conflict, with contemporary mujtahids' evaluations retaining a concern to rebut the Akhbārī assertion of the total authenticity of the 'Four Books'. See, for instance, al-Khūʾī, *Muʿjam*, 1:26.

13 For more on al-Mufīd's criticisms of al-Ṣadūq, see Chapter 2.

14 For example, Newman, *Formative Period*; Bar-Asher, *Scripture and Exegesis*; Amir-Moezzi and Ansari, 'Perfecting a Religion: Remarks on al-Kulaynī and his Summa of Traditions', in *The Silent Qur'an and the Speaking Qur'an: Scriptural Sources of Islam Between History and Fervor*, ed. Mohammad Ali Amir-Moezzi (New York; Columbia University Press, 2015), 124–60. While Amir-Moezzi names al-Mufīd as the point where this distinct, earlier form of Imāmīsm was extinguished, in practice the last author in whose work he decisively identifies its presence is al-Kulaynī. A partial exception is Sander's *Charisma und Ratio*, which aims to demonstrate continuity from al-Barqī through to al-Mufīd. However, this interest in continuity ends up diminishing his interest in al-Ṣadūq, only going so far as to affirm him as a transitional figure between the older hadith scholars and al-Mufīd. See Sander, *Charisma und Ratio*, 165–6.

15 The events surrounding al-ʿAskarī's death have been the subject of a considerable number of studies over the past three decades. This increasing volume of scholarship notwithstanding, beyond the facts of al-ʿAskarī's death and the eventual acceptance

of the narrative of two occultations and four emissaries over the course of the fourth/tenth century, the history of this development in the Imāmī community is deeply contentious, and the question of when exactly the several components of what became the standard position became generally accepted is not easy to answer. By the time al-Kulaynī completed *al-Kāfī* in the 320/930s, the doctrine of a twelfth, hidden, messianic imam seems established; however, the eventual orthodoxy regarding the emissaries may not have solidified until the close of the fourth/tenth century. See Hossein Modarressi, *Crisis and Consolidation in the Formative Period of Shi'ite Islam: Abū Ja'far Ibn Qiba Al-Rāzī and His Contribution to Imāmite Shī'ite Thought* (Princeton: Darwin Press, 1993); Etan Kohlberg, 'Imamiyya to Ithnā-'Ashariyya; Verena Klemm, 'Die Vier Sufarā' Des Zwölften Imam Zur Formativen Periode Der Zwölferšī'a', *Die Welt Des Orients* 15 (1984): 126–43;' Hussein Abdulsater, 'Dynamics of Absence: Twelver Shi'ism during the Minor Occultation', *Zeitschrift Der Deutschen Morgenländischen Gesellschaft* 161/2 (2011): 305–34; Said Amir Arjomand, 'The Crisis of the Imamate and the Institution of Occultation in Twelver Shiism: A Sociohistorical Perspective', *International Journal of Middle East Studies* 28/4 (1996): 491–515; 'The Consolation of Theology: Absence of the Imam and Transition from Chiliasm to Law in Shi'ism', *The Journal of Religion* 76/4 (1996): 548–71; 'Imam Absconditus and the Beginnings of a Theology of Occultation: Imami Shi'ism Circa 280–90 A. H./900 A. D', *Journal of the American Oriental Society* 117/1 (1997): 1–12; Amir-Moezzi, *Divine Guide*; Edmund Hayes, 'The Envoys of the Hidden Imam: Religious Institutions and the Politics of the Twelver Occultation Doctrine', PhD Thesis, University of Chicago, 2015; Ansari, *L'imamat*.

16 Muḥammad b. Ya'qūb al-Kulaynī, *al-Kāfī*, (Tehran: Dār al-Kutub al-Islamiya, 1388 sh), 1:178–9.

17 Imāmī literature presents multiple accounts of these child-imams' miraculous demonstrations of their adequacy to the task. In these very accounts, however, it is the scholars of the community who examine the imam, asking him questions about doctrine and adjudicating the perfection of his answers. See Modarressi, *Crisis and Consolidation*, 32–3.

18 For discussions of the transition from visible to hidden imam see Modarressi, *Crisis and Consolidation*, 3–105; Ansari, *L'imamat*, ix–42; Hayes, 'The Envoys of the Hidden Imam'; Arjomand, 'Crisis'; '*Imam Absconditus*'; 'The Consolation of Theology'. All of these authors' analyses show the transition to have been a gradual one, the network of scholars and financial agents around the imam wielding steadily increasing authority in comparison to their ostensive master.

19 For the development of the office of the *safīr*, see Klemm, 'Die Vier Sufarā'; Abdulsater, 'Dynamics of Absence'; Omid Ghaemmaghami, *Encounters with the Hidden Imam in Early and Pre-Modern Twelver Shī'ī Islam* (Leiden: Brill, 2020), 102–5.

20 A notable voice in this regard is that of al-Kulaynī's student al-Nu'mānī, who states that the imams prophesied the confusion and despair that would follow

the occultation, and therefore the very fact that Imāmīs find the doctrine of the Hidden Imam bewildering is proof that it is true. Muḥammad b. Ibrāhīm al-Nuʿmānī, *al-Ghayba* (Beirut: Muʾassasat al-Aʿlamī li'l-Maṭbūʿāt, 2013), 147–55.

21 Even al-Kulaynī includes material foretelling that the imam will have two occultations (a concept that had already circulated among Wāqifis). Al-Kulaynī, *al-Kāfī*, 1:339 (hadith no. 12). This concept of a major and minor occultation, meanwhile, is already strikingly developed in his student, al-Nuʿmānī. See Ghaemmaghami, *Encounters*, 88.

22 There is, for instance, no sign of the occultation in al-Barqī's *al-Maḥāsin* or in al-Ṣaffār al-Qummī's *Baṣāʾir al-darajāt*. See Ghaemmaghami, *Encounters*, 23.

23 The starting point for accounts of these beliefs as originating from the imams themselves remains Ali Amir-Moezzi, *Divine Guide*. The contrasting view, meanwhile, is argued in Modarressi, *Crisis and Consolidation*, 19–51.

24 Newman, *Formative Period*, 67–93.

25 Modarressi, *Crisis and Consolidation*, 79–105.

26 See for instance Melchert, 'The Imamis Between Rationalism and Traditionalism'. Melchert argues persuasively that it is precisely this traditionist/rationalist axis that is most effective at differentiating currents in Imāmī thought in this period. A similar model is demonstrated by Gleave, one which again achieves substantial differentiation of scholars according to their attitudes to text and reason. Comparing a set of hadith compendia from al-Kulaynī to al-Ṭūsī, Gleave points out a clear trajectory of development between the compilers, with each compiler more willing to supplement hadiths with his own views, summaries and commentary than those of previous generations. Thus, al-Kulaynī gives almost no material beyond (albeit meticulously ordered) hadiths, al-Ṣadūq gives hadiths alongside his own regular summaries and asides, while al-Mufīd and al-Ṭūsī (al-Ṭūsī's *Tahdhīb al-aḥkām* supplying commentary on and expansion of al-Mufīd's *al-Muqniʿ*) give full discussion of technical problems, conflicting reports and so on. The resultant picture is of a clear, steady increase in the role of reason between al-Kulaynī and al-Mufīd. Gleave's evidence is valuable, but we must avoid drawing the conclusion that this was a trajectory followed by all (it is clear that some earlier scholars like Ibn Abī ʿAqīl were of a more rationalist persuasion than al-Ṣadūq, who flourished a little later). See Gleave, 'Between Ḥadīth and Fiqh,' 352, 360–1, 381–2.

27 Other Shīʿī groups, it must be remembered, boasted imams who were very much alive and well. The Ismāʿīlī Fāṭimids had swept to power in North Africa in the first half of the fourth/tenth century, finally conquering Egypt in 358/969, in whom their Ismāʿīlī followers revered both a temporal ruler and a divinely appointed imam (other Ismāʿīlī groups did continue in opposition to the Fāṭimid

imamate, most prominently the Qarāmiṭa). The Zaydīs, meanwhile, had seen the rise of successful (if usually short-lived) imamates in Yemen and northern Iran, and unlike the Imāmīs maintained a concept of the imamate as something that could be established at any time by a legitimate claimant, rather than as a distant eschatological event.

28 For a detailed account of these developments as they proceeded over al-Ṣadūq's lifetime, see Brown, *Canonization*, 99–206.

29 An illustrative text in this regard is al-Barqī's book of *rijāl* (commonly called *Rijāl al-Barqī*). While Sunnī works on *rijāl* from the same period discuss in some detail which narrators can be relied upon and which cannot, *Rijal al-Barqī* as it survives provides only a list of the companions of each imam, with no evaluation of their merits as transmitters. See Ansari, *L'imamat*, 28.

30 Devin Stewart, 'Muḥammad b. Jarīr al-Ṭabarī *al-Bayān ʿan uṣūl al-aḥkām* and the Genre of *Uṣūl al-fiqh* in Ninth-Century Baghdad', in *Abbasid Studies: Occasional Papers of the School of Abbasid Studies, Cambridge, 6–10 July 2002, orientalia lovaniensia analecta 135*, ed. James Montgomery (Leuven: Peeters Publishers, 2002), 347–8; *The Disagreements of the Jurists: A Manual of Islamic Legal Theory* (New York: New York University Press, 2015), xxiii–xxviii.

31 For the establishment of the *madhhab* within Sunnī Islam during this period, see Christopher Melchert, *The Formation of the Sunni Schools of Law, 9th-10th Centuries C.E.* (Leiden: Brill, 1997), 87–178; Hallaq, *Origins and Evolution*, 150–77. Stewart couches this adoption of the *madhhab* within a broader schema in which the Imāmīya have historically had three options available to them in responding to this attempted imposition and exclusion by the Sunnī majority: conformance to consensus, adoption of consensus or rejection of consensus. See Stewart, *Islamic Legal Orthodoxy*, 52–9.

32 For a discussion of these figures, see Stewart, *Islamic Legal Orthodoxy*, 137–43, 163–5.

33 For the development of an Imāmī *madhhab* as such through the middle to late Buwayhid period, see Stewart, *Islamic Legal Orthodoxy*, 111–69.

34 Stewart, *Islamic legal Orthodoxy*, 61–9, 100–9.

35 This is supported by al-Ṭūsī, who says of al-Mufīd that he held the headship (*riʾāsa*) of the Imāmīya, a title he does not mention in connection with any earlier scholar. See al-Ṭūsī, *Fihrist*, 442. The same position, moreover, is accorded him by Ibn al-Nadīm (*Fihrist*, 279).

36 Melchert, *Sunni Schools*, 87–115.

37 See ʿAlī b. Ismāʿīl al-Ashʿarī, *Maqālāt al-islāmīyīn wa'khtilāf al-muṣallīn*, ed. Muḥammad Muḥyī al-Dīn ʿAbd al-Ḥamīd (Beirut: al-Maktaba al-ʿAṣrīya, 1990), 88–9; al-Nawbakhtī, *Firaq al-shīʿa*, 2.

38 Denunciations of the Shīʿī sciences of hadith as having developmentally lagged behind those of the Sunnīs remains a feature of anti-Shīʿī polemical writings until the present. See, for example Zakarīyā Barakāt, 'Radd shubahāt ḥawla ʿilm al-ḥadīth ʿinda al-Shīʿa,' https://www.aqaed.com/faq/3123/, n. d., accessed August 30 2021.

39 Modarressi employs this periodization, and at least for this first century it is an extremely valuable means of conceptualizing Imāmī intellectual developments. See Hossein Modarressi, *An Introduction to Shīʿī Law: A Bibliographical Study* (London: Ithaca Press, 1984), 23–58.

40 A better understanding of the Imāmī approach to hadith criticism in the decades before al-Mufīd is a commonly acknowledged desideratum in the study of this period of Shīʿī thought and of Muslim thought more generally, offering as it might insights both into the clearly unusual nature of the Imāmīya in the transformative century after the death of al-ʿAskarī, and into the early history of *uṣūl al-fiqh* as a whole. See Stewart, *Disagreements*, xxviii.

Chapter 2

1 Given the potential insight they might provide into al-Ṣadūq's *fiqh*, it is unfortunate that none of the sessions in *al-Amālī* have a solidly legal focus; it is not entirely clear whether this is a result of active policy or other factors (including chance).

2 Al-Ṣadūq, *al-Faqīh*, 1:3–5.

3 Muḥammad b. al-Ḥasan al-Ṭūsī, *ʿUddat al-uṣūl*, ed. Muḥammad Mahdī Najaf (Qum: Muʾassasat Āl al-Bayt li'l-Ṭibāʿa wa'l-Nashr, 1983), 1:1–138; Even al-Kulaynī offers a brief summary of his methods of authentication, while the Ismāʿīlī al-Qāḍī al-Nuʿmān even gives a Shīʿī critique of Sunnī models of consensus. See Stewart, *Disagreements*, 130–79; al-Kulaynī, *al-Kāfī*, 1:8–9.

4 Al-Kulaynī, *al-Kāfī*, 1:5–9.

5 ʿUbayd Allāh al-ʿUkbarī (Ibn Baṭṭa), *al-Sharḥ wa'l-ibāna ʿalā uṣūl al-sunna wa'l-diyāna*, ed. Riḍā b. Naʿsān Muʿṭī (Medina: Maktabat al-ʿUlūm wa'l-Ḥikam, 2002), 117–20.

6 Ḥanafī authors such as Naṣr b. Muḥammad al-Samarqandī (d. 373/983) in this period produced legal manuals in which scriptural proof-texts of any sort are only an occasional appearance. See Naṣr b. Muḥammad al-Samarqandī, *Khizānat al-fiqh*, ed. Muḥammad ʿAbd al-Salām Shāhīn (Beirut: Dār al-Kutub al-ʿIlmīya, 2005). As Gleave notes, even when al-Ṣadūq does write in his own prose, this is often heavily dependent upon the wording of traditions. Gleave, 'Between Ḥadīth and Fiqh', 361.

7 This fact suggests an important corrective to Gleave, who identifies a steady increase in scholars' willingness to juxtapose their own rulings with hadiths between al-Kulaynī and al-Ṭūsī. Taking *al-Faqīh* as its sole sample of al-Ṣadūq's legal writing, this model neglects the fact that al-Ṣadūq's own voice is much more prominent in his other legal writings – in this regard, at least, there is little difference between *al-Hidāya* and al-Mufīd's *al-Muqniʿa*. See Gleave, 'Between Ḥadīth and Fiqh', 381–2, *passim*.
8 Gleave, 'Between Ḥadīth and Fiqh', 356–60.
9 Such methodically addressed questions include that of fasting when one is unsure of the date, or the minimum age at which fasting is required. See al-Ṣadūq, *al-Faqīh*, 2:80–4.
10 Al-Ṣadūq *al-Faqīh*, 2:72–7.
11 Ibid., 2:126–33, 392–401.
12 Ibid., 2:136 (hadith nos. 2145, 2146).
13 Ibid., 1:12.
14 For example, al-Ṣadūq, *al-Faqīh*, 1:34–8.
15 For example, Muḥammad b. Muḥammad al-Mufīd, *Taṣḥīḥ al-iʿtiqād bi-ṣawāb al-intiqād* (Beirut: Dār al-Kitāb al-Islāmī, 1983), 27, 30, 32, 34, 39.
16 Al-Najāshī, *Rijāl*, 373–5.
17 It is a hindrance in assessing the status of these works that the burgeoning Imāmī *rijāl* literature of the fifth/eleventh century does not usually cite earlier *rijāl* works. It is true that nobody seems to have authored a commentary on al-Ṣadūq's *miṣbāḥ* works, such as al-Ṭūsī did with al-Kashshī, but in his own *Kitāb al-rijāl* al-Ṭūsī gives little acknowledgement of al-Kashshī's work or any other as a regular source, a style held in common with the *rijāl* works of al-Najāshī and Ibn al-Ghaḍāʾirī. Once again, systematic changes in Imāmī jurisprudence in the decades following al-Ṣadūq's death may here obscure the nature and importance of his works on related subjects.
18 Al-Ṭūsī, *Fihrist*, 157, al-Najāshī, *Rijāl*, 372.
19 See, for instance, al-Najāshī's entry on Muḥammad b. Masʿūd al-ʿAyyāshī (*Rijāl*, 335).
20 See, for example, al-Ṣadūq, *Kamāl al-dīn*, 105–6; *ʿUyūn*, 2:24; *Maʿānī al-akhbār* (Beirut: Muʾassasat al-Tārīkh al-ʿArabī, 2009), 272.
21 Al-Ṣadūq, *Kamāl al-dīn*, 31–157.
22 Al-Ṣadūq, *al-Iʿtiqādāt*, 369. Another instance are three chapters in *ʿUyūn* which al-Ṣadūq announces as concerning, respectively, *majmūʿ* ('collected'), *manshūr* ('widespread') and *mutafarriq* ('various') hadiths. These titles seem to give a glimpse of al-Ṣadūq's terminology in grouping hadiths, and potentially of his criteria for doing so. Unfortunately, while the absence of any writings wherein he expands upon these terms' meanings makes certainty impossible, closer examination

indicates little to suggest a technical distinction between the overall content of the chapters. See al-Ṣadūq, *ʿUyūn*, 1:246–81, 2:5–80.

23 For instance, in *al-Tawḥīd*. See Chapter 4, 94.

24 A controversial follower of Jaʿfar al-Ṣādiq, Hishām numbers among a handful of his disciples who engaged in theological debates, apparently with some success. This seems to have placed him on potentially thorny ground regarding his relationship to his master. Reports suggest that taking too much theological initiative earned the rebuke of al-Ṣādiq, and his record is further complicated by apparent animosity between him and Mūsā al-Kāẓim, whom he followed only after disappointment with his older brother ʿAbd Allāh. What is certain is that he was a prolific narrator, and this results unsurprisingly in a rather ambiguous status among later Imāmī scholars, who are faced with accounts of his lauded service to the imams and of his rich body of narrations from them, but also of his attracting their censure. See Muḥammad b. ʿUmar al-Kashshī, *Rijāl al-Kashshī* (Tehran: Sāzmān-i Chāp wa Intishārāt, 1382 sh), 329–48.

25 Al-Ṣadūq, *al-Tawḥīd* (Beirut: Muʾassasat al-Aʿlamī li'l-Maṭbūʿāt, 2006), 104–12.

26 See Chapter 4.

27 Elsewhere in the same work, al-Ṣadūq actually includes hadiths in praise of Hishām, with no attempt to reconcile them with those denouncing him. Al-Ṣadūq, *al-Tawḥīd*, 132–4.

28 Al-Kashshī, *Rijāl*, 215–38, 238–45, 245–9.

29 Ibid., 349–52, 447–9.

30 Ibid., 387–94.

31 For example, al-Ṣadūq, *al-Faqīh*, 1:35–6 (hadith no. 80); see also Chapter 4, 92, 108.

32 These chapters address, respectively, hadiths that concern specifics (*mufassara*) and generalities (*mujmala*). The very shortest chapters in the book, their terse pronouncements are pure jurisprudence. Al-Mufīd adds an amendment to the second one (some things are known by the intellect to be wrong even in the absence of revealed prohibition) but leaves the first without criticism, clearly recognizing and engaging the brief pronouncements as legal theory. To an extent, they constitute another of those glimpses of an unpreserved methodology found across al-Ṣadūq's work, but these examples are especially puzzling and frustrating. This is, first, because they are even rarer for touching on an area of jurisprudence concerning not the authenticity of hadiths but the legal consequences of the linguistic technicalities in the texts thereof, constituting almost the only time we see al-Ṣadūq engaging these questions in such terms. Second, there is the enigma of their presence in *al-Iʿtiqādāt*, for the discussion of such methodological matters in a creed is, as Fyzee notes, most irregular. See Asaf A. A. Fyzee, *A Shi'ite Creed* (Tehran: World Organization for Islamic Services, 1982), 157. The

combination of their isolated subject matter and their extreme terseness makes a glaring contrast with the didactic, theological tone of the rest of the work.

33 Al-Ṣadūq, *al-I ʿtiqādāt*, 377–8.

34 Ibid., 379.

35 Ibid., 379–87.

36 The fact that this hadith clearly does not address the task of the fourth/tenth-century hadith scholar does not escape the notice of al-Mufīd, who finds much to criticize in this element of the chapter. He laments precisely al-Ṣadūq's failure to discuss how one separates authentic hadiths from false, how one discerns texts upon which one must act from those upon which one must not. Sporting as it does such gaping lacunae, he declares that al-Ṣadūq's treatment of the topic is valueless. He first directs the reader to his other works wherein he discusses the problem in depth, but nonetheless then affixes a discussion of the topic as long as any in *Taṣḥīḥ*, clearly unable to conclude while leaving the matter so lamentably undiscussed as al-Ṣadūq has done. As if to assert his point, he finishes by noting that al-Ṣadūq's hadith of ʿAlī and Sulaym is from untrusted sources and is for the most part impermissible to act upon. For his part, al-Ṣadūq makes conspicuous efforts to affirm the truth of the story. While *al-I ʿtiqādāt*'s proof-texts are usually single reports supplied without *isnād*, at the end of this hadith al-Ṣadūq includes numerous corroborating stories of how Sulaym and those who heard the hadith from him subsequently met later imams, who confirmed that they continue to transmit Muḥammad's knowledge perfectly as God promised they would. Al-Mufīd, *Taṣḥīḥ*, 123–6.

37 It dates at least as far back as al-Kulaynī (see al-Kulaynī, *al-Kāfī*, 1:62–4). Studies of early Shīʿī theology and imamology vary considerably over the extent to which material in hadith compendia like those of al-Barqī and al-Kulaynī is deemed to represent the views of earlier Shīʿīs. Amir-Moezzi, (*Divine Guide*; 'Remarques'), Lalani and others take an optimistic view, treating these later sources as fundamentally reliable portrayals of the second/eighth-century imams' teachings. See Arzina Lalani, *Early Shīʿī Thought: The Teachings of Imam Muḥammad al-Bāqir* (London: I. B. Tauris, 2000). Even among studies that take a more critical approach to the sources, however, such as Kohlberg and Modarressi, there is a broad consensus that the belief in the imam's indispensable presence dates from before the turn of the third/ninth century. See Kohlberg, '*al-Uṣūl al-arbaʿumiʾa*', 128–66; Hossein Modarressi, *Tradition and Survival: A Bibliographical Survey of Early Shīʿite Literature Volume I* (Oxford: Oneworld, 2003), xiii–xviii, *passim*.

38 Gleave ('Between Ḥadīth and Fiqh', 374) suggests that al-Ṣadūq was aware of *isnād*-related discussions but did not consider them important; what we see here is, more precisely, that he considered other matters more important, and indeed that it was important not to overemphasize *isnād* criticism.

39 Al-Ṣadūq, *al-I ʿtiqādāt*, 371–6.

40 Ansari also suggests that al-Ṣadūq's *Muṣādaqat al-ikhwān* is based upon a work of his father. Ansari, *L'imamat*, 23.

41 Ibn Bābawayh the Elder, *al-Imāma wa'l-tabṣira*, 7–9.

42 Ibid., 9–11. For overviews of this use of *taqīya* for hermeneutical purposes, albeit without reference to its elaboration by Ibn Bābawayh the Elder, see Maria M. Dakake, 'Hiding in Plain Sight: The Practical and Doctrinal Significance of Secrecy in Shi'ite Islam', *Journal of the American Academy of Religion* 74/2 (2006): 324–55', at 349–52; Etan Kohlberg, 'Some Imami-Shīʿī Views on *Taqiyya*', *Journal of the American Oriental Society* 95/3 (1975): 395–402, at 397–8.

43 Ibn Bābawayh the Elder, *al-Imāma wa'l-tabṣira*, 10–11.

44 Ibid., 11–17.

45 This is not to say that the matter of the occultation ceased to have any bearing on jurisprudence. In later centuries, for instance, the authority of the consensus of Twelver jurists would be argued on the basis that the Hidden Imam was presumed to be among them. See Stewart, *Islamic Legal Orthodoxy*, 143–73; Amjad Shah, 'The Concept of Ijmāʿ in Imami Uṣūl al-Fiqh', PhD Thesis, Edinburgh University, 1999, 39, 94–5, 116, 248, 306–8.

46 Al-Ṣadūq does evoke his father's concept of an existentially necessary *taqīya*, but crucially this is no longer in the context of a discussion of hadith criticism but of the occultation – a matter to which the idea of God concealing matters for humanity's benefit retains an obvious pertinence here. Unlike *al-Imāma wa'l-tabṣira*, meanwhile, *Kamāl al-dīn* is a text that engages extensively with questions of authenticity and transmission. When it comes to refuting the Wāqifīya's claims about al-Kāẓim, al-Ṣadūq does not entertain hadiths that support them, rather focussing on amassing testimonies to al-Kāẓim's death and so refuting any notion that he lives on in occultation. See al-Ṣadūq, *Kamāl al-dīn*, 43–5, 67–9.

47 It is worthy of note in this regard that nowhere in the extant literature of this period does an Imāmī compiler make what would appear to be the single greatest claim to authority for a book of hadith at the start of the occultation: that the imam is hidden, and therefore only accessible by means of his recollected hadith. Rather, we see again and again books introduced by the sentiment that the imams' knowledge is the way to salvation and deliverance from bewildering disagreement, sometimes along with a brief assertion that the book's transmitted hadiths are sound. See, for example al-Kulaynī, *al-Kāfī*, 1:5–9; Muḥammad b. al-Ḥasan al-Ṣaffār al-Qummī, *Baṣāʾir al-darajāt* (Qum: Ṭalīʿat al-Nūr, 1429 h), 8–23; ʿAlī b. Ibrāhīm al-Qummī, *Tafsīr al-Qummī* (Qum: Muʾassasat al-Kitāb li'l-Ṭibāʿa wa'l-Nashr, 1404 h), 1:1–29. This absence of such an apparently obvious argument may be due to the gradual nature of the transition to occultation (hadith had, after all, been transmitted during the imams' lifetimes), but in light of what is explored here it seems likely that the uncomfortable nature of this truth also contributed to its remaining unexpressed.

48 See Hallaq, *Origins*, 122–8.

49 This echoes the criticism of using anomalous (*shawwādh*) texts that al-Mufīd levels against al-Ṣadūq in *Taṣḥīḥ*, 39.

50 Jaʿfar b. Muḥammad Ibn Qūlawayh, *Kāmil al-ziyārāt* (Beirut: Muʾassasat al-Aʿlamī li'l-Maṭbūʿāt, 2009), 6.

51 Al-Qummī, *Tafsīr al-Qummī*, 1:4.

52 Al-Kulaynī, *al-Kāfī*, 1:8.

53 Al-Ṣadūq, *al-Faqīh*, 12–14. It is true that *al-Faqīh*'s status as a legal manual might make it especially necessary for al-Ṣadūq to vouch for his sources, unlike, for example, the more miscellaneous compendia studied in Chapter 3. Such a possibility does not erase the anomaly, however. After all, al-Qummī's *tafsīr* and Ibn Qūlawayh's *ziyāra* manual are not legal encyclopaedias, yet they begin with guarantees of their contents. Meanwhile, al-Ṣadūq's *al-Tawḥīd* specifically opens with the challenge of non-Imāmīs criticizing the contents of the imams' hadith, directly inviting a defence centred around the affirmation of the authenticity of some hadiths at the expense of others. Such a defence, however, is nowhere to be seen. See Chapter 4.

54 See Modarressi, *Introduction*, 32–9.

55 Al-Kulaynī, *al-Kāfī*, 1:67–8. The last step is sometimes treated as petty, polemical absurdity, but later Imāmī jurists understand it as a logical engagement with the fact of the imams' *taqīya*: since the imams are known to sometimes speak in *taqīya*, then a tradition that is in agreement with Sunnī practice could have been uttered for dissimilatory purposes, while a statement that contradicts Sunnīs is less explicable in these terms, and therefore more likely to reflect the Imam's real view. See Kohlberg, '*Taqiyya*', 397–8.

56 Al-Kulaynī, *al-Kāfī*, 1:62–7. Bayhom Daou supplies an interesting attempt to extract the details of al-Kulaynī's attitude to hadiths and other sources of law from this section of *al-Kāfī*. Tamima Bayhom-Daou, 'The Imami Shīʿī Conception of the Imam and the Sources of Religious Doctrine in the Formative Period: from Hishām b. al-Ḥakam (d. 179 A.H. to Kulīnī (d. 329 A.H.)', PhD Thesis, SOAS, 1996, 194-209.

57 Though this is the case when it comes to individual terms like *mujmal* and *tawātur*, it has been noted by Madelung with regard to al-Ṣadūq's theology and by Gleave with regard to his legal writing in *al-Faqīh* that his approach is demonstrably shaped by the content of the hadiths upon which he relies. See Madelung, 'Imamism and Mu'tazilite Theology', 17; Gleave, 'Between Ḥadīth and Fiqh', 361.

58 Melchert makes an interesting observation of the Imāmī 'semi-rationalists', as he calls them (among whom he includes al-Ṣadūq), that they are eager to label themselves as traditionist but in practice they are quite willing to argue. This

is certainly the case with al-Ṣadūq, who gives unflinchingly stark injunctions about the forbidden nature of dialectic and argumentation (*al-Tawḥīd*, 497–504; *al-Iʿtiqādāt*, 94–7), but can be found reasoning at length in polemical contexts (*Kamāl al-dīn*, 31–157). This would be well explained by what is hypothesized here of Imāmīs who were ideologically compelled to uphold a vision of the imams' reported words as the sovereign authority, even as the imam himself used to be, while being practically compelled to defend and support those words with textual criticism and reasoned argument. See Melchert, 'The Imamis Between Rationalism and Traditionalism', 247.

59 For example, al-Mufīd, *Taṣḥīḥ*, 55.

60 For Ibn Bābawayh the Elder and al-Kulaynī as representatives of the competing schools of Qum and Rayy, see Ansari, *L'imamat*, 18–36. As noted earlier, though al-Ṣadūq ultimately moved to Rayy, his intellectual foundations remained in Qum. See Ansari, *L'imamat*, 65–7.

61 This account suggests an emendation to Modarressi's model, which cuts across teacher–student relationships. In his schema, al-Kulaynī is a traditionist but his student is an intermediate, while Ibn Bābawayh the Elder is an intermediate but al-Ṣadūq remains a traditionist (Modarressi, *Introduction*, 32–39). Gleave presents a more linear account, with the role of the scholar's own legal reasoning acquiring a steadily greater presence in legal writing between al-Kulaynī and al-Ṭūsī (Gleave, 'Between Ḥadīth and Fiqh', 352, 360–1, 381–2). While this pattern is drawn between a self-confessedly restricted set of sources, it broadly holds true for the model suggested here, across divisions between different scholarly networks. Thus, al-Ṣadūq is more open to discussing *isnād* criticism than his father, and Ibn Qūlawayh shows greater engagement therewith than al-Kulaynī, even while both pairs of scholars – Qummī and Rāzī – share a continuity of disagreement with the approach of the other scholarly genealogy.

62 Al-Ṣadūq left a significant legacy as a hadith scholar, especially in Khurāsān (see Ansari, *L'imamat*, 69–71), but the dearth of sources prevents speculation regarding how this may have shaped continuing attitudes to technical questions, and whether those for whom he was an important source of hadith preserved aspects of his methodology.

63 In terms of extant works, examples include the Ḥanafī Aḥmad b. ʿAlī al-Jaṣṣāṣ's (d. 370/985) *al-Fuṣūl fī al-uṣūl*, or the lengthy treatment of jurisprudence (*al-Sharʿīyat*) in the Muʿtazilī al-Qāḍī ʿAbd al-Jabbār b. Aḥmad al- Hamadhānī's (d. 415/1024) *al-Mughnī*. See Stewart, 'Muḥammad b. Jarīr al-Ṭabarī', 347–8; Melchert, *Sunni Schools*, 87–155.

64 Stewart remarks that studies, indeed definitions of Shīʿism have too often focussed on imamology (alongside theology of which it is considered part) at the expense of questions of jurisprudence, in which Twelver Shīʿism at least is also highly

distinctive. While this is surely true, the preceding analysis shows us that in the fourth/tenth century jurisprudence and imamology are not easily separated. See Stewart, *Islamic Legal Orthodoxy*, 6, 13–14.

65 See Musa, *Ḥadīth as Scripture*, 31–68. Unlike later disputes between traditionists and rationalists and like al-Ṣadūq, these thinkers were justifying hadith on an existential level, against voices who would deny it any substantial validity. Beyond these similarities, of course, al-Ṣadūq and these Sunnī authors faced very different kinds of opposition, and the ways in which they were compelled to justify their respective proof-corpora differed accordingly.

66 As noted, Newman has documented a conspicuous decline in interest in al-Ṣadūq's works among Imāmīs after the Buwayhid period. See Newman, 'The Recovery of the Past', 112–5.

Chapter 3

1 Al-Ṣadūq, *al-Khiṣāl* (Qum: Muʾassasat al-Nashr al-Islāmī, 1429 h), 264, 444–5.

2 Despite the evidence surveyed in this chapter, al-Ṣadūq's relationship with *adab* has received no scholarly attention. No doubt as a result of the prominent place his works hold in the Imāmī legal and theological canon, and their lack of a place in canons of *adab*, he has been viewed exclusively as the property of the histories of Imāmī law and theology.

3 It is an emerging consensus that *adab* eludes exhaustive definition. The noun *adab* had a number of meanings in the fourth/tenth-century context, foremost among them good manners, moral education (often equated to the Greek παιδια) and sound literary and philological knowledge. These difficulties of definition are, moreover, compounded not only by the term's eventful philological history in the early centuries of Islam (before the kinds of writing examined in this chapter appeared) but also by its shifting, diverse use in the modern period. For discussions of its meanings past and present, see Bonebakker, 'Adab and the Concept of Belles-Lettres', in *Abbasid Belles Lettres*, ed. Julia Ashtiany, T. M. Johnstone, J. D. Latham and R. B. Serjeant, 16–30 (Cambridge: Cambridge University Press, 1990); Hilary Kilpatrick, '*Adab*', in *Encyclopedia of Arabic Literature*, ed. Julie Scott Meisami, and Paul Starkey (London: Routledge, 1998): 53–56, at 56; 'A Genre in Classical Arabic Literature: The *Adab* Encyclopedia', in *Proceedings, union européenne des arabisants et islamisants: 10th Congress, Edinburgh, 9–16 September 1980*, ed. Robert Hillenbrand, 34–42 (Edinburgh: Edinburgh University Press, 1982), 34–9; Orfali, *The Anthologist's Art*, 29–37; Daniel Beaumont, '*Min Jumlat al-Jamādāt*. The Inanimate in Fictional and *Adab* Narrative', in *On Fiction and Adab in Medieval*

Arabic Literature, ed. Philip F. Kennedy, 55–68 (Wiesbaden: Harrassowitz Verlag, 2005), 55.

4 'Culture' seems as close to a one-word translation of *adab*'s conception in the abstract as can be found. Culture has the advantage of evoking, like *adab*, a property that can be acquired; one could seek to acquire or impart *adab* just as one might seek to become more cultured or render others so. The two terms, moreover, have considerable conceptual overlap: much of what falls under *adab*'s semantic field (poetry, manners, even philological scholarship) is also covered by that of culture. Nonetheless, these overlaps have their inevitable limits, and the word falls short of a straight translation of *adab*. See Hilary Kilpatrick and Stefan Leder, 'Classical Arabic Prose Literature: A Researchers' Sketch Map', *Journal of Arabic Literature* 23/1 (1992): 2–26, 18–23, Bonebakker, 'Adab and the Concept of Belles-Lettres', 19–24.

5 For the importance and nature of the anthology in *adab* literature, see Kilpatrick, 'A Genre'; Kilpatrick and Leder, 'Classical Arabic Prose Literature', 15–18, 20–3; Orfali, *The Anthologist's Art*, 1–33.

6 Khalidi, *Islamic Historiography: The Histories of Mas'udi* (Albany: State University of New York Press, 1975), 83–130; Orfali, *The Anthologist's Art*, 29–32.

7 While *adab* literature in earlier centuries had been the property of a fairly select group, most prominently secretaries of the chancery (*kuttāb*, sg. *kātib*), over the ʿAbbāsid period it became a literature in which an increasingly diverse range of authors engaged. This development saw a corresponding expansion of *adab* works' intended audience, and what had once been a literature written by the court for the court had become by al-Ṣadūq's day a discourse that often sought as wide a readership as possible. See Khalidi, *Islamic Historiography*, 96.

8 For example, Khalidi, *Islamic Historiography*, 96–111.

9 See A. Dietrich, 'Ibn Abi 'l-Dunyā', in *Encyclopaedia of Islam, 2nd edition*, ed. P. Bearman, Th. Bianquis, C. E. Bosworth, E. van Donzel, and W. P. Heinrichs, Consulted online September 30, 2017 at http://referenceworks.brillonline.com/entries/encyclopaedia-of-islam-2/ibn-abi-l-dunya-SIM_3046?s.num=0&s.f.s2_parent=s.f.cluster.Encyclopaedia+of+Islam&s.q=ibn+abi+al-dunya; Kilpatrick, '*Adab*', 55, Kilpatrick and Leder, 'Classical Arabic Prose Literature', 20.

10 Sperl highlights not only the shared pedagogical concern of *adab* and hadith scholarship but also 'a similar conception of the edifying power of speech'. Stefan Sperl, 'Man's "Hollow Core": Ethics and Aesthetics in Hadith Literature and Classical Arabic *adab*', *BSOAS* 70/3 (2007): 459–86, at 465–6.

11 Nuha Alshaar, *Ethics in Islam: Friendship in the Political Thought of Al-Tawhidi and His Contemporaries* (London: Routledge, 2014), 59–98; Wadād al-Qāḍī, 'Abū Ḥayyān al-Tawḥīdī: A Sunnī Voice in the Shīʿī Century', in *Culture and Memory in Medieval Islam: Essays in Honour of Wilferd Madelung*, ed. Farhad Daftary and Josef

W. Meri, 128–62 (London: I. B. Tauris, 2003). Referring to al-Barqī's work, Vilozny cites the lack of humour and reliance exclusively on Imāmī hadith as barriers to their being appreciated as *adab*, but the studies cited here do not suggest that those would necessarily be disqualifying factors. Roy Vilozny, *Constructing a Worldview: al-Barqī's Role in the Making of Early Shīʿī Faith* (Turnhout: Brepols, 2017), 27–8.

The question of the admissibility of the religious into *adab* touches on a further debate about the applicability of the sometime description of such literature as 'humanist'. Goodman offers a transhistorical image of classical Islamic humanism that is paradigmatically opposed to a thoroughly negative image of religiosity and fanaticism. The studies of Arkoun and Bergé of al-Miskawayh and al-Tawḥīdī respectively, as well as Kraemer's study of the Buwayhid period in general, are more restrained, giving detailed examinations of particular trends within Buwayhid thought, such as a focus on the individual, an enfranchising of models of reason and a willingness to overlook differences of religious affiliation, as well as the relationship between these ideas and the Greek philosophical heritage. A more 'sober' image of this dichotomy is presented by Makdisi, who distinguishes humanism, defined as philology and the literary arts, from scholasticism, by which is meant matters of law. See Lenn Goodman, *Islamic Humanism* (Oxford: Oxford University Press, 2003); Mohammed Arkoun, *Contribution à l'étude de l'humanisme arabe au IVe/Xe siècle: Miskawayh (320/325-421)–(932/936-1030) philosophe et historien* (Paris: J. Vrin, 1970); Marc Bergé, *Pour un humanisme vécu: Abū Ḥayyān al-Tawḥīdī: essai sur la personnalité morale, intellectuelle et littéraire d'un grand prosateur et humaniste arabe, engagé dans la société de l'époque bouyide, à Bagdad, Rayy et Chiraz, au IVe-Xe siècle (entre 310/922 et 320/932-414/1023)* (Damascus: Institut français de Damas, 1979); Joel Kraemer, 'Humanism in the Renaissance of Islam: A Preliminary Study', *Journal of the American Oriental Society* 104/1 (1984): 135–64. The applicability of the term 'humanism' to such contexts has also been challenged, for instance in Alexander Key, 'The Applicability of the Term 'Humanism' to Abū Ḥayyān Al-Tawḥīdī', *Studia Islamica* 100–101 (2005): 71–112.

12 Sperl, 'Man's "Hollow Core"', 466.

13 See, for instance, Aḥmad b. Muḥammad Ibn ʿAbd Rabbih, *al-ʿIqd al-farīd*, ed. Mufīd Muḥammad Qamīḥa (Beirut: Dār al-Kutub al-ʿIlmīya, 1983), 1:4–7; Abū Ḥayyān al-Tawḥīdī, *al-Baṣāʾir wa'l-dhakhāʾir* (Beirut: Dār al-Yaqīn, 1964), 1:11–15; Manṣūr b. al-Ḥusayn al-Ābī, *Nathr al-Durr* (Beirut: Dār al-Kutub al-ʿIlmīya, 2008), 1:22–5.

14 One example is al-Miskawayh's compendium *al-Ḥikma al-khālida* ('The Eternal Wisdom'), which is presented as based around counsels of the ancient Persian sage Awshanj (Hushang) to his king – the oldest text of wisdom known, al-Miskawayh tells us, dating from just after the great flood. This is the prime exemplar of a wisdom that is archetypal and eternal, to which are then appended later examples,

including some from the Prophet Muḥammad. See Aḥmad b. Muḥammad al-Miskawayh, *al-Ḥikma al-khālida* (Cairo: Maktabat al-Nahḍa al-Miṣrīya, 1952), 5–6 and *passim*. This eternal aspect is a question of quality as well as origins, such that al-Miskawayh explicitly links the contents and message of *al-Ḥikma al-khālida* to that of his principal work on ethics, *Tahdhīb al-akhlāq* (*al-Ḥikma al-khālida*, 25). The primordial command, both works declare, is 'Know thyself'. Aḥmad b. Muḥammad al-Miskawayh, *Tahdhīb al-akhlāq* (Beirut: American University of Beirut, 1966), 2; *al-Ḥikma al-khālida*, 23–5. For a discussion of al-Miskawayh's view of prophecy, see Arkoun, *Philosophe et Historien*, 315–28.

15 See Azartash Azarnoosh and Mansur Sana'i, 'Al-Ābī, Abū Saʿd Manṣūr b. al-Ḥusayn', in *Encyclopaedia Islamica*, ed. Wilfred Madelung, and Farhad Daftary, Consulted online September 30, 2016 at http://referenceworks.brillonline.com/entries/encyclopaedia-islamica/al-abi-abu-sad-mansur-b-al-husayn-SIM_0079?s.num=0&s.q=al-abi. Al-Ābī, it is clear, was a generation or two younger than al-Ṣadūq, but he certainly knew Ibn ʿAbbād, and the two speak one another's praises. Despite some sources identifying him as an Imāmī, his writings make fairly plain that he was a Zaydī; his surviving compendium *Nathr al-durr* presents a category of 'the imams from the Prophet's house' that follows a distinctly Zaydī pattern, including various heroic figures of ʿAlid descent and many Zaydī imams, while omitting many Imāmī imams. See al-Ābī, *Nath al-durr*, 1:328–91.

16 A notable case in this regard is Ibn al-Nadīm. The famous bibliographer is regularly identified as an Imāmī and, indeed, knew of and saw al-Mufīd, and lists some important third/ninth-century Imāmī works. Other indicators, however, place him in a very different intellectual landscape to al-Mufīd and al-Ṣadūq. Ibn al-Nadīm notes al-Mufīd's eminence but does not list any of his works, nor does he know of al-Kulaynī or *al-Kāfī*, a work that had become a cornerstone of Imāmī scholarship in Baghdad and beyond. Concerning al-Ṣadūq himself – his exact contemporary – Ibn al-Nadīm's knowledge is extremely vague. He includes an entry for ʿAlī Ibn Bābawayh, al-Ṣadūq's father, and, a little later, another entry for one Muḥammad b. ʿAlī b. al-Ḥusayn, author of an *al-Hidāya* who may be al-Ṣadūq; however, identification cannot be certain since Ibn al-Nadīm gives no indication that this figure is indeed the son of Ibn Bābawayh the Elder, and accords him only a single work. Overall, Ibn al-Nadīm's knowledge of Imāmī legal and theological scholarship is, for a bibliographer, extremely patchy. See Muḥammad b. Isḥāq Ibn al-Nadīm, *al-Fihrist* (Beirut: Dār al-Maʿrifa, n. d.), 274–79, 308–14; Bayard Doge, *The Fihrist of Al-Nadīm: A Tenth-Century Survey of Muslim Culture* (New York: Columbia University Press, 1970), 1:xviii–xx. Also see Devin Stewart, 'Ibn al-Nadīm's Ismāʿīlī Contacts', *Journal of the Royal Asiatic Society* 19/1 (2009): 21–40; 'The Structure of the Fihrist: Ibn Al-Nadim as Historian of Islamic Legal and Theological Schools', *International Journal of Middle East Studies* 39/3 (2007): 369–87, at 375–9.

17 Al-Ṣadūq narrates his own debates in the presence of Rukn al-Dawla in *Kamāl al-dīn* and in the surviving text of *Majālis ma ʿa Rukn al-Dawla*, as well as recounting a shorter though entirely positive interaction in *ʿUyūn* (2:312). His *ʿUyūn* is dedicated to Ibn ʿAbbād and al-Tawḥīdī recounts that at some point Ibn ʿAbbād banished him (this, of course, indicates a certain level of interaction between the two, albeit less positive than that aspired to in the dedicatory introduction to *ʿUyūn*). See al-Tawḥīdī, *Akhlāq al-wazīrayn*, 166–7.

18 Abū Ḥayyān al-Tawḥīdī, *Risālat al-ṣadāqa wa'l-ṣadīq* (Damascus: Dār al-Fikr, 1964), 203, 291; *Akhlāq al-wazīrayn*, 254–5. Al-Tawḥīdī only names his source as Ibn Bābawayh, leaving open the possibility that he is referring to al-Ṣadūq's father, but the fact that al-Tawḥīdī was in Rayy on and off between 358/968 and 370/980, the middle of al-Ṣadūq's career and after his father's death, makes it much more likely that his source is Ibn Bābawayh the younger.

19 For example, al-Ṣadūq, *ʿUyūn*, 25.

20 For example, al-Ṣadūq, *Kamāl al-dīn*, 277.

21 Books of 'firsts' constitute a particular genre of *adab* compendium, in which were listed for the curiosity and betterment of those who would be cultured anecdotes concerning the first precedents of activities and events as diverse as the first person to be stoned for adultery, the first person to draw lots for a godly cause, the first person to hire Turkic soldiers and the first person to pledge allegiance to ʿAlī. The best-known surviving such compendium by a contemporary of al-Ṣadūq is the *al-Awāʾil* of Abū Hilāl al-ʿAskarī. The book of 'lasts' is a less common phenomenon for obvious reasons, and in later literature sometimes appears discussing mystical and eschatological themes. We can, alas, only guess as to what al-Ṣaduq made of the genre.

22 For wisdom literature's significance in and relation to *adab* literature, see Dimitri Gutas, 'Classical Arabic Wisdom Literature: Nature and Scope', *Journal of the American Oriental Society* 101/1 (1981): 55–7, 62–9; Kilpatrick, '*Adab*', 55; Kilpatrick and Leder, 'Classical Arabic Prose Literature', 4.

23 See Alshaar, *Ethics in Islam*.

24 *Al-Khiṣāl*'s organizing theme of number is shared by a contemporary *adab* compendium, Abū Manṣūr al-Thaʿālibī's collection of poetic gobbets *Bard al-akbād fī al-aʿdād*. See Orfali, *The Anthologist's Art*, 49.

25 We know even less of al-Barqī's life than we do of al-Ṣadūq's, such that we can only speculate on the kind of contacts that these works evidence. See Vilozny, *Constructing a Worldview*, 22–4.

26 These include books on maths, grammar, poetry and history. See al-Najāshī, *Rijāl*, 74–5.

27 Al-Barqī is a regular presence in al-Ṣadūq's *asānīd*, and in *al-Faqīh* al-Ṣadūq names al-Barqī's *al-Maḥāsin* as one of the sources of *al-Faqīh*. There are two further

books from *al-Maḥāsin* upon which al-Ṣadūq seems to have built directly, namely *ʿIqāb al-aʿmāl* (Deeds and their Punishments) and *Thawāb al-aʿmāl* (Deeds and their Rewards), and the bibliographical record shows many other pairs of similar works by the two authors, one or both of which is lost (al-Barqī's fondness for cryptic titles notwithstanding). The extant works show that this emulation goes far beyond choice of titles, with sizeable portions and sometimes the majority of the material in al-Barqī's books appearing in the parallel work by al-Ṣadūq. Al-Ṣadūq's commentary on al-Barqī's *al-Rijāl*, meanwhile, is the only recorded incident of his having written a commentary on the work of a named author. See al-Ṣadūq, *al-Faqīh*, 13–14.

28 Roy Vilozny, 'A Concise Numerical Guide for the Perplexed Shiite: Al-Barqī's (d. 274/888 or 280/894) *Kitāb al-Aškāl wa-l-qarāʾin*', *Arabica* 63/1–2 (2016): 64–88', at 69.

29 Vilozny suggests a number of explanations for al-Barqī's having composed these works as he has, primarily their situation in the pre-Buwayhid, pre-canonical phase of Imāmī hadith, al-Barqī's having borrowed an *adabī* form for his hadith compendia, the influence of Middle Persian traditions of wisdom literature (itself a common feature of *adab* literature), and Imāmī customs for the dissemination of knowledge among the faithful, including ensuring that secret knowledge is not made available to the uninitiated. This chapter's analysis clearly has much in common with the hypothesized borrowing from wisdom literatures, and we shall have cause to engage with the possibility of dissimilation in what follows. See Vilozny, *Constructing a Worldview*, 27–8, 163–208.

As for the notion that this is a 'pre-canonical' form of compilation, its common use between al-Barqī and al-Ṣadūq must complicate this suggestion somewhat. Buwayhid Imāmī scholars from al-Ṣadūq to al-Ṭūsī addressed with a formative vigour the question of how the Imāmī hadith corpus was to be approached and routinized, but that process is already thoroughly in evidence before the Buwayhids in al-Kulaynī (while in Sunnī hadith literature it well predates al-Barqī). What we see in al-Ṣadūq's usage of these forms, then, is not the absence of later, 'canonizing' modes of hadith compilation, but the authorial choice to compile differently.

30 See, for example, Abū Ḥanīfa al-Nuʿmān b. Muhammad al-Qāḍī al-Nuʿmān, *Sharḥ al-akhbār fī faḍāʾil al-aʾimma al-aṭhār* (Muʾassasat al-Nashr al-Islāmī, 1431 h), 3:435–510.

31 For developments of these ideas in the centuries prior to al-Ṣadūq, see Maria Massi Dakake, *The Charismatic Community: Shi'ite Identity in Early Islam*, (Albany: State University of New York Press, 2008), 103–251; Newman, *Formative Period*, 67–93, 174–7, 193–201.

32 For example, Aḥmad b. Muḥammad al-Barqī, *al-Maḥāsin* (Beirut: al-Majmaʿ al-ʿĀlamī li-Ahl al-Bayt, 2011), 1:226–47; al-Ṣaffār, *Baṣāʾir al-darajāt*, 27–32.

33 Bar-Asher and Newman convincingly link this isolationist outlook and the elaborate cosmology that accompanied it to the hostile environment of the pre-Buwayhid period. Bar-Asher in particular outlines a set of identifying features of pre-Buwayhid Imāmīsm as exhibited in exegetical writings, among which is a virulently hostile attitude to non-Shīʿīs. Newman, *Formative Period*, 67–93; Bar-Asher, *Scripture and Exegesis*, 71–86.

34 Al-Ṣadūq, *Faḍāʾil*, 192–3, 199 (hadith no. 10). Though al-Ṣadūq does not include cosmological material in these books, such hadiths do appear elsewhere in his writings, as we shall see in what follows. This, of course, only underscores the significance of his decision to exclude them from the three works discuss here.

Much has been made of the beliefs enunciated in the pre-Buwayhid literature on this subject and their significance (most prominently in Amir-Moezzi, *Divine Guide*), but even here it is arguable that the ethics of brotherhood are more important to the third/ninth-century compilers than the metaphysical specifics of their texts. In al-Barqī's *al-Maḥāsin*, for instance, the author's focus seems often to be on ethical implications, rather than asserting any particular cosmology as an article of faith. In the first chapter of the *Kitāb al-ṣafwa* in *al-Maḥāsin*, the subject of which is God's creation of the believers from his light, of the four hadiths therein only two describe the creation of believers from God's light; the other two declare, respectively, that believers are infused with God's spirit, and that they have an unspecified, special relationship with God. In contrast to these cosmological discrepancies, all four hadiths contain similar imperatives to treat believers with respect – a comparative unanimity that presumably reflects the priorities of the compiler. See al-Barqī, *al-Maḥāsin*, 1:223–4.

35 Al-Ṣadūq, *Ṣifāt al-shīʿa*, in *Muṣannafāt al-Ṣadūq*, ed. Editorial Committee, Maktabat Pārsā (Qum: Maktabat Pārsā, 2008), 131–88, at 142–3.

36 Al-Ṣadūq, *Muṣādaqat al-ikhwān*, in *Muṣannafāt al-Ṣadūq*, 233–92, at 252 (hadith no. 2), 266–7 (hadith no. 2).

37 Al-Tawḥīdī, *al-Ṣadāqa waʾl-ṣadīq*, 203, 291. For the concept of friendship in *adabī* writings of the period, see Alshaar, *Ethics in Islam*, 178 and *passim*; Kraemer, *Humanism in the Renaissance of Islam*, 103–206; Arkoun, *Philosophe et historien*, 303–6.

38 Similarly, in many of the hadiths in *Ṣifāt* the Prophet or imam speaks not of the qualities of the Shīʿī but those of the believer (*muʾmin*), again blurring the distinction between a sealed Shīʿī identity and adherence to widely recognized standards of piety.

39 The book's full title is *Kitāb ʿilal al-sharāʾiʿ waʾl-aḥkām waʾl-asbāb* – 'the causes of laws, rulings and causalities'.

40 Al-Ṣadūq, *ʿIlal*, 10–11, 17–22, 171–4, 282–3, 286, 296, 311–12.

41 Al-Ṣadūq, *Maʿānī*, 315, 280–1.

42 See al-Ṣadūq, *al-Khiṣāl* (Qum: Mu'assasat al-Nashr al-Islāmī, 1429 h), 240–3. We need not infer from this that al-Kulaynī was ignorant of or disinterested in such matters, indeed biographical sources state that to the contrary he was widely educated in a much greater range of subjects, such as poetry and lexicography, than are discussed in *al-Kāfī*. See Amir-Moezzi and Ansari, 'Perfecting a Religion', 139–41.

43 Franz Rosenthal, *Knowledge Triumphant: The Concept of Knowledge in Medieval Islam* (Leiden: Brill 2007), 252–98; Alshaar, *Ethics in Islam*, 46–8, 69, 77–82.

44 Al-Ṣadūq, *al-Khiṣāl*, 374, *'Ilal*, 314–5, 328–9. *'Ilal* does contain large, continuous sections dealing with prayer, purity, fasting and pilgrimage, but these are not demarcated as such.

45 Al-Ṣadūq, *'Ilal*, 334.

46 *Ma'ānī*, of course, evokes the voluminous scholarly literature on scriptural hermeneutics, but *'Ilal*, too, stands opposite a variety of more systematic works that seek to explain the meanings behind legal rulings, including the Ṣūfī al-Ḥakīm al-Tirmidhī's (d. 318/930) *Ithbāt al-'ilal* ('Establishing Causes'), the Ismā'īlī al-Qāḍī al-Nu'mān's (d. 363/974) *Ta'wīl al-da'ā'im* ('Interpretation of the Pillars') and the Shāfi'ī Muḥammad b. 'Alī al-Qaffāl's (d. 365/976) *Maḥāsin al-sharī'a fī furū' al-shāfi'īya* ('The Benefits of the *Sharī'a* in Shāfi'ī Applied Law'). Despite this contrast, *'Ilal* has remained popular over the centuries among authors who see in it a more paradigmatic sort of guidance than its structure suggests. In particular, a genealogy of scholars stretching from al-Shahīd al-Thānī (d. 965/1557–966/1558) to Rūḥullāh Khomeini (d. 1989) have found therein confirmation of their esoteric understandings of prayer. See Ruhollah Khomeini, *The Mystery of Prayer*, Trans. Amjad H. Shah Naqavi (Leiden: Brill, 2015), xxii–xl.

47 Ibn Qūlawayh, *Kāmil al-ziyārāt*, 6–7.

48 Al-Tanūkhī, *Nishwār al-muḥāḍara*, ed. 'Abūd al-Shālijī (Beirut: Dār Ṣādir, 1995), 1:12. See also al-Ābī, *Nathr al-durr*, 1:22–3.

49 Alsaduq, *Kamāl al-dīn*, 667–8.

50 Al-Ṣadūq, *al-Khiṣāl*, 329; *'Ilal*, 547.

51 Al-Ṣadūq, *'Ilal*, 339.

52 Ibid., 342.

53 Ibid., 195.

54 Ibid., 334.

55 Al-Ṣadūq, *al-Khiṣāl*, 258–9, 298–9, 385–6. There may be a certain amount of humour in the pun of *al-Khiṣāl*'s title in this regard. In his preface, al-Ṣadūq juxtaposes the word '*al-khiṣāl*' (with its dual meaning) alongside the word *a'dād* which unambiguously means 'numbers'. Yet we know that the reader searching for information about numbers is destined for disappointment, the numbers in *al-Khiṣāl*'s narrations seldom playing a pivotal role in the reports therein. Rather, it

is 'qualities' that dominate the vast majority of the book's material, with any given number yielding a list of enumerated virtues and vices the numerical delineation of which does little to obscure their similarity with those of a different number. There can be little doubt that when al-Ṣadūq promises a work concerning 'The praised numbers and qualities/quantities', he was aware of the numerological literature this would call to mind for many readers, and we may therefore detect a hint of parody, even satire in his promising the mysteries of numbers only to deliver solid, improving sermons on a numerical theme.

56 Al-Ṣadūq, *al-Khiṣāl*, 497–9, 502, 530–1, 534–5.

57 Ibid., 509–23.

58 Ibid., 523.

59 Al-Ṣadūq, *Maʿānī*, 56–63.

60 Al-Ṣadūq, *ʿIlal*, 336–8.

61 In a further nod to polemical strategies, several of these hadiths are narrated from ʿAbd Allāh b. ʿAbbās and ʿAbd Allāh b. ʿUmar, companions revered by Sunnīs. Al-Ṣadūq, *ʿIlal*, 309–10.

62 Ibid., 332–4.

63 Ibid., 267.

64 Al-Raḍī's *Nahj al-Balāgha*, for instance, has continued to be the subject of commentaries by non-Shīʿī from its composition until the present.

65 As discussed previously, Newman has illustrated that al-Ṣadūq's writings declined in popularity even in the Shīʿī world in the centuries after his lifetime, and he has no discernible currency among *adab* writers for the remainder of the ʿAbbāsid era. Newman, 'Recovery of the Past', 112–15.

66 Al-Ṣadūq, *al-Mawāʿiẓ*, 293.

67 Vilozny reads al-Barqī's *al-ʿIlal* as undertaking to illustrate the principle that 'God has done nothing without cause', and indeed that the imams are privy to such causes, but neither al-Barqī nor al-Ṣadūq in their respective *ʿIlal*s say as much. Roy Vilozny, 'Réflexions sur le *Kitāb al-ʿilal* d'Aḥmad b. Muḥammad al-Barqī', in *Le shīʿisme imāmite quarante ans après: hommage à Etan Kohlberg*, ed. Mohammad Ali Amir-Moezzi, Meir M. Bar-Asher, and Simon Hopkins, 417–35 (Belgium: Brepols, 2009), 417.

68 Alshaar, *Ethics in Islam*, 94, 158–86 and *passim*; Roy Mottahedeh, *Loyalty and Leadership in an Islamic Society* (London: I. B. Tauris, 1998), 41–62; Salah Natij, 'La nuit inaugurale de *Kitāb al-Imtāʿ wa-l-muʾānasa* d'Abū Ḥayyān al-Tawḥīdī: une leçon magistrale d'adab', *Arabica* 55/2 (2008): 227–75, at 247.

69 Translation here supplied in G. J. H. van Gelder, 'Mixtures of Jest and Earnest in Classical Arabic Literature: Part II', *Journal of Arabic Literature* 23/3 (1992): 169–90, at 170.

70 For relations between these two understandings of *taqīya*, see Kohlberg, '*Taqiyya*', 306–401; Lynda Clarke, 'The Rise and Decline of Taqiyya in Twelver Shiʿism', in

Reason and Inspiration in Islam: Theology, Philosophy and Mysticism in Muslim Thought, ed. Todd Lawson, 46–63 (London: I.B. Tauris, 2005), 46–54. For an extended look at the first, see Dakake, 'Hiding in Plain Sight'.

71 Al-Ṣadūq, *al-I'tiqādāt*, 343.

72 Al-Mufīd, *Taṣḥīḥ*, 115–16. Al-Mufīd also remarks that al-Ṣadūq is clearly not a proponent of such total *taqīya* given his own record of proclaiming Imāmī doctrine in his writings and teaching, though this does not imply that al-Ṣadūq was never in situations where more discretion was called for.

73 Al-Ṣadūq's transitional status in this regard has often been noted; see Kohlberg, '*Taqiyya*', 400; Clarke, '*Taqiyya*', 56.

74 Clarke, '*Taqiyya*', 46–55; Dakake, 'Hiding in Plain Sight', 326–35; Orkhan Mir-Kasimov, 'Techniques de garde du secret en Islam', *Revue de l'histoire des religions* 2 (2011), 274–9.

75 Kohlberg, '*Taqiyya*, 401–2.

76 Though less common, later Imāmī authors do recognize writing for a Sunnī audience as a potential context for *taqīya*. See Kohlberg, '*Taqiyya*', 401–2.

77 See Dakake, 'Hiding in Plain Sight', 325.

78 See Chapter 5, 120-1.

79 A further philological dimension to this overlap may be found in the dual meaning of the term *'āmma*, 'masses; commoners'. Imāmīs of this period use the term to denote non-Shī'īs, with Shī'īs being termed the '*khāṣṣa*' ('elite'), but the *'āmma* were also the mass of less educated people whom the community-minded *adīb* hoped to educate. Both senses were deeply derogatory. We may thus see in al-Ṣadūq's appropriation of *adab*'s aspiration to educate the *'āmma* ('the common people'), reconceived as an effort to educate the *'āmma* ('non-Shī'īs'), a play on the dual meaning of the term among Shī'īs and an underscoring its uncomplimentary aspects as generalized across both meanings. For a discussion of the negative connotations of the *'āmma* in Buwayhid literature, see Sinan Antoon, *The Poetics of the Obscene in Premodern Arabic Poetry: Ibn al-Ḥajjāj and Sukhf* (London: Palgrave Macmillan, 2014), 128–32.

80 Hugh Kennedy, 'The late 'Abbāsid pattern, 945–1050', in *The New Cambridge History of Islam*, ed. Chase F. Robinson (Cambridge: Cambridge University Press, 2010), 360–94, at 387–93; Donohue, *The Buwayhid Dynasty*, 103, Busse, *Chalif Und Grosskönig*, 429–30; Kraemer, *Humanism and the Rennaissance of Islam*, 39–44. While al-Ṣadūq gives multiple rationales for *taqīya* and occultation, his stated principal reasoning for both remains fear of oppression; it is for fear of this misguided majority this the imam hides, and it is that same fear that bids his Shī'a hide until he returns. See al-Ṣadūq, *Kamāl al-dīn*, 507–9.

81 'Abd Allāh b. Muslim Ibn Qutayba, *'Uyūn al-akhbār* (Beirut: al-Maktab al-Islāmī, 2008) 1:3. Over the third/ninth and fourth/tenth centuries, *adab* literature had

broadened its horizons beyond purely courtly audiences, but the paradigm outlined here still held firm in Buwayhid Rayy.

82 Mottahedeh, *Loyalty and Leadership*, 82–96.

83 Van Gelder, 'Part II', 174. *Adab* compendia frequently contain humorous, perhaps risqué material, but they just as frequently accompany these light-hearted elements with pointed apologies for their inclusion. See Ibn Qutayba, *ʿUyūn al-akhbār*, 1:3–10; al-Ābī, *Nathr al-durr*, 1:22; G. J. H. van Gelder, 'Mixtures of Jest and Earnest in Classical Arabic Literature: Part I', *Journal of Arabic Literature* 23/2 (1992): 83–108, especially at 6, 89–95.

84 See Mottahedeh, *Loyalty and Leadership*, 82–96; Natij, 'Nuit inaugurale', *passim*; Alshaar, *Ethics in Islam*, 94, 124–31.

85 See, for example, Chapter 4, 110–111.

86 Al-Tawḥīdī, *Akhlāq al-wazīrayn*, 166–7.

87 Al-Ābī, al-Sharīf al-Raḍī and al-Sharīf al-Murtaḍā (let alone al-Miskawayh) all leaned heavily towards the dominant Muʿtazilī thinking of the court, and held high office therein. Al-Ābī was Majd al-Dawla's vizier, while al-Raḍī and al-Murtaḍā held in succession the syndicate of the Ṭālibids of Baghdad.

88 See al-Ṣadūq, *Kamāl al-dīn*, 117–18; *Munāẓarat al-malik Rukn al-Dawla li'l-Ṣadūq Ibn Bābawayh*, ed. Jawād al-Warad (Beirut: Dār al-Ḥujja al-Bayḍāʾ, 2010). Al-Ṣadūq certainly is the narrator in *Kamāl al-dīn*, and may well be in *Majālis maʿa Rukn al-Dawla*. Indeed, the fact that we see him using such a device of self-narration elsewhere, alongside the fact that the *Majālis maʿa Rukn al-Dawla* are consistently counted as a work by al-Ṣadūq himself, indicates as much, though other possibilities cannot be discounted given the uncertain state of this text. See Ansari, 'Bar rasī'.

89 *ʿUyūn* is far larger than any preceding work on al-Riḍā's life, and accordingly in the Twelver tradition its contents have remained the basis of almost all subsequent works on the subject. Cooperson, *Classical Arabic Biography*, 76–98.

90 Al-Ṣadūq, *ʿUyūn*, 1:105–38. Another point where al-Ṣadūq conspicuously works to offer a rationalist portrait of the imam is his presentation of hadiths from al-Riḍā about cause and effect (*ʿilal*). Unlike what we have seen in *ʿIlal*, in *ʿUyūn* chapters on the subject showcase the imam's rationality, supplying wise interpretations of points of law or, indeed, upholding the doctrine of God's justice in questionable moments of prophetic history such as the presumed drowning of infants during Noah's flood. See al-Ṣadūq, *ʿUyūn*, 2:81 (hadith no. 2), 91 (hadith no. 28).

91 Al-Ṣadūq, *ʿUyūn*, 2:221–42.

92 Al-Ṣadūq, *ʿIlal*, 336–8.

93 Al-Ṣadūq, *ʿUyūn*, 1:225–9. For Ibn ʿAbbād's confessional identity and his corresponding attitudes to patronage, see Erez Naaman, *Literature and the Islamic Court: Cultural Life under al-Ṣāḥib Ibn ʿAbbād* (London: Routledge, 2016), 4, 22–59.

94 Al-Ṣadūq, *ʿUyūn*, 2:179–83.
95 Ibid., 1:244.
96 Ibid., 2:296–8.

Chapter 4

1 Al-Ṣadūq, *al-Tawḥīd*, 21–2.
2 The most prominent representatives of this approach are the studies by McDermott, Sander and Madelung, all of which largely engage *al-Tawḥīd* as a source of al-Ṣadūq's theology, citing material across the book according to individual reports' pertinence to particular doctrines, with minimal interest in how material in one part of *al-Tawḥīd* may interact with another. Instances of where such an approach is particularly misleading will be pointed out over the course of this chapter.
3 Kraemer, *Humanism and the Rennaissance of Islam*, 72–3. 'Literalism' (*ḥashw*), closely associated with *tashbīh*, is listed among the intellectual crimes for which al-Ṣadūq and other traditionists were banished by Ibn ʿAbbād in the account supplied by al-Tawḥīdī. See al-Tawḥīdī, *Akhlāq al-wazīrayn*, 166–7.
4 See, for instance, their utility in matters regarding the occultation of the twelfth imam in Chapter 5.
5 Al-Ṣadūq, *al-Iʿtiqādāt*, 41–2. Very occasionally, al-Ṣadūq refers to the threat of inauthentic hadiths and their unscrupulous narrators (for example al-Ṣadūq, *al-Tawḥīd*, 354, hadith no. 12), but never in a way that is harnessed into *al-Tawḥīd*'s core apology.
6 Al-Ṣadūq, *al-Tawḥīd*, 24–5 (hadith nos. 8, 10).
7 Ibid, 37.
8 Ibid., 31, 128, 145.
9 For example, ibid., 53 (hadith no. 10), 80 (hadith no. 28), 131, 142 (hadith no. 14).
10 For example, ibid., 90–4, 159.
11 Ibid., 21.
12 Ibid., 132–4 (hadith no. 1), 137 (hadith no. 5), 139 (hadith no. 9).
13 Gleave discusses the use of this compiler's technique in al-Ṣadūq's *al-Faqīh* as well as in al-Kulaynī's *al-Kāfī*. Gleave, 'Between Ḥadīth and Fiqh', 353–73. See also Amir-Moezzi and Ansari, 'Perfecting a Religion', 154; Burge, 'Reading Between the Lines', 179–88.
14 We are told first that just as God can contain within the space of the eyeball all the images of the heavens and the earth that the eye can see, so he can also contain the universe within an egg. However, a few reports later the reply seems to be a negative one: 'God cannot be called lacking in power, and what greater power is there than his who could so shrink the universe and so magnify an egg?' The implication is surely that he could not, but the fact that he could do so if only in violation of the 'no enlarging/shrinking' clause is testament enough to his omnipotence. Another

report simply answers in the negative, prohibits the attributing of impotence to God and leaves it at that. Al-Ṣadūq, *al-Tawḥīd*, 132–4 (hadith no. 1), 137 (hadith no. 5), 139 (hadith no. 9).

15 Ibid., 124–6 (hadith nos. 16, 17, 20).

16 Again, we should recall that al-Ṣadūq uses just such a strategy when it suits him in *al-I῾tiqādāt*, warning readers that unorthodox-looking hadiths may be inauthentic. We have seen in Chapter 2 how al-Ṣadūq is ambivalent about such assertions, and in the more ambitious context of *al-Tawḥīd* he shows how productively they may be thrown aside.

17 Al-Ṣadūq, *al-Tawḥīd*, 131.

18 Ibid., 221, 259.

19 Al-Ṣadūq is already evoking combative contrast with Mu῾tazilī accounts of such matters. See, for instance, al-Ḥasan Ibn Mattawayh, *al-Tadhkira fī aḥkām al-jawāhir wa'l-a῾rāḍ*, ed. Sāmī Naṣr Luṭf, and Fayṣal Badīr ῾Ūn (Cairo: Dār al-Thaqāfa, 1975), 400–31.

20 Al-Ṣadūq, *al-Tawḥīd*, 244–5 (hadith no. 1).

21 See John Turner, *Inquisition in Early Islam: The Competition for Political Authority in Abbasid Empire* (London: I. B. Tauris, 2013), 1–14.

22 Al-Ṣadūq, *al-Tawḥīd*, 246 (hadith no. 5).

23 The angel in question, the hadith narrates, prays as follows: 'Glory to God who dulls the heat of this fire lest it melt this ice, and who dulls the chill of this ice lest it extinguish the heat of this fire. O God, you who unite fire and ice, unite the hearts of the believers, your servants, in obedience to you.' Al-Ṣadūq, *al-Tawḥīd*, 308 (hadith no. 5).

24 Al-Ṣadūq, *al-Tawḥīd*, 309 (hadith no. 8).

25 One need look no further than al-Mufīd for a rationalist condemnation of al-Ṣadūq's use of such material; *al-I῾tiqādāt* regularly employs hadith to illustrate cosmic entities and processes such as the soul and the descent of revelation; al-Mufīd, accordingly, steps in each time to declare that these matters are unknowable in such terms, and that such hadiths are not to be relied upon. Al-Mufīd, *Taṣḥīḥ*, 59–73, 86–90, 99–101. Al-Mufīd's own account of the cosmos is utterly Mu῾tazilī in character and, indeed, his writings are a valued source for Mu῾tazilī views on the subject. See McDermott, *Theology*, 214–15.

26 For Ḥanbalī usage of very similar material to illustrate the greatness of God, see, for example, Muḥammad b. Isḥāq Ibn Mandah (d. 395/1004–5), *Kitāb al-tawḥīd*, ed. ῾Alī al-Faqīhī (Medina: al-Jāmi῾a al-Islāmīya bi'l-Madīna, 1989), 1:113ff.

27 *῾Aql* has received a number of translations among scholars of Shī῾ism, ranging from 'the intellect' to 'hiero-intelligence'. 'Reason', meanwhile, is usually avoided, with readers of its usage in many early Shī῾ī sources having contended that *῾aql* constitutes something more than cold rationality. See, Amir-Moezzi, *Divine Guide*, 6–13; Karim Douglas Crow, 'The Role of *al-῾Aql* in Early Islamic Wisdom with

Reference to Imam Jaʿfar al-Ṣādiq', PhD Thesis, McGill University, 1996, *passim*; al-Kulaynī, *al-Kāfī*, 1:10–29. In al-Ṣadūq's usage here, conversely, *ʿaql* clearly refers to reason conceived as the faculty at work in independent reasoning and analogy, hubristic challenges to the authority of text to which al-Ṣadūq was firmly opposed.

28 This is not to claim that al-Ṣadūq was influenced by Ibn Ṭufayl's *Ḥayy b. Yaqẓān*, written as it was many decades later.

29 Madelung characterizes *al-Tawḥīd* as an attempt to minimize disagreement with the Muʿtazilīs. Though he does point out some areas where al-Ṣadūq diverges from Muʿtazilī positions, these are characterized as isolated disagreements of doctrine. Similarly, McDermott describes al-Ṣadūq's preference to discourage controversy, noting his strong words on *taqīya* in *al-Iʿtiqādāt* and a number of conciliatory theological positions expressed in his works. Neither scholar engages chapter 32 of *al-Tawḥīd* or those that surround it. See Madelung, 'Imamism and Mu'tazilite Theology', 17–19; McDermott, *Theology*, 315–22.

30 Madelung notes that it is in these areas that al-Ṣadūq is in his sharpest disagreement with the Muʿtazila, on no less pivotal a notion than the central Muʿtazilī creed of God's justice (the same justice to which al-Ṣadūq pays enthusiastic lip service in chapter 5 discussed earlier). These conclusions, however, are based almost entirely on *al-Iʿtiqādāt* rather than *al-Tawḥīd*'s treatment of this topic. The reasons for this are not hard to see, for while *al-Iʿtiqādāt* gives brief, definitive answers on points like free will and human agency (al-Ṣadūq, *al-Iʿtiqādāt*, 59–66, 75–9, 85–7), *al-Tawḥīd* is open to the same criticism that once prompted Madelung to reject *al-Kāfī* as a viable source of theological thought: it presents only amassed hadiths that do not constitute full answers to theological questions. See Madelung, 'Imamism and Mu'tazilite Theology', 19–20, 29. More recently, Madelung has revised his view of *al-Kāfī*'s utility. See W. Madelung, 'Early Imāmī Theology as Reflected in the *Kitāb al-Kāfī* of al-Kulaynī,' in *The Study of Shiʿi Islam: History, Theology and Law*, ed. Gurdofrid Miskinzoda and Farhad Daftary, 465–74 (London: I. B. Tauris, 2014), at 465.

31 For Imāmī scholars' gradual rapprochement with Muʿtazilīs regarding *badāʾ* over the next two generations, see Hussein Ali Abdulsater, *Shi'i Doctrine, Mu'tazili Theology: al-Sharīf al-Murtaḍā and Imami Discourse* (Edinburgh: Edinburgh University Press, 2017), 201–2.

32 See McDermott, *Theology*, 329–33. *Badāʾ* was reportedly first invoked by al-Mukhtār in the first/seventh century, to explain the loss of battles in which he had told his followers in advance that God had promised them victory. While undoubtedly contentious from its inception, the idea has a clear persistence in Shīʿī and later in Imāmī circles. The second locus classicus of the doctrine is the death of Ismāʿīl the son of Jaʿfar al-Ṣādiq, who is widely narrated to have been designated by al-Ṣādiq as his successor before unfortunately predeceasing him. Thus told, the story casts obvious doubt on al-Ṣādiq's inspired knowledge and the divine provenance of his office. If the imams are appointed by God's will (let alone marked

as such since the dawn of creation), how could al-Ṣādiq make such a clear error in appointing a successor? One answer proffered was *badāʾ*: God simply changed his mind. Al-Mufīd laments (*Taṣḥīḥ*, 50), that when it comes to *badāʾ* the Imāmīs are slaves to traditions. In this complaint we see a theologian who has minimal tolerance for the concept of *badāʾ* acknowledging its tenacious presence in the Imāmī hadith corpus. Al-Ṣadūq, meanwhile, is also on the defensive in *al-Iʿtiqādāt*, but unlike al-Mufīd, he blames misunderstandings about *badāʾ* not on thoughtless following of the hadith but on the ignorance and malice of the Imāmīya's opponents. Al-Ṣadūq, *al-Iʿtiqādāt*, 90.

33 This meticulous dexterity with which al-Ṣadūq here orders his material, tradition by tradition, is exactly the explicatory precision the absence of which was so conspicuous in the first section.

34 See note 32 to this chapter.

35 '*Mā badā lillāh badāʾ kamā badā lahu fī Ismāʿīl*'.

36 Al-Ṣadūq, *al-Tawḥīd*, 366 (hadith no. 7).

37 In the chapter on God's will and intention in *al-Iʿtiqādāt* (67–74), al-Ṣadūq is vocally on the defensive, twice decrying those who misrepresent Imāmī beliefs on this point out of spite, and adducing a long list of Qurʾanic verses to support his position. He further provides a long case study on the death of al-Ḥusayn, rigorously demonstrating how God's utter control over human actions does not compromise the culpability of those who killed the imam. None of these concerns, however, are visible in the chapter of the same title in *al-Tawḥīd*.

38 Madelung and especially McDermott have recounted in some detail these divergences with Muʿtazilī doctrine. See Madelung, 'Imamism and Muʿtazilite Theology', 19–20; McDermott, *Theology*, 341–52.

39 Al-Ṣadūq, *al-Tawḥīd*, 369 (hadith no. 1), 371 (hadith no. 5).

40 Ibid., 373 (hadith no. 10).

41 Ibid., 371, (hadith no. 6).

42 Ibid., 393 (hadith no. 3).

43 Ibid., 397 (hadith no. 11).

44 Ibid., 399 (hadith no. 3).

The second section's treatment of the Qurʾan's (non-)createdness is, it should be noted, very similar to al-Ṣadūq's approach to the problem of predestination in the third section. It is difficult not to see this as rather disruptive to the proposed division of *al-Tawḥīd* into three sections! Nonetheless, it remains the case that the treatment of the Qurʾan is much shorter and distinctly isolated from the later discussion of predestination, constituting only one chapter among others dealing with the meanings of God's names and so on. It therefore seems plausible to read it as working as a case study within the endeavours of the second section, rather than as a misplaced bit of the sustained discussions of predestination that make up the third.

45 Al-Ṣadūq, *al-Tawḥīd*, 419–24. McDermott (*Theology*, 349) takes this discussion of the meanings of *qaḍāʾ* as a concession to the need for intellectual enquiry, and thus a retraction of al-Ṣadūq's oft-expressed disavowal of any discussion of the question, a reading which in turn contributes to his hypothesis that *al-Tawḥīd* is a later work than *al-Iʿtiqādāt* and *al-Hidāya*, written after al-Ṣadūq had been influenced by his rationalist neighbours at Rayy. This reading only seems viable if one is to disallow any coherence between al-Ṣadūq's various statements and cited hadiths across *al-Tawḥīd*, not least the fact that this statement of polyvalence immediately follows a formidable set of hadiths disavowing speculation on this matter. Conversely, as this chapter's analysis makes clear, these multiple meanings of qaḍāʾ are not a self-defeating acquiescence to speculation, but an illustration of the futility of confident judgements regarding both this matter of doctrine and the hadiths themselves.

46 Al-Ṣadūq, *al-Tawḥīd*, 425 (hadith no. 33).

47 Ibid., 426–7.

48 Ibid., 431 (hadith no. 8).

While McDermott (*Theology*, 349–50) discusses al-Ṣadūq's position on the fate of deceased infants, he does not cite this passage of *al-Tawḥīd*, despite its being by far al-Ṣadūq's most extensive discussion of the problem. This omission is noteworthy as it illustrates the limits of reading *al-Tawḥīd* purely as a doctrinal text. To do so is to find little in this chapter other than contradictions, with different descriptions of the Day of Judgement being presented which in turn may be variously interpreted to conflict with al-Ṣadūq's professed views on free will and predestination. When, however, one reads the text, as it announces itself, as a defence of the imams' traditions, the utility of these colourful, inconsistent eschatologies at this juncture in the text becomes apparent.

49 Al-Ṣadūq, *al-Tawḥīd*, 405 (hadith no. 10).

50 Ibid., 408 (hadith no. 16).

51 Ibid., 437 (hadith no. 2).

52 Ibid., 503 (hadith no. 29).

53 Indeed, in the account of al-Ṣadūq's own debates at the court of Rukn al-Dawla, we see exactly the same mode of debate. Al-Ṣadūq, as the account tells it, vanquishes his opponent simply by bringing forth hadiths that soundly and irrefutably contradict the latter's argument. See, for example, al-Ṣadūq, *Majālis maʿa Rukn al-Dawla*, 31–6.

54 As al-Riḍā berates the Zoroastrian priest he demands how, if he believes in Zoroaster and his miracles on the basis of hadiths, he can reject hadiths that prove the status of other, more Abrahamic prophets. This reasoning is reproduced almost verbatim in al-Ṣadūq's argument for belief in the Hidden Imam in *Kamāl al-dīn*. See al-Ṣadūq, *Kamāl al-dīn*, 34, 85, 113–14, 117, 134, etc.

55 Al-Ṣadūq, *al-Tawḥīd*, 481–2.

56 See also Cooperson, *Classical Arabic Biography*, 95–6.

57 For the importance of ʿAbbāsid persecution in al-Ṣadūq's vision of the occultation and its causes, see al-Ṣadūq, *Kamāl al-dīn*, 507–8 (hadith nos. 7–10).

58 As remarked upon in the preceding notes, both Madelung and McDermott have emphasised al-Ṣadūq's conciliatory attitude towards the Muʿtazila in *al-Tawḥīd*. McDermott, moreover, argues that the book's concessions to Muʿtazilī thought represents a later stage of al-Ṣadūq's thinking than *al-Hidāya* and *al-Iʿtiqādāt* (McDermott, *Theology*, 323, 341–52). In both cases, we have seen that this hypothesis is built upon isolated elements within the book; conspicuously, neither author engages with these resolutely combative closing portions of *al-Tawḥīd*, nor, indeed, with its middle section. Though *al-Tawḥīd*'s *asānīd* do suggest that it is a later work, more evidence is required to prove support for any hypothesis of a departure from the content of al-Ṣadūq's creeds. See Madelung, 'Imāmism and Mu'tazilite Theology', 17–19; McDermott, *Theology*, 315–22.

Chapter 5

1 An early version of some of the arguments of this chapter is contained in George Warner, 'Buddha or Yūdhāsaf? Images of the Hidden Imam in al-Ṣadūq's *Kamāl al-dīn*', *Mizan: Journal for the Study of Muslim Societies and Civilizations* 2/1 (2017).

2 Ibn Bābawayh the Elder's *al-Imāma wa'l-tabṣira* introduces itself as a work on the occultation, but while it discusses the question at length in its introduction, the remaining chapters of the text as it has come down to us do not discuss the twelfth imam. This is almost certainly because the work either was left incomplete or has been incompletely preserved, though some have suggested that the text indicates that Ibn Bābawayh the Elder was in fact a Wāqifī and did not accept the doctrine of twelve imams. This latter suggestion is rendered unlikely by the extensive body of texts to the contrary that al-Ṣadūq narrates from his father in *Kamāl al-dīn*. The Nuṣayrī al-Ḥusayn b. Ḥamdān al-Khuṣaybī's (d. 346/957 or 358/968) *al-Hidāya al-kubrā* speaks of twelve imams and give details of the occultation of the twelfth, as does pseudo-Masʿūdī's *Ithbāt al-waṣīya*, which seems to date from the fourth/tenth century. Ṭihrānī in *al-Dharīʿa* lists a great many books entitled *Kitāb al-ghayba*, but there were doubtless many more discussions of the topic under less obvious titles, not least many of the *Kitāb al-imāma*s that Ṭihrānī lists from the period.

3 Al-Ṣadūq, *Kamāl al-dīn*, 33–4. This exercise of drawing parallels between prophets and imams is an early (though not the first) instance of a tenacious Shīʿī and especially Imāmī preoccupation in this period. See Judith Loebenstein, 'Miracles in Šīʿī Thought: A Case Study of the Miracles Attributed to Imam Gaʿfar al-Ṣādiq',

Arabica 50 (2003): 199–244, at 235–7, 241–2; Matthew Pierce, *Twelve Infallible Men: The Imams and the Making of Shi'ism* (Cambridge, MA: Harvard University Press, 2016) 92, 108–9, 120, 130–2, 144–6; Khalid Sindawi, 'The Donkey of the Prophet in the Shīʿite Tradition', *Al-Masāq: Journal of the Medieval Mediterranean* 18 (2006): 87–98; 'Noah and Noah's Ark as the Primordial Model of Shiʿism in Shiʿite Literature', *Quaderni di Studi Arabi* 1 (2006): 29–48.

4 Al-Ṣadūq, *Kamāl al-dīn*, 74.

5 Here I must disagree with Yoshida, who states that al-Ṣadūq relies on the unusual operations of *Kamāl al-dīn* at the expense of any 'straightforward' discussion, neglecting the bibliographical evidence that al-Ṣadūq provided such discussions elsewhere. See Kyoko Yoshida, '*Qiṣaṣ* Contribution to the Theory of *Ghayba* in Twelver Shīʿism'. *Orient* 44 (2009): 91–104', at 97–8.

6 Al-Ṣadūq, *Kamāl al-dīn*, 34–49.

7 Ibid., 79.

8 Ibid., 62–75, 112.

9 The introduction contains several lengthy citations from earlier Imāmīs, often scholars of *kalām* like Ibn Qiba al-Rāzī, in debate over various aspects of the Imāmī view of the imamate and occultation. Though Sunnīs are referred to, the primary opponents of these arguments are Zaydīs and Muʿtazilīs, the former of whom al-Ṣadūq describes as 'our fiercest opponents' (*Kamāl al-dīn*, 157). These opponents often lay into the textual basis of the Imāmī arguments, accusing them of questionable interpretations and of lacking sufficient material to claim *tawātur*, among other things.

This is an important aspect of *Kamāl al-dīn* in that it manifests different polemical priorities to those of earlier Imāmī occultation literature. Al-Nuʿmānī's *Kitāb al-ghayba* directs itself primarily against Ismāʿīlī and especially Fāṭimid claims (al-Nuʿmānī, *al-Ghayba*, 179, 240–5), while both he and al-Kulaynī are recorded as authoring works against the Ismāʿīlīs (al-Najāshī, *Rijāl*, 361, 367). By contrast, *Kamāl al-dīn*'s fiercest engagement with Ismāʿīlī ideas is when Zaydī opponents cite the Ismāʿīlī genealogy of imams as a foil against the Imāmī claims (al-Ṣadūq, *Kamāl al-dīn*, 100–4). This shift in concerns reflects the history and geography of the three authors. Ismāʿīlī fortunes around Rayy and Qum declined sharply after 332/943, making them much less of a threat for al-Ṣadūq than they had been for al-Kulaynī. Al-Nuʿmānī, meanwhile, was active further west, placing him much closer to the Fāṭimid conquests that caused him concern. For the Ismāʿīlīs in Rayy see Stern, 'Early Ismā'īlī Missionaries', 79–80.

10 While al-Ṣadūq cites unnamed sources (for example *Kamāl al-dīn*, 93–4), elsewhere he names his sources, making *Kamāl al-dīn* a valuable repository of earlier fourth/tenth-century Imāmī theology. Most prominent in this regard are the lengthy quotations of Abū Sahl al-Nawbakhtī and of Ibn Qiba al-Rāzī,

including the latter's polemics against named Zaydī scholars, who are also cited at some length. (*Kamāl al-dīn*, 83–93, 118–57). Indeed, the quotations of Ibn Qiba in *Kamāl al-dīn* form the basis of Modarressi's groundbreaking study of him. See Modarressi, *Crisis and Consolidation*, 133–244.

11 Al-Ṣadūq, *Kamāl al-dīn*, 82; Muḥammad b. al-Ḥasan al-Ṭūsī, *al-Ghayba* (Beirut: Manshūrāt al-Fajr, 2012), 13, 143, *passim*.

12 The reliability of reports is, of course, crucial if their quantity is to have any value, and al-Ṣadūq certainly does not suggest that quantity supersedes the reliability of individual *asānīd*. Rather, his focus on the quantitative question of *tawātur* allows him to leave the matter of reports' comparative reliability largely implicit.

13 Al-Ṣadūq, *Kamāl al-dīn*, 114–15. The context of this detail is also thoroughly defensive. Al-Ṣadūq registers the voices interrogating whether the *tawātur* of reports confirming the Prophet's miracles is not rather stronger than that with which he affirms the occultation, responding with the intimation that those traditionists (*aṣḥāb al-ḥadīth*) who narrate such prophetic miracles as the splitting of the moon could not, in fact, muster more than three reports, contrary to his opponent's fancy that they could draw on ten or more.

14 Al-Ṣadūq, *Kamāl al-dīn*, 34, 85, 113–14, 117, 134 etc. For this role of the Brahmins in Islamic thought as those monotheists who reject all Abrahamic prophets, see Norman Calder, 'The Barāhima: Literary Construct and Historical Reality', *BSOAS* 57/1 (1994): 40–51.

15 Al-Ṣadūq, *Kamāl al-dīn*, 138. Al-Ṣadūq references the complaint of an antagonist that the Imāmīya have their own trusted sources just as every group does, and that the existence of such sources is not enough to make their testaments binding upon everyone.

16 Al-Ṣadūq, *Kamāl al-dīn*, 111, 157.

17 Here *shīʿa* stands as the Arabic word for a group of followers, as distinct from its common English usage, capitalized as a proper noun denoting a particular Muslim denomination.

18 Also frequently evoked are a group of hadiths in which Muḥammad states that the *qāʾim* will exhibit the *sunna* of one or more previous prophets, many of which will involve concealment, for example Moses's concealed birth or Muḥammad's use of the sword. See for example al-Ṣadūq, *Kamāl al-dīn*, 58, 176–7, 184.

19 Muhammad b. Muhammad al-Mufīd, *al-Irshād* (Beirut: Muʾassasat Āl al-Bayt li-Iḥyāʾ al-Turāth, 2008), 2:342–3.

20 Ibid., 2:342–3.

21 Al-Mufīd, *al-Fuṣūl al-ʿashara fī al-ghayba* (Qum: al-Muʾtamar al-ʿĀlamīya li-Alfīyat al-Shaykh al-Mufīd, 1993), 81–2.

22 Al-Nuʿmānī, *al-Ghayba* 65, 79–85. Al-Nuʿmānī refers to these texts as hadiths narrated by the *ʿāmma*, 'the masses', the usual Imāmī moniker for Sunnīs.

23 It should be emphasized that both these authors, like al-Nuʿmānī, focus on affirming more basic components such as the number of imams being twelve, rather than the historical minutiae of the twelfth imam's birth and disappearance.

24 Donner has noted the remarkable unanimity with which the early Islamic historical tradition agreed on the Muslim community's narratives of origins, pointing to the great extent to which writers in the third/ninth and fourth/tenth centuries were constrained from any attempt to generate new narratives by a redoubtable body of widely known earlier material. See Fred Donner, *Narratives of Islamic Origins: The Beginning of Islamic Historical Writing* (Princeton: Darwin Press, 1998), 286–7. On the widespread acceptance and polemical use of the Ghadīr Khumm traditions in the early period, see Dakake, *Charismatic Community*, 33–48.

Al-Ṣadūq himself makes some effort to tie the Hidden Imam into more recognizable history, giving an account of how the ʿAbbāsids, quite convinced that al-ʿAskarī had a son, made great, conspicuous and widely documented efforts to find him (*Kamāl al-dīn*, 76–7, 506). This account, however, is not recorded either by non-Imāmī historians or by even historians who were favourable to the Imāmī position. Al-Masʿūdī, for example, whose interests in Imāmī beliefs are nowhere clearer than when he notes the twelfth imam's birth as apparent fact, makes no mention of an ʿAbbāsid response. See ʿAlī b. al-Ḥusayn al-Masʿūdī, *Murūj al-dhahab* (Beirut: al-Maktaba al-ʿAṣrīya, 2005) 4:160.

25 We will look at the instabilities in al-Ṣadūq's material in detail later on in the chapter. Al-Kulaynī's corpus is a more sober one than al-Ṣadūq's, excluding almost all accounts of believers actually meeting the imam, but his hadiths are still punctuated by incomplete *asānīd* and the highly miraculous. Al-Kulaynī, *al-Kāfī*, 1:514–25. Characteristically, all of al-Mufīd's accounts of the Hidden Imam in *al-Irshād* are found in *al-Kāfī*. Al-Mufīd, *al-Irshād*, 2:351–4.

26 Al-Ṣadūq, *Kamāl al-dīn*, 169–71.

27 Ibid., 173–6, 180, 189–90.

28 While any direct precursor has yet to be identified, other Shīʿīs were certainly making use of similar material at around al-Ṣadūq's time. As *Kamāl al-dīn*'s own title illustrates, comparable works might be invisible in the bibliographical record. The most similar extant text to *Kamāl al-dīn* in terms of its use of *qiṣaṣ* texts, and one that may well be earlier, is pseudo-Masʿūdī's *Ithbāt al-waṣīya*. It puts a similar corpus to a similar effect, though the focus is less on the twelfth imam and more on establishing patterns between the lives of all the imams and those of past prophets. Unlike *Kamāl al-dīn*, *Ithbāt al-waṣīya* also lacks any pertinent statement of purpose or method. Its uncertain date and authorship, meanwhile, render questions of influence between the two books difficult to answer – the very similarity between *Ithbāt al-waṣīya* and *Kamāl al-dīn* is a significant piece of evidence for dating

it. *Ithbāt al-waṣīya*'s *asānīd* point to a date in the first half of the fourth/tenth century, narrating from such late-third/ninth-century figures as Saʿd b. ʿAbd Allāh al-Ashʿarī and ʿAbd al-Raḥmān b. Jaʿfar al-Ḥimyarī, but a later date is far from impossible; indeed, the work's *qiṣaṣ* texts lack full *asānīd* altogether. If nothing else, the book attests to a circulation of Imāmī-influenced *qiṣaṣ* texts around the time al-Ṣadūq was writing. For discussions of *Ithbāt al-waṣīya*'s provenance (albeit rather more focussed on the fact that al-Masʿūdī probably didn't write it than on who did), see Charles Pellat, 'Masʿūdī et l'imamisme', in *Le shi'isme imamite*, ed. Robert Brunschvig, 69–90 (Paris: Presses universitaires de France, 1970); Khalidi, *Islamic Historiography*, 136–42. For an account of the very different use to which Ismāʿīlīs of the period were putting such material, see David Hollenberg, *Beyond the Qurʾān: Early Ismāʿīlī Taʾwīl and the Secrets of the Prophets* (Columbia: University of South Carolina Press, 2016), 79–125. Yoshida notes in his discussion of *Kamāl al-dīn* that stories about al-Khiḍr, at least, appear in Shīʿī literature in the mid-fourth/tenth century, a contention for which he cites Franke, who, in turn, cites *Kamāl al-dīn* as the earliest exemplar. See Yoshida, '*Qiṣaṣ*', 94; Patrick Franke, *Begegnung mit Khiḍr: Quellenstudien zum Imaginären im traditionellen Islam* (Beirut: Orient-Institut Beirut, 2000), 11; also note 3 to this chapter.

29 Al-Ṣadūq, *Kamāl al-dīn*, 231.

30 *Naṣṣ* had long been a cornerstone of Imāmī imamology. An imam was known to be the imam on the basis of his infallibility and knowledge, but also through his having been explicitly named as the next imam by his predecessor. See al-Ṣadūq, *Kamāl al-dīn*, 46; Rodrigo Adem, 'Classical Naṣṣ Doctrines in Imami Shīʿism: On the Usage of an Expository Term', *Shi'i Studies Review* 1 (2017): 42–71.

31 The emphasis on *tawātur* regarding *naṣṣ*-texts in particular is also deployed by al-Nuʿmānī. Al-Nuʿmānī, *al-Ghayba*, 97–140.

32 Al-Ṣadūq, *Kamāl al-dīn*, 470–1.

33 The two instinctive translations of this term correlate closely with al-Ṣadūq's two probative methods, his use of *dalāla* shifting between 'sign' and 'proof' in different contexts. When *tawātur* is emphasized the *dalāla* appears as proof, the miracle by which the imam is confirmed as such. Elsewhere in *Kamāl al-dīn*, however, we see the faithful in search of 'signs' of the imam, such as might direct them towards him.

34 Prominent examples of this *dalāʾil al-nubuwwa* genre include works by al-Qāḍī ʿAbd al-Jabbār, Abū Nuʿaym, al-Iṣfahānī (d. 430/1038) and Aḥmad b. al-Ḥusayn al-Bayhaqī (d. 458/1066).

35 Both al-Kulaynī's *al-Kāfī* and al-Khuṣaybī's *al-Hidāya al-kubrā* feature extensive collections of reported miracles identified as the imams' *dalāʾil*. See al-Kulaynī, *al-Kāfī*, 1:439–525; al-Ḥusayn b. Ḥamadān al-Khuṣaybī, *al-Hidāya al-kubrā* (Damascus: Muʾassasat al-Balāgh, 2005), 209, 214, 234 etc.

36 For example, al-Ṣadūq, *Kamāl al-dīn*, 515 (hadith no. 9), 521, 528 (hadith no. 28).

37 McDermott, *Theoogy*, 112–14; Loebenstein, 'Miracles', 206–10; al-Qāḍī ʿAbd al-Jabbār b. Aḥmad al-Asadābādī, *al-Mughnī fī abwāb al-tawhīd wa-al-ʿadl* (Cairo: Ishrāf Duktūr Ṭaha Ḥusayn, 1962), 15:247–56. While al-Ṣadūq has made it clear in his introduction that he is talking primarily to a Shīʿī readership, we need look no further than that same introduction to learn that there were Shīʿī, indeed Imāmī voices who shared the Muʿtazilī view on this matter. In one of al-Ṣadūq's long citations of Ibn Qiba al-Rāzī, we see the latter state his view that the imams cannot have knowledge of the unseen. Al-Ṣadūq, *Kamāl al-dīn*, 140. Al-Mufīd, too, cites Muʿtazilī incredulity at Imāmī claims about the occultation and the imam's longevity in particular, himself not admitting the broader array of wonders that al-Ṣadūq presents in *Kamāl al-dīn*. Al-Mufīd, *al-Fuṣūl al-ʿashara*, 81–2, 91–2.

38 For example, al-Ṣadūq, *Kamāl al-dīn*, 463–4 (hadith nos. 1, 4).

39 Al-Ṣadūq, *Kamāl al-dīn*, 480.

40 Ibid., 457, 474, 503.

41 Ibid., 474–6, 528.

42 See p. 85 of Chapter 3 and p. 77 of Chapter 3 for examples of al-Ṣadūq in, respectively, more and less cautions mode on this issue. In *al-Iʿtiqādāt*, meanwhile, he is clear that the imams can perform miracles. Al-Ṣadūq, *al-Iʿtiqādāt*, 294.

43 Al-Mufīd, *al-Irshād*, 355–67.

44 It seems the receipt of a letter from the Hidden Imam is not in and of itself enough to constitute a *dalāla*; rather, there must be some further miraculous element to the story. Al-Ṣadūq and al-Kulaynī narrate reports in which a believer corresponds with the imam without any wondrous occurrence, but such reports are absent from the collection al-Ṣadūq offers here. In al-Kulaynī's case, too, the report in question is not in his chapter on the twelfth imam's *dalāʾil* but in a chapter regarding *khums*. Al-Ṣadūq, *al-Faqīh*, 2:102 (hadith no. 2010); al-Kulaynī, *al-Kāfī*, 1:545 (hadith no. 12). For an alternative reading of the significance of these encounters, see Mohammad Ali Amir-Moezzi, *The Spirituality of Shi'i Islam: Beliefs and Practices* (London: I. B. Tauris, 2010), 431–60.

45 Al-Ṣadūq, *Kamāl al-dīn*, 467, 470, 549.

46 See, for instance, Abū Ḥanīfa b. al-Nuʿmān al-Qāḍī al-Nuʿmān, *Iftitāḥ al-Daʿwa*, ed. Farḥāt Dashrāwī (Tunis: al-Sharika al-Tūnisīya li'l-Tawzīʿ, 1986), 4; for Ismāʿīlī criticism of the Imāmī doctrine of occultation, see Ghaemmaghami, *Encounters*, 91–3. The Muʿtazilī al-Qāḍī ʿAbd al-Jabbār counts narrated absurdities as a lamentable feature of Shīʿī thought, including Imāmī thought, a characteristic attitude to which al-Mufīd's writings on the occultation respond directly. See note 37 to this chapter; al-Qāḍī ʿAbd al-Jabbār, *al-Mughnī*, 20.ii:172, 188, *passim*.

47 This is exactly what al-Mufīd does in his own use of *qiṣaṣ* texts and *muʿammarūn* texts, deploying them in answer to the specific question of the imam's longevity,

without resorting to any expansion of the imam's biography beyond this single detail. Al-Mufīd, *al-Fuṣūl al-ʿashara*, 83–103.

48 Al-Nuʿmānī, *al-Ghayba*, 114, *passim*.

An important element of these texts is the lack of any overt distinction between the lesser and greater occultations. Other Imāmī authors are willing to admit witnesses to the imam in the lesser occultation (not least the emissaries) but not the greater, but al-Ṣadūq makes no such distinction. Ghaemmaghami has argued convincingly that all of al-Ṣadūq's encounter narratives are datable to the minor occultation, but does not observe how this only highlights al-Ṣadūq's obfuscation of any difference between the two – though he was surely aware of this aspect of his texts, he does not point it out, let alone seek to draw theological implications from it. A reading of these texts as constituting an assertion that the Hidden Imam cannot be encountered in the greater occultation is, therefore, highly implausible; rather, al-Ṣadūq suppresses this element of the texts the better to suggest the continuing possibility of meeting the imam. See Ghaemmaghami, *Encounters*, 105–32.

49 Al-Ṣadūq, *Kamāl al-dīn*, 380 (hadith no. 34), 385 (hadith no. 49), 468 (hadith nos. 7, 8).

50 Ibid., 175–6.

51 Al-Ṣadūq, *Kamāl al-dīn*, 468 (hadith no. 10). Though al-ʿAmrī's account is evocative, it should be noted that al-Ṣadūq's material does not restrict sightings to the imam's emissaries.

52 Al-Ṣadūq, *Kamāl al-dīn*, 473 (hadith no. 19), 503–4, 513–14.

53 Curiously, this narrative appears twice in modern editions of *Kamāl al-dīn*, once in the chapter on those who met the Hidden Imam and once, more incongruously, in the chapter on those who received written messages from him. Ghaffārī acknowledges this discrepancy in his edition; see al-Ṣadūq, *Kamāl al-dīn*, 522.

54 For example, al-Ṣadūq, *Kamāl al-dīn*, 202–3, 223–7.

55 Ibid., 188–90.

56 Ibid., 462–506.

57 Ibid., 158–64.

58 For al-Ṣadūq's typically absolute views on prophetic infallibility, see al-Ṣadūq, *al-Iʿtiqādāt*, 304–7. In *al-Tawḥīd*, meanwhile, he characteristically intervenes to ensure that his hadiths are not read as contradicting this doctrine. See for example al-Ṣadūq, *al-Tawḥīd*, 128.

59 Al-Kulaynī, *al-Kāfī*, 1:178–9.

60 Al-Ṣadūq, *Kamāl al-dīn*, 169.

61 Ibid., 194–232. Outside the Imāmīya, the idea of such a gap is a common and long-standing one. Indeed, other Imāmī groups seem to have believed that God could remove his *ḥujja* if angered. See al-Nawbakhtī, *Firaq al-shīʿa*, 87.

62 Al-Ṣadūq, *Kamāl al-dīn*, 684–8.

63 Ibid., 173, 193.

64 Ibid., 433.

65 See Andrew George, *The Babylonian Gilgamesh Epic: Introduction, Critical Edition and Cuneiform Texts* (Oxford: Oxford University Press, 2003), 54–70.

66 Bray has also explored this concept of myth and mythography, understood as the creation and manipulation of images and motifs that have a particularly pervasive and semantically fertile presence in a given literary context, in ʿAbbāsid literature, focussing on the *adīb* Ibn ʿAbd Rabbih. See Julia Bray, 'Abbasid Myth and the Human Act', in *On Fiction and Adab in Medieval Arabic Literature*, ed. Philip F. Kennedy, 1–49 (Wiesbaden: Harrassowitz Verlag, 2005).

67 Al-Ṣadūq, *Kamāl al-dīn*, 465–8.

68 Ibid., 422–3.

69 Ibid., 191.

70 Though it is only with al-Ṣadūq's generation that the problem of the imam outliving a normal human lifespan becomes inevitable, the concern to persuade the faithful that his return was not imminent seems to have been longstanding – it is already emphatically there in al-Nuʿmānī. Crucially, it seems to have been widely accepted by Shīʿīs that the *qāʾim* would appear as a heroic youth; the claim of the first Fāṭimid imam-caliph to be the returning *qāʾim* is said to have been met with suspicion on account of his having reached the advanced age of 35. Heinz Halm, *The Empire of the Mahdi: The Rise of the Fāṭimids* (Leiden: Brill, 1996), 159–60.

71 Al-Ṣadūq, *Kamāl al-dīn*, 582, 586.

72 Al-Ṣadūq's source cannot be known for certain – he once names it as 'The Book of *Muʿammarūn*', but gives no author. A probable though possibly indirect source is the *Kitāb al-muʿammarīn* of Sahl b. Muḥammad al-Sijistānī (d. 255/869), with which al-Ṣadūq's selection has a great deal of material in common.

73 Al-Ṣadūq, *Kamāl al-dīn*, 578, 581.

74 Ibid., 575, 581.

75 Ibid., 601.

76 Ibid., 557, 578–81.

77 Ibid., 564.

78 Ibid., 556–9, 601.

79 Ibid., 558–9.

80 Ibid., 578. Tellingly, al-Ṣadūq inserts no such objection earlier on in *Kamāl al-dīn* when Alexander, at the end of his wanderings, comes across a land where there live descendants of Moses's people in a perfect society, with whom Alexander elects to dwell for the rest of his days. *Kamāl al-dīn*, 433–5.

81 Al-Ṣadūq, *Kamāl al-dīn*, 480–1.

82 The printed text of *Kamāl al-dīn* renders the name Ḥammādawayh; however, Khuramawayh b. Aḥmad b. Ṭūlūn, ruler of Egypt, is clearly meant.

83 Al-Ṣadūq, *Kamāl al-dīn*, 588–90.

84 Ibid., 561, 568–9.

85 Unlike the son of Aḥmad b. Ṭūlūn, the Buddha, from whose title the word Yūdhāsaf ultimately derives, is a long way from any historical memory that al-Ṣadūq might be party to. Yūdhāsaf becomes Josephat in European contexts, a figure of legend with similarly little self-conscious connection to any Buddhist milieu. Although other Arabic versions of the story are nearer the mark in their location of dots with *Būdāsf* (as followed by Gimaret), and though it is not apparent whether the shift from b to y comes from al-Ṣadūq or a later scribe, to 'correct' the text would be to impose a quite fictitious notion that al-Ṣadūq or the scribe was somehow mistaken in giving the name Yūdhāsaf to the protagonist of this text's wondrous adventures, when in fact Yūdhāsaf is perfectly named to perform the task intended for him. It seems judicious, then, to leave him as he is.

Not only is al-Ṣadūq's recourse to such material highly unusual in the works of an Imāmī *faqīh*, but his Yūdhāsaf texts in fact include a number of narratives that are not preserved in any Buddhist source. This has drawn some attention to these texts and their provenance, but not thus far to their role in *Kamāl al-dīn* itself. See Warner, 'Buddha or Yūdhāsaf?', 18. Gimaret undertook to produce a translation and edition of *Kitāb Bilawhar wa Būdāsf*, based on a manuscript of *Kamāl al-dīn* and other Arabic exemplars of the story. See Daniel Gimaret, *Kitāb Bilawhar wa Būdāsf* (Beirut: Dar el-Mashreq, 1972). Stern and Walzer give a translation and analysis of those stories in the text that are unknown in any Buddhist source, and Matar examines an instance of continued interest in the text for later Shīʿī readers. Zeina Matar, 'The Buddha Legend: A Footnote from an Arabic Source', *Oriens* 32 (1990): 440–2; S. M. Stern, and Sophie Walzer, *Three Unknown Buddhist Stories in an Arabic Version* (Oxford: Cassirer, 1971). For an analysis of the potential sources of the text in *Kamāl al-dīn*, see François de Blois, 'On the Sources of the Barlaam Romance, or How Buddha Became a Christian Saint', in *Literarische Stoffe und ihre Gestaltung in mitteliranischer Zeit Kolloquium anlässlich des 70. Geburtstages von Werner Sundermann*, ed. Christiane Reck, Desmond Durkin-Meisterernst, and Dieter Weber, 7–26 (Wiesbaden: Dr Ludwig Reichert Verlag, 2009).

86 Some manuscripts omit the *isnād* entirely. See al-Ṣadūq, *Kamāl al-dīn*, 603.

87 Al-Ṣadūq, *Kamāl al-dīn*, 603.

88 Al-Ṣadūq is rather ambiguous regarding whether the Yūdhāsaf stories are to be considered equivalent to the *muʿammarūn* texts in terms of their value. He refers to 'this hadith [the Yūdhāsaf stories] and what else in this book resembles it', (*Kamāl al-dīn*, 667) and then again to 'this hadith [the Yūdhāsaf stories] and those of the reports (*akhbār*) of the *muʿammarūn* that resemble it' (*Kamāl al-dīn*, 668),

as aiming to attract curious readers, but goes no further in determining which of his other texts this might include.

89 India has a history of playing the role of the exotic other in ʿAbbāsid literature. This receives abundant illustration in the *ʿAjāʾib al-Hind* of Buzurg b. Shahriyār (d. 342/954), whose exotic tales must represent a much more widespread popular literature along similar lines now lost to us. A different perspective comes from al-Bīrūnī at the start of his laboriously researched work on India, where he vents not a little frustration at people's credulity with regard to this subject matter. See Muḥammad b. Aḥmad al-Bīrūnī, *Taḥqīq mā li'l-Hind* (Qum: Intishārāt-i Bīdār, 1418 h), 1–6.

90 See Bray, 'ʿAbbasid Myth'.

91 See especially al-Ṣadūq, *Kamāl al-dīn*, 641–5.

92 In his short chapter on the reason (*ʿilla*) for the occultation, al-Ṣadūq gives ten hadiths that offer a variety of explanations, including that the imam should be hidden so that he is not be compelled to give allegiance to any other, and that he is hidden out of fear of being killed. Further reasons are meanwhile suggested sporadically across the text. Al-Ṣadūq, *Kamāl al-dīn*, 507–9.

93 Al-Ṣadūq, *Kamāl al-dīn*, 463; Q 2:260.

94 Q 17:65.

95 See al-Ṣadūq, *Kamāl al-dīn*, 417–23, 561–2. A magisterial survey of al-Khiḍr's appearances and figurings in Islamic literature is supplied by Franke in his *Begegnung mit Khiḍr*. As mentioned earlier, Franke in fact notes *Kamāl al-dīn* as the first known instance of al-Khiḍr's being put to use in Shīʿī literatures. Yoshida has also observed al-Khiḍr's role in *Kamāl al-dīn*, as well as supplying a valuable comparison with his role in the writings of al-Mufīd and al-Ṭūsī on the occultation. Franke, *Begegnung mit Khidr*; Yoshida, '*Qiṣaṣ*'.

96 Al-Ṣadūq, *Kamāl al-dīn*, 123, 510, 676–7.

97 For example, al-Ṣadūq, *Kamāl al-dīn*, 91, 284, 368, 458, 469. In a number of such instances (though by no means all), the name Muḥammad is written with the letters of 'Muḥammad' separated in their isolated forms (m-ḥ-m-d), clearly in a gesture of dissimilation. The gesture is an interesting one in that it requires little imagination to deduce the name being represented, though may, in its reduction of the name to voiceless consonants, evoke the notion that it should be written but not uttered. Unfortunately, the early history of this device and its pertinence to al-Ṣadūq is difficult to study. It is self-evidently extremely susceptible to the whims of copyists, who might join the letters up or separate them depending on their sensibilities, be they the copyists of al-Ṣadūq's own written sources or those of the manuscripts of *Kamāl al-dīn* over the past millennium. Only an autograph manuscript from al-Ṣadūq's own hand or one endorsed by him – both unlikely eventualities – could clarify his own position on the matter. The device is shared

with other works on the Hidden Imam, for example, al-Kulaynī, *al-Kāfī*, 1:514 (hadith no. 1).

98 This ambivalence between including hadiths that prohibit naming the imam and including other hadiths that do exactly that is common to al-Ṣadūq and other early occultation literature. See, al-Nuʿmānī, *al-Ghayba*, 103, 166–7, 212–17; al-Kulaynī, *al-Kāfī*, 332–3, 514 (hadith no. 1). The apparent contradiction may reflect a distinction between naming the imam out loud and writing his name, though this is not clearly enunciated.

99 Al-Ṣadūq, *Kamāl al-dīn*, 466–7, 522–3.

100 For example, ibid., 509–12 (hadith nos. 1, 3, 4). Dakake has also explored this interplay between secrecy and the written word in the broader context of early Shīʿī literature. See Dakake, 'Hiding in Plain Sight', 347–9.

101 For example, al-Ṣadūq, *Kamāl al-dīn*, 473.

102 While it is true that in the encounter narratives this vision, of course, precedes an actual encounter with the imam, *Kamāl al-dīn*'s stories are not short of believers receiving messages in the forms of dreams and visions. See *Kamāl al-dīn*, 559.

103 Al-Ṣadūq, *Kamāl al-dīn*, 529.

104 Ibid., 32–3.

105 Yoshida interprets this aspect of *Kamāl al-dīn* somewhat in reverse, describing al-Ṣadūq's use of the al-Khiḍr narrative as serving to support his view that the imam's occultation is prefigured in the occultations of earlier figures (Yoshida, '*Qiṣaṣ*', 95). This casts the occultations of previous prophets as something that al-Ṣadūq has set out a priori to prove, whereas in fact they evidently function as a means towards al-Ṣadūq's primary objective of convincing the reader that the current occultation, that of the twelfth imam, is real.

106 The Yūdhāsaf texts, for instance, end with Yūdhāsaf himself transforming from seeker to sage, such that he himself may go forth as 'an imam for the people who may call them to paradise'. al-Ṣadūq, *Kamāl al-dīn*, 663–7.

107 It is worth recalling the explicit denial in *al-Tawḥīd* of humanity's ability to deduce even such essential truths as these without a *ḥujja*. See Chapter 4, 102.

That al-Ṣadūq exploits the ambiguity of hadith compilation should not surprise us. Atomizing readings of hadith literature are not a modern invention; rather, hadiths never ceased to be in circulation and to have meaning beyond any one setting a compiler put them in – their centrifugal meaning as Burge puts it (Myth, Meaning and the Order of Words, 216–21ff.). Compilers, especially compilers of hadith, know that their agency more often than not remains concealed behind the greater authority of the words that they transmit, and use this to their advantage, as has been observed of a number of premodern authors. See Tokatly, 'The *A'lām al-ḥadīth* of al-Khaṭṭābī', 60, 87, Burge, 'Jalāl al-Dīn al-Suyūṭī', 299, Hodgson, *The Venture of Islam*, 1:353–8.

Bibliography

Primary sources

Ibn ʿAbd Rabbih, Aḥmad b. Muḥammad. *Al-ʿIqd al-farīd*. Ed. Mufīd Muḥammad Qamīḥa. Beirut: Dār al-Kutub al-ʿIlmīya, 1983.

Al-Ābī, Manṣūr b. al-Ḥusayn. *Nathr al-Durr*. Beirut: Dār al-Kutub al-ʿIlmīya, 2008.

Ibn Abī al-Dunyā, ʿAbd Allāh b. Muḥammad. *Majmūʿat al-rasāʾil*. Beirut: Dār al-Nadwa al-Islāmīya, 1988.

Al-Asadābādī, al-Qāḍī ʿAbd al-Jabbār b. Aḥmad al-Hamadhānī. *al-Mughnī fī abwāb al-tawhīd wa'l-ʿadl*. Cairo: Ishrāf Duktūr Ṭaha Ḥusayn, 1962.

Al-Asadābādī, ʿAbd al-Jabbār b. Aḥmad al-Hamadhānī. *Tathbīt Dalāʾil al-Nubuwwa*. Beirut: Dār al-ʿArabīya, 1966.

Al-Ashʿarī, ʿAlī b. Ismāʿīl. *Maqālāt al-islāmīyīn wa'khtilāf al-muṣallīn*. Ed. Muḥammad Muḥyī al-Dīn ʿAbd al-Ḥamīd. Beirut: al-Maktaba al-ʿAṣrīya, 1990.

Al-ʿAskarī, Abū Hilāl al-Ḥasan b. ʿAbd Allāh. *al-Awāʾil*. Damascus: Wizārat al-Thaqāfa wa'l-Irshād al-Qawmī, 1975.

Ibn Bābawayh, ʿAlī b. al-Ḥusayn ('Ibn Bābawayh the Elder'). *al-Imāma wa'l-tabṣira min al-ḥayra*. Qum: Madrasat al-Imām al-Mahdī, 1985.

Ibn Baṭṭa, ʿUbayd Allāh al-ʿUkbarī. *al-Sharḥ wa'l-ibāna ʿalā uṣūl al-sunna wa'l-diyāna*. Ed. Riḍā b. Naʿsān Muʿṭī. Medina: Maktabat al-ʿUlūm wa'l-Ḥikam, 2002.

Barakāt, Zakarīyā. 'Radd shubahāt ḥawla ʿilm al-ḥadīth ʿinda al-Shīʿa.' https://www.aqaed.com/faq/3123/, n.d., accessed August 30 2021..

Al-Barqī, Aḥmad b. Muḥammad. *al-Maḥāsin*. Beirut: al-Majmaʿ al-ʿĀlamī li-Ahl al-Bayt, 2011.

Al-Bayhaqī, Ibrāhīm b. Muḥammad. *Al-Maḥāsin wa'l-Masāwī*. Beirut: Dār Ṣādir, 1960.

Al-Bīrūnī, Muḥammad b. Aḥmad. *Taḥqīq mā li'l-Hind*. Qum: Intishārāt-i Bīdār, 1418 h.

Ibn al-Ghaḍāʾirī, Aḥmad b. al-Ḥusayn. *al-Rijāl*. Ed. Muḥammad Riḍā al-Ḥusaynī al-Jalālī. Qum: Dār al-Ḥadīth, 1380 sh.

Al-Jaṣṣāṣ, Aḥmad b. ʿAlī. *al-Fuṣūl fī al-uṣūl*. Kuwait City: Wizārat al-Awqāf wa'l-Shuʾūn al-Islāmīya, 1994.

Al-Kashshī, Muḥammad b. ʿUmar. *Rijāl al-Kashshī*. Tehran: Sāzmān-i Chāp wa Intishārāt, 1382 sh.

Al-Khuṣaybī, al-Ḥusayn b. Ḥamadān. *al-Hidāya al-kubrā*. Damascus: Muʾassasat al-Balāgh, 2005.

Al-Kulaynī, Muḥammad b. Yaʿqūb. *al-Kāfī*. Tehran: Dār al-Kutub al-Islāmīya, 1388 sh.

Ibn Mandah, Muḥammad b. Isḥāq. *al-Tawḥīd*. Ed. ʿAlī al-Faqīhī. Medina: al-Jāmiʿa al-Islāmīya bi'l-Madīna, 1989.

Al-Masʿūdī, ʿAlī b. al-Ḥusayn. *Murūj al-dhahab*. Beirut: al-Maktaba al-ʿAṣrīya, 2005.

Ibn Mattawayh, al-Ḥasan al-Najrānī. *al-Tadhkira fī aḥkām al-jawāhir wa'l-a'rāḍ*. Ed. Sāmī Naṣr Luṭf, and Fayṣal Badīr 'Ūn. Cairo: Dār al-Thaqāfa, 1975.

Al-Māwardī, 'Alī b. Muḥammad. *Adab al-dunyā wa'l-dīn*. Cairo: al-Dār al-Miṣīya al-Lubnānīya, 2014.

Al-Miskawayh, Aḥmad b. Muḥammad. *Al-Ḥikma al-khālida*. Cairo: Maktabat al-Nahḍa al-Miṣrīya, 1952.

Al-Miskawayh, Aḥmad b. Muḥammad. *Tahdhīb al-akhlāq*. Beirut: American University of Beirut, 1966.

Al-Mufīd, Muḥammad b. Muḥammad. *al-Masā'il al-ṣāghānīya*. Qum: al-Mu'tamar al-'Ālamīya li-Alfīyat al-Shaykh al-Mufīd, 1993.

Al-Mufīd, Muḥammad b. Muḥammad. *al-Muqni'a*. Qum: al-Mu'tamar al-'Ālamīya li-Alfīyat al-Shaykh al-Mufīd, 1993.

Al-Mufīd, Muḥammad b. Muḥammad. *al-Fuṣūl al-'ashara fī al-ghayba*. Qum: al-Mu'tamar al-'Ālamīya li-Alfīyat al-Shaykh al-Mufīd, 1993.

Al-Mufīd, Muḥammad b. Muḥammad. *Taṣḥīḥ al-i'tiqād bi-ṣawāb al-intiqād*. Beirut: Dār al-Kitāb al-Islāmī, 1983.

Al-Mufīd, Muḥammad b. Muḥammad. *al-Irshād*. Beirut: Mu'assasat Āl al-Bayt li-Iḥyā' al-Turāth, 2008.

Al-Murtaḍā, al-Sharīf 'Alī b. al-Ḥusayn. *Amālī al-Murtaḍā: Ghurar al-fawā'id wa durar al-qalā'id*. Qum: Dhawā al-Qurbā, 1435 h.

Ibn al-Nadīm, Muḥammad b. Isḥāq. *al-Fihrist*. Beirut: Dār al-Ma'rifa, n. d.

Al-Najāshī, Aḥmad b. 'Alī. *Rijāl al-Najāshī*. Beirut: Sharikat al-A'lamī li'l-Maṭbū'āt, 2010.

Al-Nawbakhtī. *Firaq al-shī'a*. Istanbul: Jamī'at Mustashriqīn Almānīya, 1931.

Al-Nu'mānī, Muḥammad b. Ibrāhīm. *al-Ghayba*. Beirut: Mu'assasat al-A'lamī li'l-Maṭbū'āt, 2013.

Al-Qāḍī al-Nu'mān, Abū Ḥanīfa al-Nu'mān b. Muḥammad. *Sharḥ al-akhbār fī faḍā'il al-a'imma al-aṭhār*. Mu'assasat al-Nashr al-Islāmī, 1431 h.

Al-Qāḍī al-Nu'mān, Abū Ḥanīfa al-Nu'mān b. Muḥammad. *Iftitāḥ al-Da'wa*. Ed. Farḥāt Dashrāwī. Tunis: al-Sharika al-Tūnisīya li'l-Tawzī', 1986.

Ibn Qūlawayh, Ja'far b. Muḥammad. *Kāmil al-ziyārāt*. Beirut: Mu'assasat al-A'lamī li'l-Maṭbū'āt, 2009.

Al-Qummī, 'Alī b. Ibrāhīm. *Tafsīr al-Qummī*. Qum: Mu'assasat al-Kitāb li'l-Ṭibā'a wa'l-Nashr, 1404 h.

Ibn Qutayba , 'Abd Allāh b. Muslim. *'Uyūn al-akhbār*. Beirut: al-Maktab al-Islāmī, 2008.

Al-Raḍī, al-Sharīf Muḥammad b. al-Ḥusayn. *Khaṣā'iṣ al-a'imma*. Beirut: Mu'assasat al-A'lamī li'l-Maṭbū'āt, 2001.

Al-Raḍī, al-Sharīf Muḥammad b. al-Ḥusayn. *Nahj al-Balāgha*. Beirut: Dār al-Ḥujja al-Bayḍā', 2009.

Al-Ṣadūq (Ibn Bābawayh), Muḥammad b. 'Alī. *Mashyakhat al-faqīh*. Ed. Muḥammad Ja'far Shams al-Dīn. Beirut: Dār al-Ta'āruf li'l-Maṭbū'āt, n. d.

Al-Ṣadūq (Ibn Bābawayh), Muḥammad b. 'Alī. *Man lā yaḥḍuruhu al-faqīh*. Ed. Ḥusayn al-A'lamī. Beirut: Mu'assasat al-A'lamī li'l-Maṭbū'āt, 1986.

Al-Ṣadūq (Ibn Bābawayh), Muḥammad b. ʿAlī. *al-Tawḥīd*. Beirut: Muʾassasat al-Aʿlamī li'l-Maṭbūʿāt, 2006.

Al-Ṣadūq (Ibn Bābawayh), Muḥammad b. ʿAlī. *ʿIlal al-sharāʾiʿ*. Beirut: Muʾassasat al-Aʿlamī li'l-Maṭbūʿāt, 2007.

Al-Ṣadūq (Ibn Bābawayh), Muḥammad b. ʿAlī. *al-Mawāʿiẓ*. In *Muṣannafāt al-Ṣadūq*, edited by Editorial Committee, Maktabat Pārsā, 293–384. Qum: Maktabat Pārsā, 2008.

Al-Ṣadūq (Ibn Bābawayh), Muḥammad b. ʿAlī. *Faḍāʾil al-ashhur al-thalātha*. In *Muṣannafāt al-Ṣadūq*, edited by Editorial Committee, Maktabat Pārsā, 385–488. Qum: Maktabat Pārsā, 2008.

Al-Ṣadūq (Ibn Bābawayh), Muḥammad b. ʿAlī. *Muṣādaqat al-ikhwān*. In *Muṣannafāt al-Ṣadūq*, edited by Editorial Committee, Maktabat Pārsā, 233–92. Qum: Maktabat Pārsā, 2008.

Al-Ṣadūq (Ibn Bābawayh), Muḥammad b. ʿAlī. *Ṣifāt al-shīʿa*. In *Muṣannafāt al-Ṣadūq*, edited by Editorial Committee, Maktabat Pārsā, 131–88. Qum: Maktabat Pārsā, 2008.

Al-Ṣadūq (Ibn Bābawayh), Muḥammad b. ʿAlī. *Faḍāʾil al-shīʿa*. In *Muṣannafāt al-Ṣadūq*, edited by Editorial Committee, Maktabat Pārsā, 189–232. Qum: Maktabat Pārsā, 2008.

Al-Ṣadūq (Ibn Bābawayh), Muḥammad b. ʿAlī. *al-Iʿtiqādāt*. Ed. Imām Hādī Foundation Editorial Committee. Qum: Muʾassasat al-Imām al-Hādī, 1389 sh.

Al-Ṣadūq (Ibn Bābawayh), Muḥammad b. ʿAlī. *Maʿānī al-akhbār*. Beirut: Muʾassasat al-Tārīkh al-ʿArabī, 2009.

Al-Ṣadūq (Ibn Bābawayh), Muḥammad b. ʿAlī. *al-Amālī*. Beirut: Muʾassasat al-Aʿlamī li'l-Maṭbūʿāt, 2009.

Al-Ṣadūq (Ibn Bābawayh), Muḥammad b. ʿAlī. *Thawāb al-aʿmāl wa ʿIqāb al-aʿmāl*. Beirut: Intishārāt al-Maktaba al-Ḥaydarīya, 2009.

Al-Ṣadūq (Ibn Bābawayh), Muḥammad b. ʿAlī. *Munāẓarat al-malik Rukn al-Dawla li'l-Ṣadūq Ibn Bābawayh*. Ed. Jawād al-Warad. Beirut: Dār al-Ḥujja al-Bayḍāʾ, 2010.

Al-Ṣadūq (Ibn Bābawayh), Muḥammad b. ʿAlī. *ʿUyūn akhbār al-Riḍā*. Qum: Dhawā al-Qurbā, 1427 h.

Al-Ṣadūq (Ibn Bābawayh), Muḥammad b. ʿAlī. *al-Khiṣāl*. Qum: Muʾassasat al-Nashr al-Islāmī, 1429 h.

Al-Ṣadūq (Ibn Bābawayh), Muḥammad b. ʿAlī. *Kamāl al-dīn wa tamām al-niʿma*. Ed. ʿAlī Akbar Ghaffārī. Qum: Muʾassasat al-Nashr al-Islāmī, 1429 h.

Al-Ṣadūq (Ibn Bābawayh), Muḥammad b. ʿAlī. *al-Hidāya*. Ed. Imām Hādī Foundation Editorial Committee. Qum: Muʾassasat al-Imām al-Hādī, 1390 sh.

Al-Ṣadūq (Ibn Bābawayh), Muḥammad b. ʿAlī. *al-Muqniʿ*. Ed. Imām Hādī Foundation Editorial Committee. Qum: Muʾassasat al-Imām al-Hādī, 1390 sh.

Al-Ṣaffār, Muḥammad b. al-Ḥasan. *Baṣāʾir al-darajāt*. Qum: Ṭalīʿat al-Nūr, 1429 h.

Al-Samarqandī, Naṣr b. Muḥammad. *Khizānat al-fiqh*. Ed. Muḥammad ʿAbd al-Salām Shāhīn. Beirut: Dār al-Kutub al-ʿIlmīya, 2005.

Ibn Shahriyār, Buzurg. *ʿAjāʾib al-Hind*. Jabil: Dār wa Maktabat Bīblīyūn, 2009.

Al-Sijistānī, Sahl b. Muḥammad. *al-Muʿammarūn*. Beirut: Maktabat al-Maʿārif, 1997.

Al-Tanūkhī, al-Muḥassin b. ʿAlī. *Nishwār al-muḥāḍara*. Ed. ʿAbūd al-Shālijī. Beirut: Dār Ṣādir, 1995.

Al-Tawḥīdī, Abū Ḥayyān Muḥammad b. ʿAlī. *al-Imtāʿ wa'l-muʾānasa*. Cairo: Maṭbaʿat Lajnat al-Taʾlīf wa'l-Ṭabʿa wa'l-Nashr, 1939.

Al-Tawḥīdī, Abū Ḥayyān Muḥammad b. ʿAlī. *al-Baṣāʾir wa'l-dhakhāʾir*. Beirut: Dār al-Yaqīn, 1964.

Al-Tawḥīdī, Abū Ḥayyān Muḥammad b. ʿAlī. *Risālat al-ṣadāqa wa'l-ṣadīq*. Damascus: Dār al-Fikr, 1964.

Al-Tawḥīdī, Abū Ḥayyān Muḥammad b. ʿAlī. *Akhlāq al-wazīrayn*. Damascus: Dār Ṣādir, 1965.

Al-Thaʿlabī, Aḥmad b. Muḥammad. *Qiṣaṣ al-anbiyāʾ al-musammā bi-ʿarāʾis al-majālis*. Beirut: Dār al-Kutub al-ʿIlmīya, 2017.

Al-Ṭūsī, Muḥammad b. al-Ḥasan. *'Uddat al-uṣūl*. Ed. Muḥammad Mahdī Najaf. Qum: Muʾassasat Āl al-Bayt li'l-Ṭibāʿa wa'l-Nashr, 1983.

Al-Ṭūsī, Muḥammad b. al-Ḥasan. *al-Ghayba*. Beirut: Manshūrāt al-Fajr, 2012.

Al-Ṭūsī, Muḥammad b. al-Ḥasan. *al-Fihrist*. Qum: Maṭbaʿat al-Muḥaqqiq al-Ṭabāṭabāʾ, 1420 sh.

Secondary sources

Abdulsater, Hussein Ali. 'Dynamics of Absence: Twelver Shiʿism during the Minor Occultation'. *Zeitschrift Der Deutschen Morgenländischen Gesellschaft* 161, no. 2 (2011): 305–34.

Abdulsater, Hussein Ali. *Shi'i Doctrine, Mu'tazili Theology: al-Sharīf al-Murtaḍā and Imami Discourse*. Edinburgh: Edinburgh University Press, 2017.

Adam, Ali (trans.). *Kitāb Al-Tawḥīd: The Book of Divine Unity of Al-Shaykh Al-Ṣadūq*. Birmingham: AMI Press, 2013.

Adem, Rodrigo. 'Classical Naṣṣ Doctrines in Imāmī Shīʿism: On the Usage of an Expository Term'. *Shi'i Studies Review* 1 (2017): 42–71.

Allen, Michael. 'How *Adab* Became Literary: Formalism, Orientalism and the Institutions of World Literature'. *Journal of Arabic Literature* 43 (2012): 172–96.

Allen, Roger. *The Arabic Literary Heritage: The Development of Its Genres and Criticism*. Cambridge: Cambridge University Press, 2008.

Alsehail, Marzoug A. M. 'Ḥadīth-Amālī Sessions: Historical Study of a Forgotten Tradition in Classical Islam'. PhD Thesis, University of Leeds, 2014.

Matar, Zeina. 'The Buddha Legend: A Footnote from an Arabic Source'. *Oriens* 32 (1990): 440–2.

Alshaar, Nuha. *Ethics in Islam: Friendship in the Political Thought of Al-Tawhidi and His Contemporaries*. London: Routledge, 2014.

Amir-Moezzi, Mohammad Ali. *The Divine Guide in Early Shi'ism: The Sources of Esotericism in Islam*. Trans. David Streight. Albany: State University of New York Press, 1994.

Amir-Moezzi, Mohammad Ali. 'Remarques sur les critères d'authenticité du hadîth et l'autorité du juriste dans le shi'isme imâmite'. *Studia Islamica* 85 (1997): 5–39.

Amir-Moezzi, Mohammad Ali. *The Spirituality of Shi'i Islam: Beliefs and Practices.* London: I. B. Tauris, 2010.

Amir-Moezzi, Mohammad Ali. *The Silent Qur'ān and the Speaking Qur'ān: Scriptural Sources of Islam Between History and Fervor.* Trans. Eric Ormsby. New York: Columbia University Press, 2016.

Amir-Moezzi, Mohammad Ali, and Hassan Ansari. 'Perfecting a Religion: Remarks on al-Kulaynī and his Summa of Traditions'. In Mohammad Ali Amir-Moezzi, *The Silent Qur'an and the Speaking Qur'an: Scriptural Sources of Islam Between History and Fervor*, 125–60. Trans. Eric Ormsby. New York: Columbia University Press, 2015.

Amir-Moezzi, Mohammad Ali, and Meir M. Bar-Asher (eds.). *Le shi'isme imamite quarante ans après: hommage à Etan Kohlberg.* Turnhout: Brepols, 2009.

Ansari, Hassan. 'Bar rasī-yi matn-i munāẓara-yi Shaykh-i Ṣadūq dar majlis-i Rukn al-Dawla-yi Būyahī'. http://ansari.kateban.com/post/1418, posted 28/07/2008, accessed July 30, 2016.

Ansari, Hassan. 'Une Version Incomplète du *Kitāb al-Nubuwwa* d'al-Ṣadūq'. In *Le shi'isme imamite quarante ans après: Hommage à Etan Kohlberg*, edited by Mohammad Ali Amir-Moezzi, and Meir M. Bar-Asher, 49–53. Turnhout: Brepols, 2009.

Ansari, Hassan. 'Uṣūl-i riwāyī (4): āthār-i mafqūd-i Shaykh-i Ṣadūq, chirā wa chigūna?'. http://ansari.kateban.com/post/1735, posted February 02, 2011, accessed 30 July 2016.

Ansari, Hassan. 'The Shīʿī Reception of Muʿtazilism (I): Zaydīs'. In *The Oxford Handbook of Islamic Theology*, edited by Sabine Schmidtke, 182–94. Oxford: Oxford University Press, 2016.

Ansari, Hassan, and Sabine Schmidtke. 'The Shīʿī Reception of Muʿtazilism (II): Twelver Shīʿīs'. In *The Oxford Handbook of Islamic Theology*, edited by Sabine Schmidtke, 196–214. Oxford: Oxford University Press, 2016.

Ansari, Hassan. *L'imamat et l'Occultation selon l'imamisme.* Leiden: Brill, 2017.

Antoon, Sinan. *The Poetics of the Obscene in Premodern Arabic Poetry: Ibn al-Ḥajjāj and Sukhf.* London: Palgrave Macmillan, 2014.

Arjomand, Said Amir. 'The Crisis of the Imāmate and the Institution of Occultation in Twelver Shiism: A Sociohistorical Perspective'. *International Journal of Middle East Studies* 28, no. 4 (1996): 491–515.

Arjomand, Said Amir. 'The Consolation of Theology: Absence of the Imam and Transition from Chiliasm to Law in Shiʿism'. *The Journal of Religion* 76, no. 4 (1996): 548–71.

Arjomand, Said Amir. 'Imam Absconditus and the Beginnings of a Theology of Occultation: Imami Shiʿism Circa 280–90 A. H./900 A. D'. *Journal of the American Oriental Society* 117, no. 1 (1997): 1–12.

Arkoun, Mohammed. *Contribution à l'étude de l'humanisme arabe au IVe/Xe siècle: Miskawayh (320/325-421)–(932/936-1030) philosophe et historien.* Paris: J. Vrin, 1970.

Ashtryan, Mushegh. 'An Early Shīʿi Cosmology'. *Studia Islamica* 110, no. 1 (2015): 1–80.

Azarnoosh, Azartash, and Sana'i, Mansur. 'Al-Ābī, Abū Saʿd Manṣūr b. al-Ḥusayn'. In *Encyclopaedia Islamica*, edited by Wilfred Madelung, and Farhad Daftary, Consulted online 30 September 2016 at http://referenceworks.brillonline.com/en tries/encyclopaedia-islamica/al-abi-abu-sad-mansur-b-al-husayn-SIM_0079?s.num =0&s.q=al-abi.

Baker, Christine D. *Medieval Islamic Sectarianism*. Leeds: Arc Humanities Press, 2019.

Bar-Asher, Meir M. *Scripture and Exegesis in Early Imāmī Shiism*. Leiden: Brill, 1999.

Bayhom-Daou, Tamima. 'The Imāmī Shīʿī Conception of the Imām and the Sources of Religious Doctrine in the Formative Period: from Hishām b. al-Ḥakam (d. 179 A.H. to Kulīnī (d. 329 A.H.)'. PhD Thesis, SOAS, 1996.

Bayhom-Daou, Tamima. *Shaykh Al-Mufid*. Oxford: Oneworld, 2005.

Beaumont, Daniel. '*Min Jumlat al-Jamādāt*. The Inanimate in Fictional and *Adab* Narrative'. In *On Fiction and Adab in Medieval Arabic Literature*, edited by Philip F. Kennedy, 55–68. Wiesbaden: Harrassowitz Verlag, 2005.

Bergé, Marc. *Pour un humanisme vécu: Abū Ḥayyān al-Tawḥīdī: essai sur la personnalité morale, intellectuelle et littéraire d'un grand prosateur et humaniste arabe, engagé dans la société de l'époque bouyide, à Bagdad, Rayy et Chiraz, au IVe-Xe siècle (entre 310/922 et 320/932-414/1023)*. Damascus: Institut français de Damas, 1979.

Bishop, Eric E. F. 'Form-Criticism and the Forty-Two Traditions of an-Nawawi'. *The Muslim World* 30 (1940): 253–61.

Blecher, Joel. *Said the Prophet of God: Hadith Commentary Across a Millennium*. Oakland: University of California Press, 2018.

de Blois, François. 'On the Sources of the Barlaam Romance, or How Buddha Became a Christian Saint'. In *Literarische Stoffe und ihre Gestaltung in mitteliranischer Zeit Kolloquium anlässlich des 70. Geburtstages von Werner Sundermann*, edited by Christiane Reck, Desmond Durkin-Meisterernst, and Dieter Weber, 7–26. Wiesbaden: Dr Ludwig Reichert Verlag, 2009.

Bonebakker, S. 'Adab and the Concept of Belles-Lettres'. In *Abbasid Belles Lettres*, edited by Julia Ashtiany, T. M. Johnstone, J. D. Latham and R. B. Serjeant, 16–30. Cambridge: Cambridge University Press, 1990.

Bray (Ashtiany Bray), Julia. 'Abbasid Myth and the Human Act'. In *On Fiction and* Adab *in Medieval Arabic Literature*, edited by Philip F. Kennedy, 1–49. Wiesbaden: Harrassowitz Verlag, 2005.

Bray (Ashtiany Bray), Julia. *Abbasid Belles Lettres*. Cambridge: Cambridge University Press, 2009.

Brown, Jonathan. *The Canonization of Al-Bukhārī and Muslim: The Formation and Function of the Sunnī Ḥadīth Canon*. Leiden: Brill, 2007.

Brown, Jonathan. *Hadith: Muhammad's Legacy in the Medieval and Modern World*. Oxford: Oneworld, 2009.

Brown, Jonathan. 'Even if It's Not True, It's True: Using Unreliable Ḥadīths in Sunnī Islam'. *Islamic Law and Society* 18 (2011): 1–52.

Brunschwig, R. (ed.). *Le shî'isme imâmite: colloque de Strasbourg (6–9 Mai 1968)*. Paris: Presses Universitaires de France, 1970.

Burge, Stephen R. 'Reading Between the Lines: The Compilation of *Ḥadīṯ* and the Authorial Voice'. *Arabica* 58, no. 3–4 (2011): 167–97.

Burge, Stephen R. 'Jalāl al-Dīn al-Suyūṭī, the *Mu'awwidhatān* and the Modes of Exegesis'. In *Aims, Methods and Contexts of Qur'anic Exegesis (2nd/8th–9th/15th C.)*, edited by Karen Bauer, 277–307. London: Oxford University Press, 2013.

Burge, Stephen R. 'Myth, Meaning and the Order of Words: Reading Hadith Collections with Northrop Frye and the Development of Compilation Criticism'. *Islam and Christian-Muslim Relations* 72, no. 2 (2016): 213–28.

Burge, Stephen R. 'The Ḥadīth Literature: What is It? And Where is It?' *Arabica* 65, no. 1–2 (2018): 64–83.

Busse, Heribert, *Chalif Und Grosskönig: Die Buyiden Im Iraq* (945–1055). Würzburg: Ergon-Verlag, 1969.

Calder, Norman. 'Judicial Authority in Imami Shi'i Jurisprudence'. *Bulletin (British Society for Middle Eastern Studies)* 6, no. 2 (1979): 104–8.

Calder, Norman. 'Doubt and Prerogative: The Emergence of an Imāmī Shī'ī Theory of Ijtihād'. *Studia Islamica* 70 (1989): 57–78.

Calder, Norman. 'The Barāhima: Literary Construct and Historical Reality'. *BSOAS* 57, no. 1 (1994): 40–51.

Canard, Maurice. *Histoire de la dynastie des Hamdanides de Jazira et de Syrie*. Paris: Presses Universitaires de France, 1953.

Clarke, Lynda (ed.). *Shī'ite Heritage*. Binghamton: Global Academic Publishing, 2001.

Clarke, Lynda. 'The Rise and Decline of *Taqiyya* in Twelver Shi'ism'. In *Reason and Inspiration in Islam: Theology, Philosophy and Mysticism in Muslim Thought*, edited by Todd Lawson, 46–63. London: I.B. Tauris, 2005.

Cooperson, Michael. *Classical Arabic Biography: The Heirs of the Prophets in the Age of Al-Ma'mūn*. Cambridge: Cambridge University Press, 2000.

Coupe, Laurence. *Myth*. London: Routledge, 2008.

Crow, Karim Douglas. 'The Role of *al-'Aql* in Early Islamic Wisdom with Reference to Imam Ja'far al-Ṣādiq'. PhD Thesis, McGill University, 1996.

Daftary, Farhad. *A History of Shi'i Islam*. London: I. B. Tauris, 2013.

Daftary, Farhad, and Josef W. Meri (eds.). *Culture and Memory in Medieval Islam: Essays in Honour of Wilferd Madelung*. London: I. B. Tauris, 2003.

Daftary, Farhad, and Gurdofarid Miskinzoda (eds.). *The Study of Shi'i Islam: History, Theology and Law*. London: I. B. Tauris, 2014.

Dakake, Maria Massi. 'Hiding in Plain Sight: The Practical and Doctrinal Significance of Secrecy in Shi'ite Islam'. *Journal of the American Academy of Religion* 74, no. 2 (2006): 324–55.

Dakake, Maria Massi. *The Charismatic Community: Shi'ite Identity in Early Islam*. Albany: State University of New York Press, 2008.

Davis, Dick. *Epic and Sedition: The Case of Ferdowsi's Shahnameh*. Washington, DC: Mage, 2006.

De Smet, Daniel. 'From Khalaf (beginning of the 4th/10th century?) to Ḥasan al-Ṣabbāḥ (d. 518 H/1124 CE): Ismailism in Rayy before and under the Seljūqs'. *Der Islam* 93, no. 2 (2016): 433–59.

Dietrich, A. 'Ibn Abī 'l-Dunyā'. In *Encyclopaedia of Islam*, 2nd edition, edited by P. Bearman, Th. Bianquis, C. E. Bosworth, E. van Donzel, and W. P. Heinrichs, Consulted online September 30, 2017 at http://referenceworks.brillonline.com/entries/encyclopaedia-of-islam-2/ibn-abi-l-dunya-SIM_3046?s.num=0&s.f.s2_parent=s.f.cluster.Encyclopaedia+of+Islam&s.q=ibn+abi+al-dunya.

Doge, Bayard. *The Fihrist of Al-Nadīm: A Tenth-Century Survey of Muslim Culture*. New York: Columbia University Press, 1970.

Donner, Fred McGraw. *Narratives of Islamic Origins: The Beginning of Islamic Historical Writing*. Princeton: Darwin Press, 1998.

Donohue, John. *The Buwayhid Dynasty in Iraq 334H./945 to 403H./1012: Shaping Institutions for the Future*. Leiden: Brill, 2003.

Fadel, Mohammed. 'Ibn Ḥajar's *Hady al-Sārī*: A Medieval Interpretation of the Structure of al-Bukhārī's *Al-Jāmi' al-Ṣaḥīḥ*: Introduction and Translation'. *Journal of Near-Eastern Studies* 54 (1995): 161–97.

Franke, Patrick. *Begegnung mit Khidr: Quellenstudien zum Imaginären im traditionellen Islam*. Beirut: Orient-Institut Beirut, 2000.

Fück, Johann Wilhelm (ed.). *Ibn an-Nadīm und die mittelalterliche arabische Literatur: Beiträge zum 1. Johann Wilhelm Fück-Kolloquium (Halle 1987)*. Wiesbaden: Harrassowitz, 1996.

Fyzee, Asaf A. A. *A Shi'ite Creed*. Tehran: World Organization for Islamic Services, 1982.

George, Andrew. *The Babylonian Gilgamesh Epic: Introduction, Critical Edition and Cuneiform Texts*. Oxford: Oxford University Press, 2003.

Geries, Ibrāhīm. *Un genre littéraire arabe: al-maḥāsin wa-l-masāwī*. Paris: Maisonneuve & Larose, 1977.

Ghaemmaghami, Omid. *Encounters with the Hidden Imam in Early and Pre-Modern Twelver Shī'ī Islam*. Leiden: Brill, 2020.

Gimaret, Daniel. *Kitāb Bilawhar wa Būdāsf*. Beirut: Dar el-Mashreq, 1972.

Gleave, Robert. 'Between Ḥadīth and Fiqh: The 'Canonical' Imāmī Collections of Akhbār'. *Islamic Law and Society* 8, no. 3 (2001): 350–82.

Gleave, Robert. *Scripturalist Islam: The History and Doctrines of the Akhbārī Shī'ī School*. Leiden: Brill, 2007.

Goldziher, Ignaz. *Muslim Studies*. Trans. S. M. Stern, and C. R. Barber. Albany: State University of New York Press, 1971.

Goodman, Lenn. *Islamic Humanism*. Oxford: Oxford University Press, 2003.

Gutas, Dimitri. 'Classical Arabic Wisdom Literature: Nature and Scope'. *Journal of the American Oriental Society* 101, no. 1 (1981): 49–86.

Haider, Najam. *The Origins of the Shīʻa: Identity, Ritual, and Sacred Space in Eighth-Century Kūfa*. Cambridge: Cambridge University Press, 2011.

Haider, Najam. *Shi'i Islam: An Introduction*. Cambridge: Cambridge University Press, 2014.

Haider, Najam. *The Rebel and the Imām in Early Islam: Explorations in Early Muslim Historiography*. Cambridge: Cambridge University Press, 2019.

Hallaq, Wael B. *The Origins and Evolution of Islamic Law*. Cambridge; New York: Cambridge University Press, 2004.

Hallaq, Wael B. *Authority, Continuity and Change in Islamic Law*. Cambridge: Cambridge University Press, 2005.

Halm, Heinz. *The Empire of the Mahdi: The Rise of the Fatimids*. Leiden: Brill, 1996.

Hamdani, Sumaiya Abbas. *Between Revolution and State: The Path to Fatimid Statehood: Qadi Al-Nu'man and the Construction of Fatimid Legitimacy*. London: I.B. Tauris, 2006.

Hayes, Edmund. 'The Envoys of the Hidden Imam: Religious Institutions and the Politics of the Twelver Occultation Doctrine'. PhD Thesis, University of Chicago, 2015.

Heinrichs, Wolfhart (ed.). *Orientalisches Mittelalter*. Wiesbaden: AULA-Verlag, 1990.

Al-Ḥillī, ʿAbd al-Ḥalīm ʿŪḍ. *Mā waṣala ilaynā min Kitāb madīnat al-ʿilm li'l-Shaykh al-Ṣadūq Muḥammad b. ʿAlī b. al-Ḥusayn (t. 381 h.)*. Karbala: Dār Makhṭūṭāt al-ʿAtaba al-ʿAbbāsīya al-Muqaddasa, 2016.

Hodgson, Marshall G. S. *The Venture of Islam*. Chicago: Chicago University Press, 1974.

Hollenberg, David. *Beyond the Qurʾān: Early Ismāʿīlī Taʾwīl and the Secrets of the Prophets*. Columbia: University of South Carolina Press, 2016.

Kennedy, Hugh. 'The Late ʿAbbāsid Pattern, 945–1050'. In *The New Cambridge History of Islam*, edited by Chase F. Robinson, 360–94. Cambridge: Cambridge University Press, 2010.

Kennedy, Philip F. (ed.). *On Fiction and Adab in Medieval Arabic*. Wiesbaden: Harrassowitz, 2005.

Key, Alexander. 'The Applicability of the Term 'Humanism' to Abū Ḥayyān Al-Tawḥīdī'. *Studia Islamica*, 100, no. 101 (2005): 71–112.

Khalidi, Tarif. *Islamic Historiography: The Histories of Mas'udi*. Albany: State University of New York Press, 1975.

Khalidi, Tarif. *Arabic Historical Thought in the Classical Period*. Cambridge: Cambridge University Press, 1994.

Khomeini, Ruhollah. *The Mystery of Prayer*. Trans. Amjad H. Shah Naqavi. Leiden: Brill, 2015.

Al-Khūʾī, Abū al-Qāsim. *Muʿjam rijāl al-dīn*. Najaf: Maktabat al-imām al-Khūʾī, n. d.

Kilito, Abdelfattah. *Les Séances: Récits et codes culturels chez Hamadhânî et Harîrî*. Paris: Sindbad, 1983.

Kilpatrick, Hilary. 'A Genre in Classical Arabic Literature: The *Adab* Encyclopedia'. In *Proceedings, union européenne des arabisants et islamisants: 10th Congress,*

Edinburgh, 9–16 September 1980, edited by Robert Hillenbrand, 34–42. Edinburgh: Edinburgh University Press, 1982.

Kilpatrick, Hilary. 'Context and the Enhancement of the Meaning of Aḫbār in the Kitāb Al-Aġānī'. *Arabica* 38, no. 3 (1991): 351–68.

Kilpatrick, Hilary, and Stefan Leder. 'Classical Arabic Prose Literature: A Researchers' Sketch Map'. *Journal of Arabic Literature* 23, no. 1 (1992): 2–26.

Kilpatrick, Hilary. 'Some Late ʿAbbāsid and Mamlūk Books about Women: A Literary Historical Approach'. *Arabica* 42, no. 1 (1995): 56–78.

Kilpatrick, Hilary. 'Adab'. In *Encyclopedia of Arabic Literature*, edited by Julie Scott Meisami, and Paul Starkey, 53–56. London: Routledge, 1998.

Kilpatrick, Hilary. *Making the Great Book of Songs: Compilation and the Author's Craft in Abū al-Faraj al-Iṣbahānī's Kitāb al-Aghānī*. London: Routledge, 2003.

Kirk, G. S. *Myth: Its Meaning and Functions in Ancient and Other Cultures*. Berkeley: University of California Press, 1992.

Klemm, Verena. 'A Genre in Classical Arabic: The *Adab* Encyclopaedia'. In *Union Européenne des Arabisants et Islamisants 10th Congress, Edinburgh, September 1980, Proceedings*, edited by Robert Hillenbrand, 32–42. Edinburgh: Edinburgh University Press, 1982.

Klemm, Verena. 'Die Vier Sufarā' Des Zwölften Imām Zur Formativen Periode Der Zwölferšīʿa'. *Die Welt Des Orients* 15 (1984): 126–43.

Kohlberg, Etan. 'Some Imāmī-Shīʿī Views on *Taqiyya*'. *Journal of the American Oriental Society* 95, no. 3 (1975): 395–402.

Kohlberg, Etan. 'From Imāmiyya to Ithnā-'Ashariyya'. *BSOAS* 39, no. 3 (1976): 521–34.

Kohlberg, Etan. 'Abū Turāb'. *BSOAS* 41 (1978): 347–52.

Kohlberg, Etan. '*al-Uṣūl al-arbaʿumiʾa*''. *Jerusalem Studies in Arabic and Islam* 10 (1987): 128–66.

Kraemer, Joel L. 'Humanism in the Renaissance of Islam: A Preliminary Study'. *Journal of the American Oriental Society* 104, no. 1 (1984): 135–64.

Kraemer, Joel L. *Humanism in the Renaissance of Islam: The Cultural Revival during the Buyid Age*. Leiden: Brill, 1986.

Lalani, Arzina. *Early Shīʿī Thought: The Teachings of Imam Muḥammad al-Bāqir*. London: I. B. Tauris, 2000.

Lawson, Todd (ed.). *Reason and Inspiration in Islam: Theology, Philosophy and Mysticism in Muslim Thought: Essays in Honour of Hermann Landolt*. London: I. B. Tauris, 2005.

Lazarus-Yafeh, Hava (ed.). *The Majlis: Interreligious Encounters in Medieval Islam*. Wiesbaden: Harrassowitz, 1999.

Lecomte, Gérard. *Ibn Qutayba (mort En 276/889), L'homme, son oeuvre, ses idées*. Damascus: Institut Français de Damas, 1965.

Leder, Stefan (ed.). *Story-Telling in the Framework of Non-Fictional Arabic Literature*. Wiesbaden: Harrassowitz, 1998.

Loebenstein, Judith. 'Miracles in Šīʿī Thought: A Case Study of the Miracles Attributed to Imām Gaʿfar al-Ṣādiq'. *Arabica* 50 (2003): 199–244.

Madelung, W. 'Imāmism and Mu'tazilite Theology'. In *Le shi'isme imamite*, edited by Robert Brunschvig, 13–30. Paris: Presses universitaires de France, 1970.

Madelung, W. 'Early Imāmī Theology as Reflected in the *Kitāb al-Kāfī* of *al-Kulaynī*'. In *The Study of Shi'i Islam: History, Theology and Law*, edited by Gurdofrid Miskinzoda, and Farhad Daftary, 465–74. London: I. B. Tauris, 2014.

Makdisi, George. *The Rise of Humanism in Classical Islam and the Christian West: With Special Reference to Scholasticism*. Edinburgh: Edinburgh University Press, 1990.

Marcinkowski, Muhammad Ismail. 'Selected Aspects of the Life and Works of Al-Shaykh Al-Mufīd (336-413/498-1022)'. *Hamdard Islamicus* 23, no. 2 (2000): 41–54.

Marcinkowski, Muhammad Ismail. 'Twelver Shî'ite Scholarship and Bûyid Domination: A Glance on the Life and Times of Ibn Bâbawayh Al-Shaikh Al-Sadûq (d.381/991)'. *Islamic Culture* 76, no. 1 (2002): 69–99.

McDermott, Martin J. *The Theology of Al-Shaikh Al-Mufīd (d. 413/1022)*. Beirut: Dar al-Mashreq, 1978.

Meisami, Julie Scott, and Paul Starkey (eds.). *Encyclopedia of Arabic Literature*. London: Routledge, 1998.

Melchert, Christopher. *The Formation of the Sunni Schools of Law, 9th–10th Centuries C.E.* Leiden: Brill, 1997.

Melchert, Christopher. 'The Imāmīs Between Rationalism and Traditionalism'. In *Shī'ite Heritage: Essays on Classical and Modern Traditions*, edited by L. Clarke, 273–84. Albany, NY: SUNY Press, 2001.

Mir-Kasimov, Orkhan. 'Techniques de garde du secret en Islam'. *Revue de l'histoire des religions* 2 (2011): 265–87.

Modarressi, Hossein Tabataba'i. *An Introduction to Shī'ī Law: A Bibliographical Study*. London: Ithaca Press, 1984.

Modarressi, Hossein Tabataba'i. *Crisis and Consolidation in the Formative Period of Shi'ite Islam: Abū Ja'far Ibn Qiba Al-Rāzī and His Contribution to Imāmite Shī'ite Thought*. Princeton: Darwin Press, 1993.

Modarressi, Hossein Tabataba'i. *Tradition and Survival: A Bibliographical Survey of Early Shī'ite Literature Volume I*. Oxford: Oneworld, 2003.

Momen, Moojan. *An Introduction to Shi'i Islam: The History and Doctrines of Twelver Shi'ism*. New Haven: Yale University Press, 1985.

Montgomery, James E. (ed.). *'Abbasid Studies: Occasional Papers of the School of 'Abbasid Studies, Cambridge, 6–10 July 2002*. Leuven: Peeters, 2002.

Montgomery, James E. *Al-Jāḥiẓ: In Praise of Books*. Edinburgh: Edinburgh University Press, 2015.

Moosa, Matti. *Extremist Shiites: The Ghulat Sects*. Syracuse: Syracuse University Press, 1987.

Mottahedeh, Roy. *Loyalty and Leadership in an Islamic Society*. London: I. B. Tauris, 1998.

Mourad, Suleiman A., and James E. Lindsay. *The Intensification and Reorientation of Sunni Jihad Ideology in the Crusader Period: Ibn 'Asākir of Damascus (1105–1176) and His Age, with an edition, and translation of Ibn ʿAsākir's The Forty Hadith for Inciting Jihad*. Leiden: Brill, 2013.

Mubārak, Zakī. *ʿAbqarīyat al-Sharīf al-Raḍī*. Beirut: Dār al-jīl, 1988.

Musa, Aisha Y. *Ḥadīth as Scripture: Discussions on the Authority of Prophetic Traditions in Islam*. Basingstoke: Palgrave Macmillan, 2008.

Naaman, Erez. *Literature and the Islamic Court: Cultural Life under al-Ṣāḥib Ibn ʿAbbād*. London: Routledge, 2016.

Natij, Salah. 'La nuit inaugurale de *Kitāb al-Imtāʿ wa-l-muʾānasa* d'Abū Ḥayyān al-Tawḥīdī: une leçon magistrale *d'adab*'. *Arabica* 55, no. 2 (2008): 227–75.

Neggaz, Nassima. 'Al-Karkh: The Development of an Imāmī-Shīʿī Stronghold in Early Abbasid and Būyid Baghdad (132-447/750-1055)'. *Studia Islamica* 114 (2019): 265–315.

Newman, Andrew. *The Formative Period of Twelver Shīʿism: Ḥadīth as Discourse Between Qum and Baghdad*. Richmond: Curzon Press, 2000.

Newman, Andrew. 'The Recovery of the Past: Ibn Babawayh, Baqir al-Majlisi and Safavid Medical Discourse'. *Journal of the British Institute for Persian Studies* 50 (2012): 109–27.

Newman, Andrew. *Twelver Shiism: Unity and Diversity in the Life of Islam*. Edinburgh: Edinburgh University Press, 2013.

Orfali, Bilal. 'A Sketch Map of Arabic Poetry Anthologies up to the Fall of Baghdad'. *Journal of Arabic Literature* 43, no. 1 (2012): 29–59.

Orfali, Bilal. *The Anthologist's Art: Abū Manṣūr al-Thaʿālibī and His Yatīmat al-Dahr*. Leiden: Brill, 2016.

Pākatchī, Aḥmad (ed.). *Mawlid amīr al-muʾminīn: nuṣūṣ mustakhraja min al-turāth al-islāmī*. Qum: Bunyād-i Nahj al-Balāgha, 1382 Sh.

Pellat, Charles. 'Masʿūdī et l'imāmisme'. In *Le shi'isme imamite*, edited by Robert Brunschvig, 69–90. Paris: Presses universitaires de France, 1970.

Pierce, Matthew. *Twelve Infallible Men: The Imams and the Making of Shiʿism*. Cambridge, MA: Harvard University Press, 2016.

Pouzet, Louis. *Hermeneutique de la tradition islamique: le commentaire des Arbaʿūn al-Nawawīya de Muḥyī al-Dīn al-Nawawī (m. 676/1277): introduction, texte de arabe, traduction, notes et index du vocabulaire*. Beirut: Dar el-Machreq and Libraire Orientale, 1982.

al-Qāḍī, Wadād. 'Abū Ḥayyān al-Tawḥīdī: A Sunnī Voice in the Shīʿī Century'. In *Culture and Memory in Medieval Islam: Essays in Honour of Wilferd Madelung*, edited by Farhad Daftary and Josef W. Meri, 128–62. London: I. B. Tauris, 2003.

Qutbuddin, Tahera (trans.). *A Treasury of Virtues*. New York: New York University Press, 2013.

Reinhart, A. Kevin. 'Juynbolliana, Gradualism, the Big Bang and Ḥadīth Study in the Twenty-First Century'. *Journal of the American Oriental Society* 130, no. 3 (2010): 413–44.

Reynolds, Dwight Fletcher, and Kristen Brustad (eds.). *Interpreting the Self: Autobiography in the Arabic Literary Tradition*. Berkeley: University of California Press, 2001.

Ricoeur, Paul. *The Symbolism of Evil*. Trans. Emerson Buchanan. Boston: Beacon Press, 1969.

Rosenthal, Franz. *Knowledge Triumphant the Concept of Knowledge in Medieval Islam*. Leiden: Brill, 2007.

Sander, Paul. *Zwischen Charisma Und Ratio: Entwicklungen in Der Frühen Imāmitischen Theologie*. Berlin: K. Schwarz, 1994.

Schmidtke, Sabine (ed.). *The Oxford Handbook of Islamic Theology*. Oxford: Oxford University Press, 2015.

Sezgin, Fuat. *Geschichte des arabischen Schrifttums*. Leiden: Brill, 1967.

Shah Naqavi, Amjad. 'The Concept of Ijmāʿ in Imāmī Uṣūl al-Fiqh'. PhD Thesis, Edinburgh University, 1999.

Sindawi, Khalid. 'The Donkey of the Prophet in the Shīʿite Tradition'. *Al-Masāq: Journal of the Medieval Mediterranean* 18 (2006): 87–98.

Sindawi, Khalid. 'Noah and Noah's Ark as the Primordial Model of Shiʿism in Shiʿite Literature'. *Quaderni di Studi Arabi* 1 (2006): 29–48.

Sperl, Stefan. *Mannerism in Arabic Poetry: A Structural Analysis of Selected Texts (3rd Century AH/9th Century AD – 5th Century AH/11th Century AD)*. Cambridge: Cambridge University Press, 1989.

Sperl, Stefan. 'Man's 'Hollow Core': Ethics and Aesthetics in *Ḥadīth* Literature and Classical Arabic *adab*'. *BSOAS* 70, no. 3 (2007): 459–86.

Stern, S. M. 'The Early Ismā'īlī Missionaries in North-West Persia and in Khurāsān and Transoxania'. *BSOAS* 23, no. 1 (1960): 56–90.

Stern, S. M., and Sophie Walzer. *Three Unknown Buddhist Stories in an Arabic Version*. Oxford: Cassirer, 1971.

Stetkevych, Suzanne Pinckney. *The Mute Immortals Speak: Pre-Islamic Poetry and the Poetics of Ritual*. Ithaca: Cornell University Press, 1993.

Stewart, Devin. 'Muḥammad b. Jarīr al-Ṭabarī's *al-Bayān ʿan uṣūl al-aḥkām* and the Genre of *Uṣūl al-fiqh* in Ninth-Century Baghdad'. In *Abbasid Studies: Occasional Papers of the School of Abbasid Studies, Cambridge, 6–10 July 2002, orientalia lovaniensia analecta 135*, edited by James Montgomery, 321–49. Leuven: Peeters Publishers, 2002.

Stewart, Devin. *Islamic Legal Orthodoxy: Twelver Shiite Responses to the Sunni Legal System*. Salt Lake City: The University of Utah Press, 2007.

Stewart, Devin. 'The Structure of the Fihrist: Ibn Al-Nadim as Historian of Islamic Legal and Theological Schools'. *International Journal of Middle East Studies* 39, no. 3 (2007): 369–87.

Stewart, Devin. 'Ibn Al-Nadīm's Ismāʿīlī Contacts'. *Journal of the Royal Asiatic Society* 19, no. 1 (2009): 21–40.

Stewart, Devin (trans.). *The Disagreements of the Jurists: A Manual of Islamic Legal Theory*. New York: New York University Press, 2015.

Ṭihrānī, Āqā Buzurg. *al-Dharīʿā ilā taṣānīf al-shīʿa*. Beirut: Dār al-Aḍwāʾ, 1983.

Ṭihrānī, Āqā Buzurg. *Ṭabaqāt aʿlām al-shīʿa*. Beirut: Dār Iḥyāʾ al-Turāth al-ʿArabī, 2009.

Tokatly, Vardit. 'The *A'lām al-ḥadīth* of al-Khaṭṭābī: A commentary on al-Bukhārī's *Ṣaḥīḥ* or a polemical treatise?' *Arabica* 92 (2001): 53–91.

Turner, John. *Inquisition in Early Islam: The Competition for Political Authority in Abbasid Empire*. London: I. B. Tauris, 2013.

van Gelder, G. J. H. 'Mixtures of Jest and Earnest in Classical Arabic Literature: Part I'. *Journal of Arabic Literature* 23, no. 2 (1992): 83–108.

van Gelder, G. J. H. 'Mixtures of Jest and Earnest in Classical Arabic Literature: Part II'. *Journal of Arabic Literature* 23, no. 3 (1992): 169–90.

Vilozny, Roy. 'A Šīʿī Life Cycle according to Al-Barqī's *Kitāb Al-Maḥāsin*'. *Arabica* 54, no. 3 (2007): 362–96.

Vilozny, Roy. 'Réflexions sur le *Kitāb al-ʿilal* d'Aḥmad b. Muḥammad al-Barqī'. In *Le Shīʿisme imāmite quarante ans après. Hommage à Etan Kohlberg*, edited by Mohammad Ali Amir-Moezzi, Meir M. Bar-Asher, and Simon Hopkins, 417–35. Belgium: Brepols, 2009.

Vilozny, Roy. 'A Concise Numerical Guide for the Perplexed Shiite: Al-Barqī's (d. 274/888 or 280/894) *Kitāb al-Aškāl wa-l-qarāʾin*'. *Arabica* 63, no. 1–2 (2016): 64–88.

Vilozny, Roy. *Constructing a Worldview: al-Barqī's Role in the Making of Early Shīʿī Faith*. Turnhout: Brepols, 2017.

Vilozny, Roy. 'Transmitting Imāmī Ḥadīth, Preserving Knowledge: Remarks on Three Amālī Works of The Buwayhī Period'. *Jerusalem Studies in Arabic and Islam* 50 (2021): 167–83.

Warner, George. 'Buddha or Yūdhāsaf? Images of the Hidden Imām in al-Ṣadūq's *Kamāl al-dīn*'. *Mizan: Journal for the Study of Muslim Societies and Civilizations* 2, no. 1 (2017). https://mizanproject.org/journal-post/buddha-or-yudhasaf/

Warner, George. 'One Thousand Ḥijaj: Ritualization and the Margins of the Law in Early Twelver Shīʿī *Ziyāra* Literature'. *Journal of the American Oriental Society* 2021 (forthcoming).

Wasserstein, David J. 'The "Majlis of al-Rida": A Religious Debate in the Court of the Caliph al-Maʾmun as Represented in a Shiʿi Hagiographical Work about the Eighth Imam ʿAli ibn Musa Al-Rida'. In *The Majlis: Interreligious Encounters in Medieval Islam*, edited by Hava Lazarus-Yafeh et al., 108–19. Wiesbaden: Harrassowitz, 1999.

Winter, Stefan. *A History of the 'Alawis: From Medieval Aleppo to the Turkish Republic*. Princeton: Princeton University Press, 2016.

Yoshida, Kyoko. '*Qiṣaṣ* Contribution to the Theory of *Ghayba* in Twelver Shīʿism'. *Orient* 44 (2009): 91–104.

Index

Ibn ʿAbbād, al-Ṣāḥib 8, 69, 84–6
ʿAbbāsids 14, 34, 67, 77, 84–5, 144, 202 n.24
al-Ābī, Manṣūr b. al-Ḥusayn 69, 79–81
adab 9, 11, 20, 65–87, 110, 139
ahl al-bayt (the house of the Prophet) 5, 71, 72, 135, 140, 141
Alexander ('The Horned One') 137, 145
ʿAlī b. Abī Ṭālib (imam) 4, 34, 49, 50, 55–6, 71, 73, 77, 78, 95, 106, 107, 110, 125, 135, 146
anthropomorphism, *see tashbīh*
al-ʿAskarī, al-Ḥasan b. Muḥammad (imam) 5, 37–44, 59, 64, 117, 121, 124–5, 135
authenticity, of hadith 3, 11–12, 20, 32, 35, 41–8, 50–64, 94–5, 98, 120–6, 129–33, 138–42, 147–8
authority
  of imams 4–6, 11–12, 38–45, 58–9, 62–4, 102–3, 107–8, 111–14, 147–50
  of scholars 4–6, 13–16, 38–50, 58–9, 62–5, 146–8, 149–50

Ibn Bābawayh the Elder (father of al-Ṣadūq) 7, 39–40, 44, 47, 57–62, 108, 145, 147
badāʾ 58–9, 103–5
Baghdad 8, 10, 34, 39, 83
  Imāmī scholarship in 34, 62
al-Bāqir, Muḥammad b. ʿAlī (imam) 42, 49, 72, 145
al-Barqī, Aḥmad b. Muḥammad 41, 47, 51, 53, 70, 71, 73
bāṭin, *see* esoteric
Bilawhar and Yūdhāsaf 76, 142–4
Buddha, *see* Bilawhar and Yūdhāsaf
al-Bukhārī, Muḥammad b. Ismāʿīl 1, 5, 18, 42
Burge, Stephen 12, 16
Buwayhids 9–10, 26, 31, 34–5, 37–8, 66–9, 74, 79, 83–4, 87

chain of transmission, *see isnād*
Christian 112, 135
compilation, compilation criticism 10–21, 87, 151–2
contradiction between hadiths 48, 54–9, 61–2, 74, 97–9, 106, 131, 148
council (*majlis*)
  of al-Riḍā before al-Maʾmūn 85–6, 111–14
  of al-Ṣadūq before Rukn al-Dawla 26, 69, 84

dalāla (sign) 85, 129–35, 147
dialectic theology, *see kalām*
dissimilation, *see taqīya*

egg containing the universe (theological conundrum) 97, 116
emissaries (*sufarāʾ*, sg. *safīr*) of the Hidden Imam 5, 39–40, 44, 129–30, 134
End Times 5, 58, 120, 141
esoteric 80, 99–101, 190 n.46

Faḍāʾil al-shīʿa (book by al-Ṣadūq) 25, 70–3
Fāṭima bt. Muḥammad 4, 51, 55, 74, 110, 128
Fāṭimids 6, 164 n.30, 174 n.27, 200 n.9, 206 n.70
fatra (inter-*ḥujja* hiatus) 136
'four books' of Twelver hadith 3, 37
free will and predestination 92–4, 103–10, 116
friendship 70–3, 84

Ghadīr Khumm 34, 77, 125

Ḥanbalī 10, 48, 102

ḥayra (post-occultation confusion) 39, 57–8, 147
al-Hidāya (book by al-Ṣadūq) 23, 48, 92
Hidden Imam 5–7, 31, 37–40, 47, 57–8, 117–51
Hishām b. al-Ḥakam 18, 52, 53
ḥujja, as indispensable 4, 38, 42, 56, 63, 85, 111, 114, 120, 136, 147, 150
al-Ḥusayn b. ʿAlī (imam) 26, 33, 34, 55, 106, 114, 132, 145

ʿIlal al-sharāʾiʿ (book by al-Ṣadūq) 24, 70, 73–84, 87
imamology 4–6, 32, 41, 44–6, 55–6, 62–3, 74, 85–6, 91, 100–2, 111–14, 117–50
infallibility
  of imams 4–5, 38–9, 55–8, 60, 63, 108
  of prophets 58, 136
intercession 106
Iram (legendary city) 140, 141
al-Irshād (book by al-Mufīd) 124
Ismāʿīl b. Jaʿfar b. Muḥammad 105
Ismāʿīlī 3, 6, 10, 124, 125, 160 n.2, 200 n.9, *see also* Fāṭimids
isnād, *see* authenticity
al-Iʿtiqādāt (book by al-Ṣadūq) 23, 37, 50–1, 54–8, 81, 92, 94–5, 108, 115, 151

jabr, *see* free will and predestination
Jaʿfar b. ʿAlī 'the liar' 39, 132
al-Jawharī, Aḥmad b. ʿAyyāsh 125
jurisprudence 31, 33, 35, 40–64, 69

kalām (dialectic theology) 10, 35, 84, 91–2, 96, 100–5, 108–15.
Kamāl al-dīn wa tamām al-niʿma (book by al-Ṣadūq) 9, 24, 40, 53, 76, 77, 80, 82, 84, 117–48, 157–9
al-Kashshī, Muḥammad b. ʿUmar 17, 52–4, 62, 177 n.17
al-Kāẓim, Mūsā b. Jaʿfar (imam) 58, 85, 178 n.24, 180 n.46
al-Khazzāz, ʿAlī b. Muḥammad 125
al-Khiḍr 138, 144, 145
al-Khiṣāl (book by al-Ṣadūq) 24, 70, 73–84, 87
al-Khuṣaybī, al-Ḥusayn b. Ḥamdān 199 n.2
al-Kulaynī, Muḥammad b. Yaʿqūb 1, 2, 37, 39, 44, 48, 49, 60–2, 74, 124, 133

law 4, 43, 46–50, 78, 109–10
  legal school (*see madhhab*)
  legal theory (*see* jurisprudence)
longevity of the imam 5, 133, 138–42

Maʿānī al-akhbār (book by al-Ṣadūq) 24, 70, 73–8, 80, 87
madhhab (school of law) 21, 35–6, 43–5, 59, 63
Majālis maʿa Rukn al-Dawla (book by al-Ṣadūq) 26, 84
mahdī, *see* Hidden Imām
Mājīlawayh, Muḥammad b. ʿAlī 7, 94
al-Maʾmūn (caliph) 85–6, 100, 111–4
Man lā yaḥḍuruhu al-faqīh (book by al-Ṣadūq) 1, 3, 8, 9, 22–3, 26, 32, 46–50, 53, 61, 65
al-Mawāʿiẓ (book by al-Ṣadūq) 25, 70, 79–80, 82, 87
miracles 40–1, 77, 85, 125, 130–5, 138–42, 148
al-Miskawayh, Aḥmad b. Muḥammad 69, 185 n.14
al-Mufīd, al-Shaykh Muḥammad b. Muḥammad b. al-Nuʿmān 25, 33–7, 43, 44, 46, 50–2, 61, 62, 69, 81, 124, 130, 132
Muḥarram 34
Muʿizz al-Dawla 34
al-Muqniʿ (book by al-Ṣadūq) 23, 48
al-Murtaḍā, al-Sharīf ʿAlī b. al-Ḥusayn 33, 35, 69, 79
Muṣādaqat al-ikhwān (book by al-Ṣadūq) 25, 70–3, 82, 87
Muʿtazilī 4, 9, 10, 93, 94
  accommodation with 35, 36, 85, 94, 96, 103–4
  conflict with 84–5, 92, 100–6, 115, 120–1, 130–1

al-Najāshī, Aḥmad b. ʿAlī 8, 27, 51
naṣṣ (designation of the imam) 79, 124, 128–30, 132

al-Nuʿmānī, Ibn Abī Zaynab 117, 124–5, 130, 134
Nuṣayrī 160 n.2, 165 n.30

occultation (*ghayba*) 5–6, 10, 31–2, 37–43, 45, 47, 56–9, 61–4, 77, 111, 113, 117–50, *see also* Hidden Imam

persecution
of imams 58, 86, 114, 127, 143–4, 146
of Shīʿīs 34, 81–3, 127, 143
piety 49, 72–3, 76–7, 109–11
poetry 16, 70, 84, 86, 87, 106, 139
in *adab* literature 66–70
pre-Buwayhid (phase of Imāmī thought) 34–7, 41, 71, 81
pre-creation, of the imams and the Shīʿa 71
predestination, *see* free will and predestination
Prophet, Muḥammad 4–6, 11, 50, 51, 55–6, 58, 61, 71–4, 77, 85, 95, 106, 112, 121, 123, 125, 128, 130, 132, 135, 136, 145

qaḍāʾ *see* free will and predestination
qadar, *see* free will and predestination
qāʾim 5, 39, 58, 85, 127, 140, 141, *see also* Hidden Imam
qiṣaṣ al-anbiyāʾ, *see* stories of the prophets
Ibn Qūlawayh, Jaʿfar b. Muḥammad 36, 44, 60, 62, 74–5
Qum 7, 8, 41
Imāmī scholarship in 62
al-Qummī, ʿAlī b. Ibrāhīm 60
Qurʾan 3, 6, 126, 145
criterion for truth of hadith 61, 92
falsification of 35
interpretation of 27, 55, 92
(un)createdness of 100–1
Ibn Qutayba, ʿAbd Allāh b. Muslim 63, 83

Al-Raḍī, al-Sharīf Muḥammad b. al-Ḥusayn 25, 69, 79
rationalist/traditionist distinction 3–4, 33, 36–7, 41, 56–64, 84, 87, 91–3, 100–3, 107–8, 111–16, 123–6, 147–8, 151–2
Rayy 8–10, 34, 69, 83, 84, 86
Imāmī scholarship in 62
Ricoeur, Paul 15–16
al-Riḍā, ʿAlī b. Mūsā (imam) 8, 24, 84–6, 100, 111–14
rijāl (science of) 3, 51–63, 98, 131
rooster, supporting the heavens 99, 101
Rukn al-Dawla 26, 69, 84

al-Ṣādiq, Imam Jaʿfar b. Muḥammad 42, 52, 72, 73, 78, 103–5, 107, 129, 144
Safavids 33, 164 n.20
al-Ṣaffār al-Qummī, Muḥammad b. al-Ḥasan 37, 71
Samarra 41
school
of Imāmī thought 62
of law (*see madhhab*)
Shāfiʿī 35, 44, 48
al-Shāfiʿī, Muḥammad b. Idrīs 3–4, 63
Shīʿī century 10
Ṣifāt al-shīʿa (book by al-Ṣadūq) 25, 70–3
stories of the prophets 118, 120, 122–3, 126–30, 133–8, 141, 143, 144, 146
Sunnī
Sunnī anti-Shīʿī sentiment 10, 35, 81, 83, 135, 146
Sunnī hadith literature 1, 3–6, 22, 35, 42–5, 48, 63, 66, 68, 94, 125, 149
Sunnī legal and theological scholarship 10, 21, 35, 43–5, 48, 63, 91–2, 102–3

al-Tanūkhī, al-Muḥassin b. ʿAlī 68, 75
taqīya 55, 58–9, 78, 81–4
tashbīh 93–6, 101–2
Taṣḥīḥ al-iʿtiqād bi-ṣawāb al-intiqād (book by al-Mufīd) 37, 50–1, 124
al-Tawḥīd (book by al-Ṣadūq) 9, 22, 24, 52, 91–8, 147, 151–6
al-Tawḥīdī, Abū Ḥayyān 67, 69, 72, 79, 164 n.26
traditionist, *see* rationalist/traditionist distinction
Transoxiana 9, 47
Tus 8, 85
al-Ṭūsī, Muḥammad b. al-Ḥasan 7, 25, 26, 33, 48, 51, 53, 121
twelfth imam, *see* Hidden Imam

uṣūl al-fiqh, *see* jurisprudence
ʿ*Uyūn akhbār al-Riḍā* (book by al-Ṣadūq) 9, 24, 84–6, 114, 119

Ibn al-Walīd, Muḥammad b. al-Ḥasan b. Aḥmad 7, 44, 47
Wāqifī 39, 43, 58, 120, 124, 199 n.2
wisdom, wisdom literature 66–8, 70, 79–80, 137, 139, 144–5

Yūdhāsaf, *see* Bilawhar and Yūdhāsaf

Zaydī 3, 10, 69, 85, 120–1, 125, 175 n.27
Zaynab bt. ʿAlī b. Abī Ṭālib 132
Zoroastrian 112